Contract Law for Legal Professionals

Andrea B. Yelin
Loyola University Chicago

Prentice Hall

Boston   Columbus   Indianapolis   New York   San Francisco   Upper Saddle River
Amsterdam   Cape Town   Dubai   London   Madrid   Milan   Munich   Paris   Montreal   Toronto
Delhi   Mexico City   Sao Paulo   Sydney   Hong Kong   Seoul   Singapore   Taipei   Tokyo

Editor in Chief: Vernon Anthony
Senior Acquisitions Editor: Gary Bauer
Development Editor: Linda Cupp
Editorial Assistant: Megan Heintz
Director of Marketing: David Gesell
Senior Marketing Manager: Leigh Ann Sims
SenioMarketing Assistant: Les Roberts
Senior Managing Editor: JoEllen Gohr
Project Manager: Christina Taylor
Operations Specialist: Deidra Skahill

Senior Art Director: Diane Ernsberger
Cover Designer: Axell Designs
Cover Art: Istockphoto.com
Full-Service Project Management: S4Carlisle Publishing Services
Composition: S4Carlisle Publishing Services
Printer/Binder: Edwards Brothers
Cover Printer: Lehigh-Phoenix Color/Hagerstown
Text Font: Goudy

Library of Congress Cataloging-in-Publication Data
Yelin, Andrea B.
  Contract law for legal professionals/Andrea B. Yelin.
       p. cm.
  Includes bibliographical references and index.
  ISBN 978-0-13-613178-6 (alk. paper)
  1. Contracts—United States—Outlines, syllabi, etc. 2. Legal assistants—United States—Handbooks, manuals, etc. I. Title.
   KF801.Y45 2011
   346.7302—dc22   2009053970

10 9 8 7 6 5 4 3 2 1

Prentice Hall
is an imprint of

www.pearsonhighered.com

ISBN 10:   0-13-613178-6
ISBN 13: 978-0-13-613178-6

BRIEF CONTENTS

CONTENTS

PART III
AFTER FORMATION: PERFORMING THE AGREEMENT

PART V
CREATING THE ACTUAL AGREEMENT

CHAPTER 11

Researching and Drafting Contracts   229

APPENDIX

Click and Accept   257

PREFACE

Contract Law for Legal Professionals instructs students in all of the fundamental rules of contract law. Students will learn the basic rules and be able to understand a contract's components and spot issues in a contract. Unlike law school materials where the students glean legal rules from cases, this text will present and explain the legal rules directly in narrative format.

The text is written in a conversational style that offers an approachable format for legal professionals. By answering questions students may pose, the text contains an appropriate level of explanation and reinforcement required for paralegal students. Furthermore, there are relevant illustrations and cases for each topic, as well as reinforcement and application exercises to facilitate mastery of the concepts.

Straightforward examples and exercises reinforce the concepts introduced in each chapter. Unlike many paralegal texts that explain the rules in narrative text, this book has a topic and skill-building approach to teaching contracts. The first chapter lays a foundation on which to base the particular rules and establishes a context to understand the overall subject matter. Cases, hypotheticals, and sample contracts help illustrate the application of the topic to contract practice. By using this text, paralegals will learn how to spot and analyze contractual issues after providing a general explanation of each topic. The goal of each topic is to introduce, explain, illustrate, reinforce, and apply the concepts.

The paralegal's ultimate goal is to be able to draft simple contracts, often using customized forms, and to locate inconsistencies and issues in contracts the attorney can resolve or direct the paralegal to resolve. The paralegal will also be responsible for obtaining the necessary information to complete the contract. This text will equip the reader with all of the necessary skills to draft simple contracts and to identify contractual issues.

■ CHAPTER FEATURES

- Case Illustrations are introduced with **Guided Reading Pointers** and reinforced with **Guided Reading Questions**. Both of these direct students' reading of the decisions.
- **What a Paralegal Needs to Know** and the **Paralegal's Role** define the workplace responsibilities of the paralegal and the ethical concerns in a legal practice using the information set out in the chapter.

■ END-OF-CHAPTER EXERCISES AND MATERIALS

- **Chapter Summaries** conclude each chapter with a narrative summary and a table of the main concepts designed for use as a quick review of key chapter topics.
- **Review Questions** allow students to check their mastery of key chapter concepts.
- **Skill-Building Applications and Exercises**
  - These require students to apply the material learned in the chapter to new situations, analyze problems, and draft provisions. This section has four types of exercises and assignments:
    - **Developing Critical Thinking Skills**
    - **Creating Law Office Documents**
    - **Improving Writing Skills**
    - **Building a Portfolio**
  - **A Simulated Law Office Assignment** begins in Chapter 1, where a mock law firm is introduced to the student. Every subsequent chapter has a Simulated Law Office assignment that requires the student to produce a document.
  - **Drafting Exercises** reinforce writing techniques and help students spot common writing mistakes.
  - **The Portfolio Assignments** ask the students to create a document that indicates concept mastery and professional aptitude. Students will be able to use the documents prepared for the Portfolio Assignments in seeking employment.

■ ADDITIONAL TEXTBOOK FEATURES

- A *Glossary* at the end of the text contains all of the chapter margin definitions.
- An *Appendix* contains sample contracts for commonly encountered agreements.

■ SUPPLEMENTS PACKAGE

To access supplementary materials online, instructors need to request an instructor access code. Go to www.pearsonhighered.com/irc, where you can register for an instructor access code. Within forty-eight hours of registering, you will receive a confirming e-mail including an instructor access code. Once you have received your code, locate your text in the online catalog and click on the Instructor Resources button on the left side of the catalog product page. Select a supplement, and a log-in page will appear. Once you have logged in, you can access instructor material for all Prentice Hall textbooks.

- *An Instructor's Manual with Test Item File* provides teaching tips for each chapter and outlines the objectives each chapter presents and the skills the students are to master.
- *TestGen,* test management software, contains all of the material from the Test Item File. This user-friendly software allows instructors to view, edit, and add test questions with a few clicks of the mouse.
- *PowerPoint Lecture Presentation Package,* a ready-to-use Power-Point slideshow, is designed for classroom presentation—use "as-is," or edit to fit your individual needs.
- *Companion Website* features practice quizzes, key terms, chapter objectives, and links to online resources.
- **CourseConnect Contract Law Online Course** Looking for robust online course content to reinforce and enhance your student learning? We have the solution: CourseConnect! CourseConnect courses contain customizable modules of content mapped to major learning outcomes. Each learning objective contains interactive tutorials, rich media, discussion questions, MP3 downloadable lectures, assessments, and interactive activities that address different learning styles. CourseConnect courses follow a consistent 21-step instructional design process, yet each course is developed individually by instructional designers and instructors who have taught the course online. Test questions, created by assessment professionals, were developed at all levels of Blooms Taxonomy. When you buy a CourseConnect course, you purchase a complete package that provides you with detailed documentation you can use for your accreditation reviews. **CourseConnect courses can be delivered in any commercial platform, such as WebCT, BlackBoard, Angel, or eCollege platforms.** For more information, contact your representative or call 800-635-1579.

■ ACKNOWLEDGMENTS

Thank you to all of the wonderful people who had a part in creating this text and shaping its contents.

Thank you to Gayle Miller of the College of Lake County for putting me in touch with Gary Bauer at Pearson.

I am so grateful to the talented and dedicated editors at Pearson. Thank you to Gary Bauer for this opportunity. A very huge debt of gratitude goes to Linda Cupp for her wisdom, guidance, patience, and faith. Linda—your time, expertise, and insight carried this project through from beginning to end.

To the Loyola Law School Library, Julia Wentz, Patricia Harris, and Fred LeBaron for his expert reference assistance, thank you.

Anna Hamburg-Gal—thank you for your assistance with the Instructor's Manual; your work is invaluable. Thank you to Laree Bobo for the practical information.

Last, but certainly not least, thank you to my family—Rachel, Henry, and David—for the time and the family room to complete this project. David—a very large thank you for reading and reviewing the many pages and examples; I could not have done it without you.

Thanks to The American Law Institute for granting permission to quote and paraphrase the Restatement (Second) of Contracts and the Uniform Commercial Code.

Thank you to the reviewers of this text:

Steve Dayton,
Fullerton College

Karen McGuffee,
University of Tennessee
  at Chattanooga

Kent D. Kauffman,
Ivey Tech Community College,
  Northeast

Heidi Getchell-Bastien,
Northern Essex Community
  College

Patricia Greer,
Berkeley College

Candace Weiss,
Wharton County Junior College

Buzz Wheeler,
Highline Community College

Kathleen Mercer Reed,
The University of Toledo

Annalinda P. Ragazzo,
Bryant and Stratton College

Robert M. Donley,
Central Pennsylvania College

Brian Craig,
Globe University, Minnesota
  School of Business

Lisa Newman,
Brown Mackie College-Atlanta

■ ABOUT THE AUTHOR

ANDREA B. YELIN received a J.D. and an M.S.L.S. from Case Western Reserve University in 1985, where she concentrated in tax law and legal research. Following graduation she joined the practice of Spindell, Kemp and Kimball, concentrating in commercial law, civil litigation, and tax appeals. She began her teaching career at Loyola University Chicago in 1992 as a legal reference librarian and an instructor in the Institute for Paralegal Studies. Since 2004, Andrea Yelin has served as an adjunct professor of professional skills at Loyola University Chicago School of Law, where she teaches first-year legal writing. She is an avid writer and is the co-author of two other textbooks, *The Legal Research and Writing Handbook: A Basic Approach for Paralegals* and *Basic Legal Writing*.

Contract Law for Legal Professionals

The Fundamentals of Contracts
The Big Picture

CHAPTER 1

THE IMPORTANCE OF CONTRACTS INTRODUCTION

Contracts are agreements that bind parties. Contracts are essential to the business process by providing assurance that the agreement will be honored and can be relied upon. Uncertainty in agreements would create chaos. This is the reason why contracts are at the foundation of many types of transactions. This chapter will provide an overview of the contracts process.

You encounter a variation of a contract each and every day. When you purchase goods, you expect that the item conforms to the purpose and is of the quality promised. Even your relationship with the government is a form of contract—you are a citizen, you pay taxes, and in return you receive rights, services, and protection. Some contracts are not negotiated and some are. Most important, contracts provide the terms of the agreement, whether oral or written, on which parties can depend and seek redress when the terms are not carried out. A contract should accurately capture the agreement between the parties. Contracts are essential instruments that protect a party's **reliance** on a promise. A contract is more than a promise because a contract provides legal **remedies** when it is not fulfilled. The main point of the remedy is to put the party that did not receive the value from the contract in the position he or she would have been in if the contract had been performed.

LEARNING OBJECTIVES

After studying this chapter, you should be able to:

1. Know why contracts are important.
2. Discuss the paralegal's role in the contract process.
3. List the essential parts of a contract.
4. Understand how a contract works generally.
5. Identify the basic types of contracts.

Contract
A binding agreement between two parties, who have the capacity to contract, that has a valid offer, acceptance, and adequate consideration.

Reliance
When a party to an agreement acts because he or she trusts that the other party will perform as promised.

Remedies
When a party does not receive what was promised under the contract, a remedy is a right that the injured party can exercise.

Valid
A contract that fulfills all of the legal requirements so that it is judicially enforceable and is binding between the parties.

Contracts are everywhere. Federal, state, and local governments enter into contracts when roads are built. The Department of the Defense enters into a contract when it purchases fighter planes. You even enter into a contract when you buy a latte. You look up at the menu and select a latte for $4.00, including tax, ask the counter person for a latte, and slide the $4.00 across the counter. If you receive an espresso, instead of the latte, you would rightfully assert that you did not receive what you agreed to. Contracts also state the rights and duties between parties in cutting-edge agreements such as between egg donors and recipients, and between participants in social networking sites.

Simply stated, a contract is a binding agreement between two parties. Many contracts are oral. Many do not even contain the words "promise" and "contract." For instance, when you buy a coffee, you do not state: "I am entering into a contract for the purchase of a latte."

■ WHY CONTRACTS ARE IMPORTANT

Contracts also permit certainty so that commerce can go forward and unrelated parties who reside in different states or even different nations can enter into an agreement. Even if the parties do not know each other, the contract provides a basis for certainty so that businesses can run and transactions can occur. Additionally, contracts have remedies that prevent parties from becoming enriched due to unjust or unfair actions. Contracts have remedies so that the party who does not receive the benefit of the agreement can recover. Contacts are important because their existence permits successful commerce. Companies would not manufacture goods without the assurance that there is a **valid** contract stating the terms of the sale of the goods to a purchaser. Banks would not lend money without a contract stating that the borrower must repay the sum and binding the borrower to this obligation. Contracts permit individuals, companies, schools, and governments to take risks because they know that they will have legal rights if the contract is not performed as agreed. A contract provides more assurances than a promise, for a contract is enforced by the law.

■ THE PARALEGAL'S ROLE IN THE CONTRACT PROCESS

Paralegals play a large role not only in drafting and revising contracts but also in reviewing contracts and in spotting issues for supervising attorneys. Paralegals check to see if an agreement does, in fact, capture the promises each party makes. Often, a paralegal will be called upon to draft an initial agreement for the attorney to edit or to find and customize a form contract for the attorney to use. Paralegals will frequently use a form to write the first draft of the contract. The paralegal will use the information and notes from a client interview or negotiation to provide the contract terms. Often, the paralegal drafts the entire contract and then the supervising attorney will evaluate the content and edit accordingly. Many companies have contracts databases that paralegals manage.

Law firms often have forms files that paralegals organize; these contain the forms created by the firm, including sample contracts. Additionally, paralegals will monitor contract expiration dates that require action. Furthermore, paralegals often perform research on various contractual **provisions**. Paralegals who are self-starters and who are detail oriented will enjoy working with contracts.

Law firms and corporations employ paralegals to work with contracts. Each area of legal practice has agreements that are in the form of a contract. Contracts are found in labor law in employment agreements, in banking in loan agreements, in real estate in purchase agreements and leases, in government purchases, and in commercial law in sales agreements. Contracts assume various forms depending on the subject matter and legal discipline. Paralegals can expect to encounter contracts in their work in almost any area.

What Does a Paralegal Need to Know about Contracts?

Paralegals need to learn about the definitions of terms, components of a contract, the essentials of contractual **formation**, and issues that arise in a contract dispute. This text will introduce the paralegals to the elements of a contract, what a valid contract looks like, and issues related to contractual formation. Additionally, modification, assent, **Statute of Frauds**, third-party contracts, **performance** and discharge, third-party agreements, remedies, and illegality will be discussed in separate chapters. Also, paralegals should be aware of the sources of law that pertain to contracts. Generally, contract law is derived from state law. The attorney that you work for will guide you to the appropriate **jurisdiction**, with the applicable law, that concerns the contract issue that you are working on. Much of contract law is determined by the common law. The common law is law created by the courts and is stated in court opinions. The **Uniform Commercial Code** governs contracts concerning the sale of goods between merchants. The Uniform Commercial Code is a body of rules that concern commercial transactions with the intent to provide uniformity rather than the variations that can occur in court decisions. The Uniform Commercial Code has been adopted by every state except Louisiana. Each state has its own respective Uniform Commercial Code provisions in its state code.

Also, you will notice the precision with which the terms were selected to reflect the particular agreement and the subject area. After you acquire some experience, this will become more evident. Also, you will gain a deeper appreciation for how contracts function as a form of legal protection for parties relying on the promises contained in the agreement.

You will acquire the confidence necessary to read a contract, to spot the issues within it, and to draft simple agreements.

■ WHAT IS A CONTRACT?

In its most basic form, a contract is an agreement between two more parties where there is some sort of exchange between them and there are remedies if the contract is not performed as agreed. This trade can be for goods, services,

Provision
A condition or a point made in a contract.

Formation
Creating the contract.

Statute of Frauds
Generally, each state's statute describes when the Statute of Frauds applies to a contract. The Statute of Frauds generally requires that contracts be in writing when the subject of the contract is the sale of real estate, the contract is for the sale of goods over $500, or the contract would require more than one year to perform.

Performance
Actually doing the action that one promises in a contract.

Jurisdiction
A particular court's right to hear and to decide a case.

Uniform Commercial Code (U.C.C.)
One of the Uniform Acts drafted with the goal to make a specific area of law uniform among the fifty states. Article 2 of the Uniform Commercial Code provides the legal rules concerning the sales of goods. Article 2 (commonly called "Sales") is important because contracts are made and goods are sold across state lines. Each state adopts the U.C.C. provisions, and once the state adopts the provisions it is part of the state's code. Forty-nine states, all states except Louisiana, have adopted Article 2 of the U.C.C., which concerns sales.

land, or even a right such as an easement, or the permission to use a website. Contracts provide a form of security or insurance that the agreement will be honored and allow the parties to rely on the agreement. Because there is a body of law pertaining to contracts, parties entering into a contract have legal rights and remedies. This is the main difference between a contract and a promise, for if a contract is **breached**, then the party that suffers the breach can take legal action.

What Are the Basic Types of Contracts?

There are two basic forms of contracts: **unilateral** and **bilateral**. Unilateral contracts are essentially a promise for performance. For example: Mr. Jones will pay neighbor $10 to vacuum the house on Sunday. When neighbor completes the vacuuming, the neighbor is paid. Only one party, Mr. Jones, is binding himself to the agreement. Bilateral contracts exist when both parties make a promise, essentially a promise for a promise. For example: Parent contracts with adult son to vacuum the house on Sunday. Adult son will vacuum the house if parent treats him to a baseball game after vacuuming. Here both parties are making a promise.

All contracts, regardless of how complex, are at the root either a unilateral or a bilateral agreement.

■ WHAT ARE THE ESSENTIAL COMPONENTS OF EVERY CONTRACT?

Every contract contains an **offer**, an **acceptance**, and **consideration**. Consideration is the value of the contract to the contracting parties. This sacrifice and gain is what cements the agreement. Consideration is, in the most basic sense, a detriment to one party and a benefit to the other party. Additionally, the parties to the contract must be mentally competent and must have reached the legal age of majority in the relevant jurisdiction. Also, the contract must be legal. If the subject of the contract is illegal, the contract is **void**, which means that the contract does not have any force and the parties can not assert any rights relating to it. One cannot legally contract to commit murder or to sell banned substances.

The intent to enter into a contract is important. In a bilateral contract, both parties must agree or assent. A contract cannot be enforced if both parties do not agree to it. Also, a party cannot be induced to enter into an agreement on **fraudulent** terms.

Finally, some contracts must be in writing. Although putting an agreement in writing is not required to make a contract enforceable in many instances, a written agreement does protect the parties. Putting a contract in writing—in other words, to **memorialize** the contract—helps to ensure that the parties' agreement is clear and captures their deal. A written agreement is required according to the Statute of Frauds, generally, if the contract is for the sale of goods in excess of $500, for the sale of land, or if performance will require more than one year. Most states have a code section stating that a

Breach
Failure to perform the contract as agreed without an excuse.

Unilateral
Generally, a promise for performance.

Bilateral
A contract composed of a promise for a promise.

Offer
A clear indication that a party wants to enter into an agreement

Acceptance
Consenting to the terms of an offer

Consideration
Value given to induce a promise; sometimes the value is forsaking something.

Void
A contract without any force; a void contract is completely ineffective as a legal instrument.

Fraud or fraudulent
Intentional misstatement or misrepresentation, designed to purposely induce another's reliance, with the intent to cause the individual to part with property or to give up a legal right.

Memorialize
Formal way of stating that a contract or a note, such as a certificate of deposit, is put into writing.

contract must be in writing if it concerns real estate, the value of the goods is in excess of $500, or if it will take longer than one year to perform.

Issues arise because of the offer's form and validity, the manner of the acceptance, and the **sufficiency** of consideration. Many issues arise in one of these three areas: the offer, the acceptance, and the consideration. An issue that appears in some contracts cases is the failure to conform to the Statute of Frauds requirements.

Sufficiency
Used when determining if consideration was adequate or enough to support the promise made.

Sample Simple Contract

Mr. Haze will provide Mr. Jones with thirty (30) bales of cotton on June 30, 2006. In exchange, Mr. Jones will pay Mr. Haze $150 in total upon receiving the thirty (30) bales of cotton.

The offer is the thirty bales. Acceptance will occur on June 30, 2006, when Mr. Jones will accept the cotton. The consideration is $150 paid by Mr. Jones to Mr. Haze.

Mr. Jones will give up $150 and Mr. Haze will receive the $150. This payment is bargained for and is a detriment to Mr. Jones and a benefit to Mr. Haze. Receiving the cotton is a benefit to Mr. Jones and a detriment to Mr. Haze.

■ HOW A CONTRACT WORKS GENERALLY

At first glance, a contract appears to be a glorified promise. Closer examination reveals that promises and contracts are in fact quite different. Promises generate goodwill and are made voluntarily. However, promises do not protect the parties from disappointment or from relying on the promise to their detriment. Promises are assurances that an act will or will not be performed but offer no legal protection to either party. Often, promises are **gratuitous**. Gratuitous agreements are promises created without valuable consideration that binds the parties. Contracts contain an offer, acceptance, and consideration, provide legal protection to all parties, and allow parties to trust in an agreement, even for an exchange at a future date. Contracts function to provide legal redress and remedies to protect the parties bound by the agreement.

Gratuitous
An offer or a promise tendered without any value, or consideration, to support it.

Contracts protect all parties affected by the agreement. Contracts operate to identify the precise agreement made by the parties. Contracts should be put into writing and not only articulate the agreement between the parties but also anticipate all issues that may arise. The writing should contain proposed remedies to address the failure to perform as promised. Often, well-drafted agreements contain a provision regarding the aggrieved party's rights if a breach should occur.

Rights and Duties

Enforceable rights and duties are at the heart of any contract. Rights and duties exist regardless of whether the contract is **formal** or **informal**. A formal contract is a traditional contract following established format, such as a letter of credit or negotiable instruments. Informal contracts capture the bargain reached between the parties coupled with the parties' intent to

Formal
Historically, a formal contract is under seal; currently, it involves observing the formalities surrounding formation.

Informal
Not a formal contract but the agreement has all of the contract components.

contract. A written document is not necessary to form a binding agreement. However, a written agreement states the particular rights and duties established by the parties and serves as a resource that the parties can consult if there are any points that are of issue and require clarification. The written contract also offers both parties protection. A well-drafted contract not only articulates the deal made but represents the sum of the negotiations and the parties' **expectations**. This is why written agreements must be precisely drafted to state the exact agreement. Remember that contracts not only enforce and protect the parties' promises but also protect a party's reliance on the agreement.

Expectation
What a party plans to receive from entering into the contract.

Intent to Contract

An important part of a contract is that the parties intend to contract. There must be a **meeting of the minds**. The meeting of the minds demonstrates willingness to contract, the intention of the parties, and an agreement on the terms. A meeting of the minds occurs when both parties to a contract clearly state their respective intentions regarding the goal of the agreement.

Meeting of the minds
When both parties have the same intentions regarding the agreement and both parties agree to the substance and the terms.

Also, there must be **mutuality of obligation** whereby both parties are bound to the agreement. A written document just offers evidence of the agreement, but this evidence is very important when a party wants to assert rights under the contract or is claiming that the contract was not performed as agreed upon (breach of contract).

Mutuality of obligation
Requires that both parties are bound to the agreement.

Sample Fact Patterns

In the following situations, examine the diagram showing the promise made and the contract drafted. See how the written contract provides protection to both the promisor and the promisee. As you read through the scenarios, ask yourself how a business would function without the protection offered by contracts. Businesses must purchase supplies and hire employees in anticipation of performing duties under a contract. Also, ask yourself how individuals would be able to rely on the agreement to provide services and goods to address particular needs, when spending sums of money, without contracts.

Example

Mrs. Smith sees the president of Cast Painting, Mr. Cast, at church on Sunday. During the coffee hour, Mrs. Smith asks Mr. Cast to just paint the trim on her windowsills when he can get to it. Mr. Cast replies: "Yeah, sure."

Mr. Cast and Mrs. Smith do not write their agreement down. There is merely a verbal exchange.

The terms are vague for there is no price, no specific date, no hours of work. This agreement is merely a promise. It could be called gratuitous because no consideration was exchanged between the parties. Additionally, the agreement between Mrs. Smith and Mr. Cast is an **illusory promise**. An illusory promise occurs where the **promisor**, here Mr. Cast, suffers no consequences for failing to perform the promise.

Illusory promise
A promise where there is no recourse for either party's failure to perform or performance is at the party's discretion.

Promisor
The party making the promise.

DIAGRAM

Offer—to paint Mrs. Smith's windowsill trim

Acceptance—Mr. Cast saying: "Yeah, sure"

Intent to contract—None

Meeting of the minds—None; too many uncertainties to perform the contract.

Consideration—None; no detriment to the **promisee**. Mr. Cast did not forsake anything here.

Contract—No

Promisee
The party receiving the promise.

This exchange could be construed as an invitation for an offer or as a gratuitous promise but not as a contract. The terms are too indefinite and there is no meeting of the minds.

Example

Compare the following agreement with the gratuitous, illusory promise exchanged between Mrs. Smith and Mr. Cast.

Mrs. Smith wants to have some decorating performed on her home. She knows that Mr. Cast is the president of Cast Painting and contacts him to come to her residence to provide an estimate for the work. Mr. Cast arrives and discusses the intended project with Mrs. Smith. Mrs. Smith request to have three rooms painted: the living room, the master bedroom, and the office. Mrs. Smith also requests to have two rooms wallpapered: the kitchen and the powder room. Additionally, Mrs. Smith requests that Cast Painting paint the trim on the windowsills throughout the house. Mr. Cast tells Mrs. Smith that his work crew is available the week of October 1 and will be able to complete the entire job in five working days, arriving at 7 A.M. and ending each workday at 4 P.M. The crew will take one hour for lunch from 12 P.M. to 1 P.M. and have two fifteen-minute coffee breaks per day, one at 9:30 A.M. and the other at 2:30 P.M. Mr. Cast has a crew of three workers available the week of October 1. He needs to pay each crew member $350 per week and the foreman $400 per week. Additionally, Cast will furnish the paints and all supplies and Smith will provide the wallpaper. Cast will provide the truck to transport his crew and all tools and materials from Cast Painting headquarters to the Smith residence. Additionally, Cast has to insure the workers, the tools and the truck, and the work performed by his employees. Mrs. Smith has her own set of concerns. First, she is spending $900 on wall coverings and wants to be sure that the wall coverings are hung properly. Second, she is taking a week off from work to supervise the work. Third, she is relying on the work to be performed as expected because she is hosting a cocktail party at her residence on November 1 for the chairman of her firm, the partners, associates, and paralegals. This situation requires that the parties have legal protection to clearly state their expectations under the agreement, to enforce performance, and to remedy a failure to perform as expected.

An informal written agreement will basically be in the form of a letter containing all of the terms agreed to by the parties. Until the contract is performed it is an executory contract because the agreement has not been executed, or performed. However, both Smith and Cast are relying on the performance of the contract, so the protection provided by a document is essential. The contract letter would appear as follows:

Commitment Letter for Painting and Decorating
Cast Painting Company
1212 Main Street
Great Falls, Minnesota 54123

September 12, 2010

Mr. and Mrs. Smith
5700 Poplar Drive
Great Falls, Minnesota 54123

Dear Mr. and Mrs. Smith:

The purpose of this letter is put into writing the agreement we reached regarding painting and wallpapering of your home. As is my custom, I require a $700 deposit prior to commencing work as to ensure the painters' availability and the procurement of materials. The entire job will cost $2,500 for labor, materials, and transportation to suppliers and the residence. Payment for the services rendered must be made no later than thirty (30) days after the completion of the work.

As per our discussion, Cast Painting will paint three rooms at your residence. The three rooms to be painted are the living room, the master bedroom, and the office. Cast will also paint the windowsills throughout the home. After Mrs. Smith selects the colors, Cast Painting will supply the paints and prep materials. Cast Painting will also wallpaper two rooms at your residence, the kitchen and the powder room. Mrs. Smith will supply the wallpaper. Cast Painting will supply all necessary materials to hang the paper.

The entire decorating job will commence on October 1, 2010, and be completed in five (5) working days. A working day is 7:00 A.M. to 4:00 P.M. with an hour for lunch and two fifteen-minute coffee breaks.

Paint color will be approved after an initial swatch. Any repainting, due to dissatisfaction with the color or gloss, will be charged to Mr. and Mrs. Smith at an hourly rate of $30.00 per painter. Wallpaper will be selected and purchased by the Smiths. Any rehanging or replacement of wallpaper shall be charged to the Smiths at an hourly rate of $30.00 per painter.

Cast Painting insures their workers fully. Cast Painting will cart any debris from the premises and clean the premises at the end of the job.

Cancellation of this job within seven (7) days of performance will require forfeiting the deposit. All cancellations must be done prior to September 24.

If you are in accord with all of the above, it will be our agreement in this matter if you sign and return the enclosed copy of this letter to Cast Painting, together with your check for $700.00 as retainer.

Sincerely,

_____

Mr. Cast

d/b/a Cast Painting

Accepted:

_____

Mrs. Smith

_____

Mr. Smith

This agreement appears to capture the deal that Mrs. Smith made with Mr. Cast. Although the letter appears to be informal, it is a contract because it contains an offer, acceptance, consideration, and specific terms regarding price, duration, location, and services. However, Mrs. Smith was concerned that the work be completed, as agreed in manner and time, by October 15 so that she can get ready for the party on November 1. Mrs. Smith communicated this to Mr. Cast. This need of Mrs. Cast's, to complete the work by the party, was contemplated by the parties at the time of the contract but it was not in the written agreement. The contract reflected Cast's needs and concerns but did not fully reflect Smith's issues. When a contract is in writing, all of the oral communications made regarding the contract are considered to be embodied in the written document. Any oral communication made prior to the written agreement regarding any issue that is not in the written document, such as Smith's need to have the work completed satisfactorily, is now not part of the contract and will be very difficult to enforce later on. This is true if the written agreement represents the parties' final and complete agreement. The rule that applies here is the parol evidence rule. The parol evidence rule will be discussed in greater detail in Chapter 5.

Mrs. Smith read the contract over very carefully and decided to insert a few sentences stating that the work must be completed by October 15 and must be completed satisfactorily by October 15. Second, since the wall coverings were so costly, Smith wanted a provision stating that if the wall coverings were handled recklessly or negligently then Cast would replace the wallpaper at Cast's expense. Third, since Smith was taking five days off from work to supervise this work she wanted protection so that she would not forfeit additional vacation time beyond the five days. Smith wanted written assurance that the work would be completed in five business days and if additional time was needed to complete the job, then Cast Painting would work evenings and weekends.

The following contract represents the agreement and concerns of both parties. The writing protects both parties, captures their respective rights and responsibilities, and provides protection if either party fails to perform as promised.

Dear Mr. and Mrs. Smith:

The purpose of this letter is put into writing the agreement we reached regarding painting and wallpapering your home. As is my custom, I require a $700 deposit prior to commencing work as to ensure the painters' availability and the procurement of materials. The entire job will cost $2,500 for labor, materials, and transportation to suppliers and the residence. Payment for the services rendered must be made no later than thirty (30) days after the completion of the work.

As per our discussion, Cast Painting will paint three rooms at your residence. The three rooms to be painted are the living room, the master bedroom, and the office. Cast will also paint the windowsills throughout the home. After Mrs. Smith selects the colors, Cast Painting will supply the paints and prep materials. Cast Painting will also wallpaper two rooms at your residence, the kitchen and the powder room. Mrs. Smith will supply the wallpaper. Cast Painting will supply all necessary materials to hang the paper. If the wallpaper is damaged by Cast Painting, then Cast Painting will replace the wallpaper or compensate the Smiths for the cost of the wallpaper at the Smiths' discretion. If Cast Painting employees handle the wallpaper recklessly or negligently, then Cast Painting will replace the wallpaper or reimburse the Smiths for the cost of the wallpaper at the Smiths' discretion.

The entire decorating job will commence on October 1, 2010, and be completed in five (5) working days. A working day is 7:00 A.M. to 4:00 P.M. with an hour for lunch and two fifteen-minute coffee breaks. If the job cannot be performed within five (5) business days, Cast Painting will work on evenings and weekends to complete the work. The additional time required to complete the job will not be billed to the Smiths. Also, the job will be completed by October 15 as agreed.

Paint color will be approved after an initial swatch. Any repainting, due to dissatisfaction with the color or gloss, will be charged to Mr. and Mrs. Smith at an hourly rate of $30.00 per painter. Wallpaper will be selected and purchased by the Smiths. Any rehanging or replacement of wallpaper shall be charged to the Smiths at an hourly rate of $30.00 per painter.

Cast Painting insures their workers fully. Cast Painting will cart any debris from the premises and clean the premises at the end of the job.

Cancellation of this job within seven (7)days of performance will require forfeiting the deposit. All cancellations must be done prior to September 24.

If you are in accord with all of the above, it will be our agreement in this matter if you sign and return the enclosed copy of this letter to Cast Painting, together with your check for $700.00 as retainer.

Sincerely,

_____

Mr. Cast

d/b/a Cast Painting

Date_____

Accepted:

_____

Mrs. Smith

Date_____

Mr. Smith

Date_____

Checkpoint

1. What does a meeting of the minds demonstrate?
2. What is a gratuitous agreement?
3. Is a written document necessary to have a binding contract?
4. What do binding contracts protect?

■ TYPES OF CONTRACTS

All contracts are agreements of some sort, but each contract has unique characteristics. A contract, as you have learned, is a promise with stipulated legal components, for which there is legal protection, or remedies, if the promise is broken, not performed as agreed, or breached. At the basis, all contracts are either bilateral or unilateral, but each contract has specific features and formats. These are various: implied in fact, implied in law or quasi contracts, constructive, express, executory, oral, formal, and informal. A contract can have more than one of these unique features at the same time. For instance, a contract can be bilateral and oral or informal and unilateral. The features of the agreement formed generally determine the contract's specific qualities.

Bilateral and Unilateral

Bilateral

In its simplest form, a bilateral contract is a promise for a promise. This occurs where each party promises something to the other and receives something in return. The nature of the promise and the return promise does not have to be monetary or even physical; it can be a promise to do a certain act or to forbear, or not to do, a certain act.

Example: Town and Country Windows will provide window washing at $1.50 per window. This is a service. The window washer will visit the residence, count the windows, and arrive at a price. The homeowner responds with a suitable and convenient time to wash the windows. The parties agree to the terms—a promise to wash a certain number of windows at a specific time and place in exchange for the promise of payment for services. This is a bilateral contract.

Unilateral

A unilateral contract occurs when one party makes a promise for another party's performance. The promisor does not receive a return promise. An example of a unilateral contract is: I promise to pay you $50 if you plow the driveway after the snow. Note that the driveway plower does not have to make a return promise, just perform the stated action.

Implied in Fact and Implied in Law

Implied in Fact

Implied
Not directly stated in an agreement. Sometimes the law will intervene and create a contract on the basis of the parties' conduct, for example, when one party is unjustly enriched by the situation. This is an instance of an implied contract because the parties did not expressly create one.

Implied contracts occur when the terms are implied by the conduct of the parties. Contracts that are implied in fact are deduced from what occurred between the parties, though not directly stated. Implied-in-fact contracts are determined by the parties' conduct or behavior. Sometimes a party will act on the basis of a promise, and then there is an implied-in-fact contract. Sometimes only one or two of the contractual conditions are implied by the parties' conduct and the rest of the contract is in writing. The parties' intent is crucial when determining if there is an implied-in-fact contract. The parties must intend to enter into a contract and must indicate assent to the terms, even if the assent is not in writing.

An example of an implied-in-fact contract is: Miss Steen enters Central Printing and requests to have a fax sent. Steen sees the sign reading: "All Faxes $3.00." Steen has the fax sent but the cashier is busy and Steen motions that she will return later with the money. Steen knew that the fax would cost $3.00 and intended to pay for it. Central Printing knew that it would charge Steen $3.00 to fax the document. Central Printing had a reasonable expectation that it would be paid by Steen, the party benefiting from the service.

Implied in Law

Contracts are implied in law when injustice would occur if the terms are not enforced. These are also called constructive contracts or quasi contracts because the court will fashion a contract to enable the aggrieved party to receive the benefit from the agreement to avoid injustice. A court of equity usually addresses implied-in-law contracts. The remedy is called specific performance and results in the contract being performed as agreed. Specific performance is a remedy that puts the injured party in the position he or she would have been in if the contract had been performed. Specific performance is used when money damages are inadequate to compensate the aggrieved party. Implied-in-law contracts prevent a party from benefiting from an agreement by becoming unjustly enriched. Implied-in-law contracts permit an aggrieved party to be compensated for the value of the bargain.

Example: Mrs. Fox broke her hip. Mrs. Fox asked her neighbor to watch her home, visit her, bring supplies to the hospital, do her laundry, and transport her to the rehabilitation facility. Neighbor, a freelance writer, neglected her own work to assist Fox and even declined assignments because she was so busy helping Fox. In exchange for the neighbor's services, Mrs. Fox stated that the neighbor would be paid. Mrs. Fox never paid the neighbor for the services. By not paying the neighbor for the services, Mrs. Fox was unjustly enriched at neighbor's expense. Although the parties did not have a contract, the court can intervene, if requested, and fashion an agreement whereby neighbor would be compensated for her services and receive the value from the bargain.

Performing the Contract

Executory

An executory contract is a contract that has not yet been fully performed but the party or parties have already agreed to the terms. An executed contract exists when the subject of the contract, or the agreement, has been performed. At some point almost all contracts are executory because the contract has yet to be fully performed.

Communicating the Contract

Oral

An oral contract is an agreement that is spoken; it is not in writing. Oral contracts present many challenges when there are problems with the terms or the performance. Additionally, according to the Statute of Frauds, a contract generally must be written if it takes longer than one year to perform, if the value of the contract is greater than $500, or if it is for the sale of real estate.

Example: Don Brown offers his Buick for sale to his neighbor, Ann Jones, for $400. Ann Jones wants the car and accepts the price of $400 for the Buick. Jones tells Brown that she will get a cashier's check on Tuesday, the following week, for $400 to purchase the car. This is an oral, executory, bilateral contract. The contract is oral because it is not in writing, but spoken. It is executory because it is not yet performed. It is bilateral because it is a promise for a promise.

Written

The contract is in written form.

Express

Express contracts occur when the parties stipulate the contract terms in words, often in writing, but express contracts can also be oral.

Express
Stated directly, usually in writing but can be communicated orally.

Formal and Informal

Formal

A formal contract follows certain prescribed formalities that are very traditional. Two examples of a formal contract are a letter of credit and a negotiable instrument. These agreements have set and certain language. Traditionally, formal contracts were under seal.

Informal

Informal contracts are agreements that contain the elements of a contract but are not formal contracts with established language such as a letter of credit or a negotiable instrument, as just described. The Statute of Frauds mandates that certain requirements be observed with informal contracts if the contract is valued at over $500, takes over one year to perform, or is for the sale of real estate. Almost all contracts, except for letters of credit and negotiable instruments, are informal contracts because the terms are determined by the parties. Informal contracts are not necessarily casual agreements. Informal contracts comply with the rules of contracts.

Void and Voidable Contracts

Void

Sometimes a contract is not valid and is not binding in any way due to some illegality in formation. The contract's terms are not upheld for either party; this is a void contract. A void contract has no legal effect.

Voidable

Voidable
A contract where the aggrieved party still can obtain value but the wrongdoer cannot. For example, this occurs when a party is induced to enter into a contract on fraudulent terms. The party perpetuating the fraud cannot benefit under the agreement.

A **voidable** contract occurs when one party, generally the wrongdoer, does not benefit from the agreement but the innocent party who relies on the contract obtains the benefit of the agreement.

What a Paralegal Needs to Know about Types of Contracts

A paralegal should know the characteristics of the various types of contracts and should be aware that a single contract can be a combination of several types. See the illustration, for example, describing the transaction for the sale of the Buick between Mr. Brown and Ms. Jones. Paralegals should also be aware of the Statute of Frauds and the state's requirements regarding the Statute of Frauds. Generally, in compliance with the Statute of Frauds, a contract should be in writing if the value exceeds $500, if the contract requires more than one year to perform, or if the contract is for the sale of real estate. Understanding a contract's type enables a paralegal to determine if the contract has been performed, that is, whether the contract is executory or executed. This also helps the paralegal track the duties of the parties to see if the contract is carried out as agreed.

A paralegal should tell the attorney about the particular features in every contract. This will assist the attorney in determining the rights of the parties. The attorney should make this determination. However, a paralegal needs to understand the obligations that arise under each type of contract. Paralegals can set up a timeline or a tickler file to be aware of when performance should occur and deadlines for performance. This is important so that the aggrieved party can assert his or her rights under the contract. However, paralegals should be aware that determining a party's rights and obligations under a contract is a legal decision amounting to the unauthorized practice of law. Paralegals can, however, work under the guidance of an attorney to determine if the contract is executory or executed, that is, performed. For instance, an attorney can specifically delegate to a paralegal to follow up on a bilateral contract. The paralegal must therefore know what a bilateral contract is and understand the rights and obligations of the parties. Determining whether the contract has been performed illuminates any outstanding issues that may arise.

Reading Contracts Cases

Cases are important because the legal rule set out in the case provides guidance for attorneys. Attorneys look at prior cases, from the appropriate jurisdiction, with similar facts and issues as the issue that they are working on, to anticipate how a court will decide. This is also called relying on precedent.

Read the case from beginning to end carefully. When reading a contracts case, just as when analyzing a contracts dispute, it is important to identify the essential facts. The facts not only lay out the story but also indicate the relationship between the parties and the promises made. Close examination of the facts of the offer, the manner of acceptance, the existence of a counteroffer, and evidence of performance helps identify the causes of the contract dispute.

Note the parties to the contract. Examine the facts of the case carefully to discern the issue raised. Identify the parties by name and their role in the agreement and dispute as well as in the proceeding. Sometimes you can make a chart or draw a diagram, and this helps to keep the facts clear. Ask yourself: What is the issue here?

What was the offer? Was there a **counteroffer**? Did the parties both want to enter into an agreement? Was there an acceptance of the terms? How was acceptance indicated? Was there any payment or exchange of value—what was the consideration? Was there a specific price paid for the goods or service? Was there a time for performance? Any locations? What are the names of the parties? These are all points to think about when reading a contracts case.

Often cases illustrate how an offer can be changed by a counteroffer. Cases also illustrate how it impacts the parties when a promise is not performed as agreed. Often, when a contract is not performed as agreed, the party that depended on the agreement must figure out a way to obtain the goods or services contracted for and must look to another source to provide item. When this happens, the breaching party, the party who fails to perform the agreed action, often has to compensate the nonbreaching party for the economic difference. Often a breach-of-contract action's goal is to make the aggrieved party *whole*. The disappointed party looks to the court to arrive at a solution so that the party that depended on the contract gets the benefit of the bargain. If the aggrieved party obtains the item or service that was due under the contract from another source, this is called *cover*.

Counteroffer
An offer made in reply to an offer. A counteroffer is made in response to an offer but has different terms than the original offer.

Step-by-Step Outline of How to Read Contracts Cases

1. Read the case through. Then read the case to answer the following questions.
2. Determine the parties and their roles. Who is the plaintiff? Who is the defendant?
3. What is the question that the court is asked to decide? This is the issue.
4. What happened here? What are the facts?
5. How did the court answer the question brought before it? This is the holding.
6. Did the court use a legal rule to support its holding? What is the legal rule? Did the court support its holding with any other information? This is the court's reasoning. This is very important because you will see how the court uses the law, particularly statutes and cases, to support its holding. This helps you understand the law. You will understand how a particular legal principle is applied to a specific set of facts.
7. What is the court's order? Was the case reversed? Did the court affirm? This is the dispostion.

CASE ILLUSTRATION

Guided Reading Pointers

Focus on the details of the agreement between the Changs and First Colonial Savings Bank that follows. Pay particular attention to the role of the advertisement. In the case, the advertisement is an offer because it contains clear, definite, and precise terms. There are no terms that are left open to negotiate by the Changs. The Changs are suing First Colonial for breach of contract. Think carefully about how the court examines the breach-of-contract claim and how the court discusses the type of contract that existed between the parties.

In-class Exercise

Use the seven-step guide on how to read a contracts case to analyze the *Chang* case that follows.

Supreme Court of Virginia.
Chia T. CHANG, et al.,
v.
FIRST COLONIAL SAVINGS BANK.
Record No. 910057.

Nov. 8, 1991.

...The primary issue that we consider in this appeal is whether a newspaper advertisement constitutes an offer which, when accepted, creates a legally enforceable contract.

The litigants stipulated the relevant facts. Chia T. Chang and Shin S. Chang, who resided in the Richmond area, read the following advertisement which appeared in local newspapers on November 18, 1985. The advertisement states in part:

You Win 2 ways
WITH FIRST COLONIAL'S
Savings Certificates
1 Great Gifts 2 & High Interest

Saving at First Colonial is a very rewarding experience. In appreciation for your business we have Great Gifts for you to enjoy **NOW**— and when your investment matures you get your entire principal back **PLUS GREAT INTEREST**.

Plan B: 3 1/2 Year Investment

Deposit $14,000 and receive two gifts: a Remington Shotgun and GE CB Radio, OR an RCA 20′ Color-Trac TV, and $20,136.12 upon maturity in 3 1/2 years.

Substantial penalty for early withdrawal. Allow 4–6 weeks for delivery. Wholesale cost of gifts must be reported on IRS Form 1099. Rates shown are . . . 8 3/4 % for Plan B. All gifts are fully warranted by manufacturer. DEPOSITS INSURED TO 100,000 by FSLIC. Interest can be received monthly by check. . . .

. . . Relying upon this advertisement, the Changs deposited $14,000 with First Colonial Savings Bank on January 3, 1986. They received a color television that day from First Colonial and expected to receive the sum of $20,136.12 upon maturity of the deposit in three and one-half years. First Colonial also gave the Changs a certificate of deposit when they made their deposit.

When the Changs returned to liquidate the certificate of deposit upon its maturity, they were informed that the advertisement contained a typographical error and that they should have deposited $15,000 in order to receive the sum of $20,136.12 upon maturity of the certificate of deposit.

First Colonial did not inform the Changs nor were the Changs made aware that the advertisement contained an error until after the certificate of deposit had matured. First Colonial, however, did display in its lobby pamphlets which contained the correct figures when the Changs made their deposit.

The Changs instituted this proceeding in the general district court seeking to recover $1,312.19, the difference between the $20,136.12 amount in the advertisement and $18,823.93, the amount that First Colonial actually paid to the Changs. The general district court awarded a judgment in favor of the Changs, and First Colonial appealed that judgment to the circuit court. The circuit court held that the advertisement did not constitute an offer but was an invitation to bargain or negotiate and entered a judgment in favor of First Colonial. We awarded the Changs an appeal.

The Changs argue that when members of the public reasonably rely upon a bank advertisement which offers a specific gift and dollar amount upon maturity in return for a deposit of a sum certain, and the bank fails to notify those who made deposits of an error in the advertisement until the certificate of deposit matures, then the specific term of the advertisement constitutes an offer which, when accepted, is a binding and enforceable contract. First Colonial argues, however, that the advertisement did not constitute an offer but rather was an invitation to make an offer because the advertisement was directed to the general public and required no performance on the part of the parties to whom it was directed.

The general rule followed in most states, and which we adopt, is that newspaper advertisements are not offers, but merely invitations to bargain. *Restatement (Second) of Contracts* § 26, pp. 75–76 (1981); 1 *Corbin on Contracts* § 25, pp. 74–75 (1950). However, there is a very narrow and limited exception to this rule. "[W]here the offer is clear, definite, and explicit, and leaves nothing open for negotiation, it constitutes an offer, acceptance of which will complete the contract." *Lefkowitz v. Great Minneapolis Surplus Store, Inc.*, 251 Minn. 188, 191, 86 N.W.2d 689, 691 (1957). *See also Izadi v. Machado (Gus) Ford, Inc.*, 550 So.2d 1135, 1139 (Fla.Dist.Ct.App.1989); *Osage Homestead, Inc. v. Sutphin*, 657 S.W.2d 346, 351–52 (Mo.App.1983); *R.E. Crummer & Co. v. Nuveen*, 147 F.2d 3, 5 (7th Cir.1945); *Oliver v. Henley*, 21 S.W.2d 576, 578–79 (Tex.Civ.App.1929). As Professor Williston observed:

In any event there can be no doubt that a positive offer may be made even by an advertisement or general notice.... The only general test which can be submitted as a guide is an inquiry whether the facts show that some performance was promised in positive terms in return for something requested.

1 *Williston on Contracts* § 27, p. 65 (3d ed. 1957).

Applying these principles to the facts before us, we hold that the advertisement constituted an offer which was accepted when the Changs deposited their $14,000 with the Bank for a period of three and one-half years. A plain reading of the advertisement demonstrates that First Colonial's offer of the television and $20,136.12 upon maturity in three and one-half years was clear, definite, and explicit and left nothing open for negotiation. . .

Even though the Bank's advertisement upon which the Changs relied may have contained a mistake caused by a typographical error, under the unique facts and circumstances of this case, the error does not invalidate the offer. First Colonial did not inform the Changs of this typographical error until after it had the use of the Changs' $14,000 for three and one-half years. Additionally, applying the general rule to which there are certain exceptions not applicable here, a unilateral mistake does not void an otherwise legally binding contract. *See Newport News v. Doyle and Russell*, 211 Va. 603, 608, 179 S.E.2d 493, 497 (1971); *Foreman v. Clement*, 139 Va. 70, 80–81, 123 S.E. 336, 339 (1924). *See also* 13 *Williston on Contracts* § 1573, pp. 486–490 (3d ed. 1957).

First Colonial further argues that even if the newspaper advertisement was an offer, it was a unilateral offer unsupported by consideration, and it was withdrawn before the date the Changs deposited their $14,000. We disagree.

An offer, which is usually but not always a promise, is a manifestation of a willingness to enter into a bargain. *Restatement (Second) of Contracts* § 24, pp. 71–72. The offer identifies the bargained for exchange, *Id.*, Comment b, and creates a power of acceptance in the offeree. *Id.* § 29(1). *See Richmond Eng. Corp. v. Loth,* 135 Va. 110, 153, 115 S.E. 774, 786 (1923).

It is true that an offer that is not supported by consideration may be withdrawn any time before it is accepted. *J.B. Colt Co. v. Elam,* 138 Va. 124, 128–29, 120 S.E. 857, 858 (1924); *Crews v. Sullivan,* 133 Va. 478, 483–84, 113 S.E. 865, 867 (1922). However, First Colonial was required to communicate the withdrawal of the offer to the Changs before they accepted it. As we have noted, First Colonial did not inform the Changs that the offer had been withdrawn or that the advertisement purportedly contained a typographical error until the Bank had used their $14,000 for three and one-half years.

We also reject First Colonial's argument that the advertisement did not create a contract because there was no meeting of the minds. As we stated in *Gibney & Co. v. Arlington B. Co.,* 112 Va. 117, 70 S.E. 485 (1911):

The offerer has a right to prescribe in his offer any conditions as to time, place, quantity, mode of acceptance, or other matters, which it may please him to insert in and make a part thereof, and the acceptance to conclude the agreement must in every respect meet and correspond with the offer, neither falling within or going beyond the terms proposed, but exactly meeting them at all points and closing with these just as they stand.

Id. at 120–21, 70 S.E. at 487 (citation omitted). When the Changs tendered their $14,000 to First Colonial for three and one-half years, they complied with all of the conditions in First Colonial's offer. Hence, there was a meeting of the minds and an enforceable contract.

Accordingly, we will reverse the judgment of the circuit court and enter final judgment here in favor of the Changs for $1,312.19 plus interest.

Reversed and final judgment.

Checkpoint

1. Can a contract be executory and bilateral?
2. Can a contract be oral and bilateral?
3. Provide an example of a formal contract.
4. What is an executed contract?
5. What is an implied-in-fact contract?
6. What is an implied-in-law contract?
7. What is an express contract?

■ WHAT SOURCES OF LAW APPLY TO CONTRACTS?

Contracts generally are based on state law. The Uniform Commercial Code is adopted by the respective state and the pertinent provisions are found in the state's code. Much of contract law is still based on the common law, that is, rules derived from cases. The only exception are those rules covered by the

Uniform Commercial Code and adopted by a state's legislature as law and included in that state's code. The Uniform Commercial Code, Article 2, concerning the sale of goods, has been adopted by all of the states except for Louisiana. You can find your state's code provisions regarding the sale of goods by looking in your state code. Most contracts concerning the sale of goods are bound by the Uniform Commercial Code. The sale of goods is the main area of contracts law that is not controlled by the common law but by state statute.

Choice of Law—Which Jurisdiction's Law Applies

Choice of law
Selecting which jurisdiction's legal authority will control the contract.

Choice of law refers to selecting which jurisdiction's legal authority will be applied to the contract. The selection of the legal forum is important if there is a dispute that needs to be settled.

Generally, the state where the contract is formed determines which state's law applies. Sometimes the parties agree, in the contract, to have a particular state's law apply. This is called a *choice of law* provision. Sometimes there are ties to more than one jurisdiction, and the applicable law must be determined by the attorney or the court. For instance, the company is headquartered in Nebraska and the individual contracted to create a commercial is located in Maryland and the contract is signed in New York. A choice of law provision in the contract will determine the applicable jurisdiction's law. Choice of law is very complex and is beyond the scope of this course. However, if you ever have a choice of law question, ask the supervising attorney, for this is a legal decision.

Codes and Codification

Codes or statutes
Rules of law enacted by governmental bodies such as the U.S Congress on the federal level or the state legislature. Once the rules are enacted by the legislature, the rules are then added to the jurisdiction's code, also called statutes. The process of inserting legislation into the code is called codification. Codes are commonly called statutes.

Codes are rules of law enacted by governmental bodies such as the U.S. Congress on the federal level or the state legislature. Once the rules are enacted by the legislature, the rules are then added to the jurisdiction's code. The process of inserting legislation into the code is called codification.

The Common Law, Precedent, and Stare Decisis Case Law

Common law
Legal rules derived from judicial opinions or cases.

Legal rules derived from judicial opinions or cases make up the body of law called the **common law**. For instance, the legal point or rule from the *Chang* decision in this chapter is a common law rule that will guide legal professionals as to the law on when an advertisement is a binding offer. The law of contracts is controlled by the common law except when the subject of the contract is the sale of goods, then the respective state's Uniform Commercial Code controls.

Legal precedent
Court opinions that are used to guide the analysis of legal issues that arise subsequently that are similar to the prior decision in law and fact.

Legal precedent is composed of court opinions that are used to guide the analysis of legal issues that arise subsequently that are similar to the prior decision in law and fact. For instance, the cases cited in the *Chang* case are precedent because they are similar in law and fact to the scenario raised in *Chang* and the court looks to these decisions to guide their decision. Law cannot be made up, and courts must provide the basis for their ruling. Courts look to precedent, or prior decisions, to support their rulings. We also look to prior decisions when researching a legal issue, for that helps us predict or anticipate how a court may rule. We look for cases with similar facts, similar issues, and from the correct jurisdiction. We rely on precedent as well.

Stare decisis is a Latin phrase meaning: "let the decision stand." It is used to indicate that the courts will follow cases that have been decided. Stated differently, courts follow legal precedent.

The Restatements of Law

The **Restatements** are a scholarly work with the purpose of taking the rules from cases and organizing them in a way that works like a code. The goal is to provide a resource that will give legal professionals guidance and certainty regarding the legal rule, regardless of state, on common law issues. The work is called the Restatements because the common law rules are restated. The objective is to have researchers from all of the states use this set of rules. The Restatements also have interesting and helpful illustrations to show how the rules are used. Although the courts are not required to follow or to adopt a Restatement provision, since the Restatements are very well respected, courts and legal professionals use them to find rules on particular points. The Restatement (Second) Contracts is used widely.

The Uniform Commercial Code (U.C.C.) is one of the Uniform Acts drafted to make a specific area of law uniform among the fifty states. Article 2 of the Uniform Commercial Code provides the legal rules concerning the sales of goods. Article 2 is especially important for sales, which is commercial law, because contracts are made and goods are sold across state lines. Each state must adopt the U.C.C. provisions, and once the state adopts the provisions they are part of the state's code. Forty-nine states, all states except Louisiana, have adopted Article 2 of the U.C.C., which concerns sales.

■ THE UNIFORM COMMERCIAL CODE AND TYPES OF CONTRACTS—U.C.C. §2–204

The Uniform Commercial Code impacts contracts between merchants concerning the sale of goods. Contracts for the sale of goods between merchants are not required to have the characteristics of a specific contract type. Generally, contracts for the sale of goods may be made in any manner sufficient to show agreement. Even conduct demonstrating agreement will suffice for terms as long as both parties recognize that a contract exists. U.C.C. §2–204(1).

Additionally, the contract will exist even if one or more terms are left open as long as "the parties intended to make a contract and there is a reasonably certain basis for giving an appropriate remedy." U.C.C. §2–204(3).

A contract for the sale of goods between merchants can be implied in fact, oral, executory, or a combination of the various contract types that we explored in this chapter as long as the parties understand the terms and the terms are sufficient to demonstrate that the parties agree.

Stare decisis
A Latin phrase meaning "let the decision stand." It is used to indicate that the courts will follow cases that have been decided.

Restatements
A scholarly work with the goal of taking the rules from cases and organizing the rules in a way that works like a code. The goal is to provide a resource that will give legal professionals guidance and certainty regarding the legal rule, regardless of state, on common law issues; the Restatement (Second) Contracts is used widely.

■ BUILDING A CONTRACT

Contract Terms

The terms used in the contract make the agreement unique to the parties and the transaction. The terms, or words, must be very accurate in describing the particular promise made between the parties and identifying the parties. Often specific categories of terms are used, for instance: price, time, location, date, quantity, condition, the subject of the agreement (what the parties are contracting for), type of good or service, the parties' names or a company names, and address or real estate description.

The more specific and accurate the terms, the less confusion later. Careful and precise drafting avoids disputes. Often disputes arise due to failure to perform the contract as promised. The clearer the language in the agreement, the more guidance the parties have and the easier it is to preserve rights under the contract. The contract should embody the agreement between the parties.

In the following sample contract, there are specific terms:

The parties to the contract: Mr. Black and Mr. Jones
The subject of the agreement: sandwiches
The quantity: thirty sandwiches
The date of the exchange: June 30, 2010
The price to be paid: $150
The date on which the payment should occur: June 30, 2010
The date of performance: June 30, 2010

Mr. Black will provide Mr. Jones with thirty (30) sandwiches on June 30, 2010. In exchange, Mr. Jones will pay Mr. Black $150 in total upon receiving the thirty (30) sandwiches.

Since this is a very simple contract, many possible terms that the parties could include are omitted, such as the condition of the sandwiches (freshness), the type of sandwiches (turkey, ham, roast beef), the form of payment (cash, check, credit card), and the right to assign performance to a third party (give a person who did not sign the contract, as a party, the right to perform the duty or to receive the benefit).

Paralegals must know the essential terms required to draft an effective contract and be able to spot deficiencies and call the deficiencies to the attorney's attention. Often, it is helpful to start with a checklist or a form when beginning to draft an agreement to ensure thoroughness. Each contract should be uniquely tailored to the parties and the agreement. Knowledge of special terms used in contracts in a particular industry, what is customary, is also important. Careful, precise drafting is necessary.

Contract Terms

Certain words appear often in contracts and in cases where there is a contract dispute. Use a legal dictionary to define words that you are unfamiliar with. Three words that are used often in contracts but may be unfamiliar are discussed as examples of contract jargon. **Covenant** is commonly used to

Covenant
A promise.

mean an agreement or promise between two or more parties. **Warranty** is to promise that the stipulation in the contract is true. For instance, to warrant that the cotton is in good condition when contracting for the purchase of cotton means that the seller is promising that the cotton is in good condition. **Assumpsit** appears frequently in older contracts cases. Assumpsit is a common law action where the plaintiff is attempting to recover damages for the breach of an oral or simple contract.

Additionally, particular industries rely on words or terms that are unique to the enterprise.

Warranty
A promise that an assertion made is true. Generally used in the sale of goods to state a promise that the subject of the agreement will be of a certain condition.

Assumpsit
A common law action to recover damages for not performing; the non-performance of a contract.

■ BREACH OF CONTRACT

A breach of contract occurs when the contract is not performed as agreed by the parties. Often, one party will assert that the contract was not performed as promised. Sometimes performance is impossible. Sometimes, one party will change the terms of the contract without notifying the other party. There are many reasons why a contract can be breached.

Example: Ms. Roberta Roberts owns a bookstore. Ms. Roberts purchased three (3) reams of Christmas wrapping paper from Wrapping Paper Source to be delivered on October 15, 2010. Ms. Roberts paid $75.00 per ream for the wrapping paper. Wrapping Paper Source purchases all of the paper it sells from various companies. Ms. Roberts needed to have possession of the paper before Halloween so that she could be ready for the holiday season. On October 1, Wrapping Paper Source heard from the company manufacturing the wrapping paper, Craft Paper Co., that there was a delay in production. Wrapping Paper Source contacted Roberts immediately and said that the paper would be delivered on November 1, 2010. On November 3, Roberts called Wrapping Paper Source and asked: "where is the wrapping paper that you promised to be delivered on November 1?" The clerk at Wrapping Paper Source told Roberts that she would receive the paper by November 5. Roberts did not receive the paper on November 5. The issue here is whether there was a breach of contract. The contract was for three reams of holiday wrap to be delivered on October 15 at $75 per ream. There was a modification of the contract when the parties agreed that delivery was changed to November 1. Roberts agreed to this. However, Roberts did not receive the wrapping paper.

Roberts then had to obtain three reams of paper at a higher price per ream. Since Wrapping Paper Source did not fulfill the promise to which it had agreed, it did breach the contract. The contract was modified when Roberts agreed to the later delivery date. When Wrapping Paper Source could not deliver the paper on the date agreed, Wrapping Paper Source did not fulfill its agreement. Since Roberts depended on receiving the paper at a certain time, she was forced to purchase the paper elsewhere at an additional cost. Roberts wanted to pass along this additional cost to Wrapping Paper Source because it did not act as promised and Roberts was depending on the company.

What were the terms of the contract?

Three reams of holiday wrap at $75 per ream to be delivered on October 15.

Then delivery was agreed, by both parties, to be on November 1.

Who were the parties?

Ms. Roberts and Wrapping Paper Source.

Notice that terms such as *date*, *quantity*, *price*, and *party* are very important. It is essential to be precise in drafting contracts.

Contracts Ensure Certainty

The Roberts example illustrates the importance of contracts in the business world. Contracts provide certainty and enable companies and businesses to make economic decisions. Contracts also provide remedies when the agreement is not performed as the parties intended. Written documents protect the parties' rights and aid a court in discerning how to enforce a contract. Courts do not like to insert contract terms later. Also, putting a contract in writing assists the court in fashioning a remedy if there is a breach.

CHAPTER SUMMARY

This chapter explored the importance of contracts and the contract's role in providing certainty and protection to the parties. Additionally, an overview of the contract and its features was explored. You will now begin to be able to identify agreements as contracts and be aware of the essential terms. Precision and accuracy in drafting are important so that the contract represents the true agreement reached by the parties.

This chapter also provided a basic framework for creating a contract from a promise. A contract represents an agreement between the parties and also provides important rights and remedies to ensure performance and to recover if performance does not occur. The essential components of any contract were explored: offer, acceptance, consideration, legality of the contract's subject, mutuality of obligation, and a meeting of the minds. These elements transform a gratuitous promise into a binding contract. Contracts are important because they provide certainty, allow parties to take risks, and permit unfamiliar parties to engage in commerce and to reach agreements.

The Fundamentals of Contracts—The Big Picture

Importance of Contracts	Essential for business and certainty when making agreements
Basic Types of Contracts	Unilateral and bilateral
Essential Components of Every Contract	Offer, acceptance, consideration, intent to contract or meeting of the minds, and mutuality of obligation

Contract as Compared to a Promise	An ordinary promise is a gratuitous agreement that is not supported by consideration. A promise, if not fulfilled, does not provide legal remedies to the aggrieved party. Contracts, if properly formed, provide legal remedies. The remedies' goal is to put the injured party in the position he or she would have been in if the contract had been performed as agreed.
Features of Contracts	Unilateral or bilateral. Additionally, all contracts can have one or more of the following features: Implied in fact or implied in law Express Executory Oral or written Formal or informal Void or voidable
Sources of Contract Law	The common law—case law State codes or statutes Uniform Commercial Code Restatements (Second) of Contracts
Essential Terms	Price, quantity, date, time for performance, amount, location, subject matter, parties' names

REVIEW QUESTIONS

1. What is a unilateral contract?
2. What is bilateral contract? What is the difference between a unilateral contract and a bilateral contract?
3. Name and describe three essential components of a contract.
4. What role does a paralegal perform in the contract process?
5. Why are contracts important?
6. What is a breach of contract?
7. What are essential terms in a contract? Name three essential terms that may be included in a contract.
8. What is a covenant?
9. What is a void contract?
10. What does a meeting of the minds demonstrate?
11. What is a gratuitous agreement?
12. Is a written document necessary to have a binding contract?
13. What do binding contracts protect?

14. What is a voidable contract?
15. Name two instances when a voidable contract occurs.
16. List two reasons why a form contract would be used.
17. List two types of terms that should generally be included in written contracts.

SKILL-BUILDING APPLICATION EXERCISE

Read over the following contract carefully. List the rights and obligations of the parties. Is this agreement a bilateral contract? Why? Describe any contract features in this agreement. For instance, is this an oral or written agreement?

Cohabitation agreement between parties with no children

THIS AGREEMENT *made and executed on July 1, 2008 by and between Patricia Lind, presently residing at 123 Main Street, Iowa City, Iowa, and James Anders, presently residing at 123 Main Street, both hereinafter collectively referred to as "the parties";*

The parties represent that neither of them is presently married, nor do either of them have any present intention of marrying; and the parties presently contemplate and have expressed a desire to reside together for an indefinite period; and in contemplation of residing together, the parties wish to enter into a written cohabitation agreement to establish any rights, interests, and claims that may accrue to each of them in the property and estate of the other as a result of their intended period of living together, and agree to accept the provisions of this Agreement in lieu of and in full discharge, settlement, and satisfaction of any and all rights, interests, and claims that each might otherwise have and acquire under the law but for this Agreement; and regardless of any legal obligation that may exist to do so, the parties have fully and completely disclosed the nature and approximate value of all of their presently existing assets, liabilities, and income to each party's satisfaction.

Patricia Lind has had the benefit of independent legal advice prior to the execution of this Agreement and *James Anders* has had the benefit of independent legal advice prior to the execution of this Agreement.

The consideration for this Agreement is the mutual promises of the parties as stated in this Agreement.

In consideration of the foregoing and intending to be legally bound hereby, the parties mutually agree as follows:

1. The parties intend that this Agreement shall supersede any and all legal rights that they might otherwise have with respect to each other under any present or future applicable court decision or statute that may tend to contravene the purpose of this Agreement.
2. Property—Any and all property acquired prior to the period of cohabitation shall remain the sole property of the original owner. Any property

acquired or earned during the period of cohabitation shall be owned jointly by Patricia Lind and James Anders.

3. Death—Each party waives the right to inherit any property acquired prior to the period of cohabitation. All property acquired during the period of cohabitation shall be inherited by the surviving cohabitant. A properly executed last will and testament shall be the vehicle ensuring the transfer of property upon the death of a cohabitant. All real property, acquired during the period of cohabitation, shall be owned in joint tenancy.

4. Chores—Each party shall perform the agreed chores. Patricia Lind shall do the laundry, grocery shopping, cooking, and dusting. James Anders shall do the dishes, yard work, take out the trash, and maintain the cars. A cleaning service shall be employed weekly to perform the cleaning of the residence.

5. Finances—All income earned by each cohabitant shall be deposited into a joint checking account. All bills will be paid with the monies from the checking account. Any excess monies, after payment of bills, exceeding $5,000, shall be invested in a joint investment account after a mutual decision regarding the investment.

Patricia Lind and James Anders state that they each entered into this agreement on her or his own free will, without duress or coercion. The parties acknowledge and represent that this Agreement has been executed by each of them free from persuasion, fraud, undue influence, or economic, physical, or emotional duress of any kind whatsoever asserted against them by the other or any other persons.

Signed and witnessed

_____

SIMULATED LAW OFFICE ASSIGNMENT

Our client, Ms. Chris Pine, is an independent art consultant. Recently Ms. Pine represented a couple, Mr. and Mrs. King. The couple wanted to purchase art at an auction. Prior to the auction, the couple requested that Pine research the pieces of art to ascertain any information that could lead to assessing the value. Additionally, the couple requested that Pine bid for them at the auction as to maintain their privacy. This entire agreement was in writing. Specifically, the couple was interested in two Calder mobiles that Pine researched and determined to be of significant value. Pine successfully bid on the two Calder mobiles at the auction for the couple. The Kings paid Pine $2,000 for her services as agreed. After the couple paid Pine and the couple received the mobiles, Pine believed that her contractual obligations were complete. What type of contract is the initial agreement? The supervising attorney requested that you write a short memo detailing the agreement between the Kings and Ms. Pine.

DRAFTING EXERCISE

The supervising attorney asks you to complete the following form for a part-time employment contract. Additionally, identify the essential terms for the attorney. Write up a list of the contract terms for each party. Your firm represents Mr. Bussell.

Mr. Bussell has a Colorado Closet Company that specializes in designing and organizing closets.

Mr. Bussell hired Sam Michaels as a carpenter to work daily from 3 P.M. to 7 P.M. installing custom closets. This time was selected due to many customers' work schedules. Mr. Michaels would be paid $25.00 per hour and work twenty hours per week. Mr. Bussell would not provide any benefits for Mr. Michaels. Mr. Bussell and Mr. Michaels agreed that Mr. Michaels would work for a total of twenty weeks beginning on January 2, 2010. Mr. Bussell would provide the tools, materials, transportation, design, and customers. Mr. Michaels would install the closets according to the design provided by Mr. Bussell.

Part-time Carpenter Agreement
Colorado Closet Company

Nature of Employment

This agreement for part-time work as a carpenter is made on [date], between [names of parties].

Mr. Bussell of Colorado Closet Company employs part-time carpenters to perform the following duties: _____.

Part-time carpenter agrees to perform the following duties: _____.

Hours of Employment

Part-time carpenter agrees to work _____ hours per week [total number of hours per week of work], from ____ to _____ daily [time of work].

Part-time carpenter agrees to work _____ weeks beginning his work on _____.

Compensation

Mr. Bussell agrees to pay part-time carpenter _____ dollars per hour.

Materials

Mr. Bussell agrees to provide: _____.

DEVELOPING CRITICAL THINKING SKILLS

Examine the following hypothetical situation. State the terms of the offer and the acceptance.

Jane Jones of XYZ Corporation is planning a lunch for the corporation's board of directors. Jones contacted Lunch Bag Catering to have Lunch Bag provide sandwiches and salad for the twelve board members as well as beverages on October 30, 2010, at 12 noon in the conference room of XYZ Corporation. Lunch Bag requested $20 per person for the food and beverage and requested that XYZ submit a deposit, of $10 per person, one month in advance. XYZ sent Lunch Bag the deposit of $120 on September 15 and it was received by Lunch Bag on September 18. On October 15, Mr. Green, of Lunch Bag, called Ms. Jones and apologized profusely that he double-booked the date and wanted to know if Ms. Jones would be comfortable if one of his colleagues in catering covered the luncheon. Ms. Jones replied that she would prefer to not have another caterer do the luncheon and would explore her options. Jones requested that Green return the deposit.

1. Is there a contract here?
2. What was the offer?
3. How was the acceptance indicated?
4. Do you think that Jones should make Green pay the difference if the luncheon would cost more if Jones books it with another catering company?

PORTFOLIO ASSIGNMENT

Acme Corporation is a large client of the firm. The president and owner of Acme, Mike Cone, asked the attorney that you work with for some advice regarding his father. Mike Cone's father, Arthur Cone, has dementia and requires a health care aide who will come to his home. Mike Cone wants to employ a male aide to care for his father. The aide should be able to live in the home and to comply with the terms of the agreement. First, determine the characteristics of this contract. Is it bilateral or unilateral? Is there a promise for a promise? Second, create a timeline for compliance with the terms to ensure that each party is complying with his respective obligations under the agreement.

HOME HEALTH CARE AIDE EMPLOYMENT CONTRACT

This employment contract is made between Michael Cone and Sam Metz.

Michael Cone is the son of the recipient of Mr. Metz's services on JANUARY 1, 2009. Mr. Arthur Cone, the father of Michael Cone, is the recipient of Mr. Metz's services. Mr. Metz shall provide for Mr. Arthur Cone's needs, desires, and wishes to ensure the care, support, attendance, skilled nursing services, and maintenance of Mr. Arthur Cone. Additionally, Mr. Metz may determine that medical care may be necessary.

Mr. Metz has stipulated that he is a Registered Nurse with five years of experience in the field of elder care.

Mr. Metz will reside in Mr. Arthur Cone's residence.

Mr. Metz will have every Saturday off duty for a period of twenty-four (24) hours.

Mr. Metz will be paid $700 every Friday.

A replacement will relieve Mr. Metz of his services every Saturday at 7:00 A.M.

To assure continuity of care, Mr. Metz agrees to work for fifty (50) weeks and then consider a renewal of the contract if Mr. Michael Cone determines that it is in the best interest of Arthur Cone.

The Offer

CHAPTER 2

INTRODUCTION—THE OFFER IN GENERAL

A contract cannot exist without an offer. The offer does not have to be written but it does have to be certain and identifiable. In its most basic form, an offer is a promise made with the expectation that a promise will be returned (bilateral contract—a promise for a promise) or that performance will occur (unilateral contract—promise for performance.) The party making the offer, the **offeror**, must intend to enter into a contract on the basis of the offer.

Restatement (Second) of Contracts § 24, defines an offer as: "An offer is the **manifestation** of willingness to enter into a bargain, so made as to justify another person in understanding that his assent to that bargain is invited and will conclude it." The intent to enter into a bargain is essential, and it is also essential to have specific terms. Additionally, the intent to enter into an agreement as well as the terms must be communicated to the person intended to accept the offer, the **offeree**. The offer may state the specific party to whom the offer is made.

In addition, the offer may state the duration for which is it valid. An offer may state that it expires within a certain period of time or is not a valid offer after a set date.

LEARNING OBJECTIVES

After studying this chapter, you will be able to:

1. Identify an offer and its various forms.

2. Understand that an offer indicates the intent to enter into a contract.

3. Discuss that a valid offer has definite, certain, and identifiable terms.

4. Understand that a valid offer identifies the party intended to receive the offer and, generally, an offer has a set time frame.

5. Identify forms that an offer can take, including irrevocable offers, option contracts, and auctions.

6. Know when an offer is no longer valid.

Offeror
The person or party extending or tendering the offer.

Manifest or manifestation
To indicate directly and plainly.

Offeree
The person or party receiving the offer.

Promisor
The person or party who makes the promise. With an offer, the promisor is usually the party extending the offer.

Promisee
The person or party who receives the promise.

An offeror is the person making the offer. This differs from a **promisor** because a promisor is a party who makes a promise but the promise may not be a valid offer. The party receiving the offer is the offeree. The offeree differs from a **promisee,** the person receiving the promise, for the promise may not have all of the components required for an offer. Although the terms may be used interchangeably, they have different legal meaning. An offer must indicate an intent to enter into an agreement, invite acceptance, have specific terms, and the offer must be communicated to the offeree (the person intended to receive the offer).

Example–Simple Statement that is an Offer: I will rake the leaves on your lawn right now for $25.00, in cash, when I am done raking.

Example–A Common Offer

THE MAGAZINE

Yes. Send me **The Magazine** for the subscription term below.
O Check circle. Send me 3 years (36 issues) for just $1.30 per issue, for a total of $46.80, payable by check or credit card prior to start of subscription.

■ OFFER INDICATING FORMAT OF ACCEPTANCE

An offer may state, directly, the form of the acceptance required but this is not necessary for a valid offer. This is expressed in Restatement (Second) of Contracts, § 30:

Form of Acceptance Invited

(1) *An offer may invite or require acceptance to be made by an affirmative answer in words, or by performing or refraining from performing a specified act, or may empower the offeree to make a selection of terms in his acceptance.*

(2) *Unless otherwise indicated by the language or the circumstances, an offer invites acceptance in any manner and by any medium reasonable in the circumstances.*

Example

In the example on page 00, The Magazine invites acceptance by the offeree checking the circle and paying by check or credit card the amount of $46.80 prior to the start of the subscription. This is an example of an offer inviting acceptance to be made by performing a specified act.

■ INTENT

Intent to enter into a contract is also an essential component of the offer. Although many parties entering into a contract do not think about its consequences, they must consider that they will be bound to the agreement, as will the other party, and that each party's rights will be enforced. An offer is an expression of the willingness to enter into a mutual undertaking, commonly referred to as *bargain*. The expression can be written, oral, or a combination. This willingness, on the part of the offeror, lends a certain seriousness to the agreement. One way the intent to enter a binding contract can be demonstrated is by pondering the right to enforce a promise as well as considering one's obligations under the agreement.

Sometimes, when parties are entering into a contract, the parties will directly state or document that they intend their agreement to be binding. The parties' intent to contract then is clear. Sometimes, though, the parties' intent must be inferred. This requires examining the circumstances surrounding the formation of the contract. The circumstances surrounding an offer are the offer itself, the offeror's intentions, and how an offeree may have to change his or her position to take an economic risk to accept the offer. The circumstances are the situation that a party is in when the offer is made and that the offeror is inviting the offeree to accept.

An offeror generally must intend to create an offer. However, this offer does not have to be written, or even spoken. It can be created through actions as well.

Both parties to an agreement must intend to be legally bound. At the outset, though, the offeror must intend to create a contract for the contractual process to begin.

Example

For instance, two twenty-one-year old fraternity brothers are playing touch football on the lawn. Fraternity Brother A says to Fraternity Brother B: "I'll bet you $1,000,000 I can throw this football 60 yards." This can be assumed to not indicate an offer, but rather bravado. Fraternity Brother A does not have a million dollars, nor does he intend to pay a million dollars to Fraternity Brother B. Oftentimes, there is no contract when it is an agreement concerning a social engagement. Fraternity touch football can be considered a social engagement. There is not a valid offer when the basis of the agreement is a joke or prank. The circumstances are examined to determine if there is an offer.

However, the intent to make an offer is determined from the standpoint of the offeree, not the offeror, and the offeror can't back out of an offer just by claiming he or she was joking.

Gratuitous Promise

Example–Social Engagements

If the Smiths invite you to dinner on Sunday and then cancel due to illness, you cannot sue for breach of contract. The Smiths' offer for dinner is a social engagement. The Smiths' invitation was gratuitous and they did not intend to create an offer that would be the basis for a contract.

Recall the example in Chapter 1 concerning Mr. Cast of Cast Painting and the gratuitous promise. Mrs. Smith sees the president of Cast Painting, Mr. Cast, at church on Sunday. During the coffee hour, Mrs. Smith asks Mr. Cast to paint just the trim on her windowsills when he can get to it. Mr. Cast replies: "Yeah, sure."

A mere verbal exchange without the intent to contract and without specific terms will not create an offer. In the gratuitous promise, Mrs. Smith did not stipulate any specific terms. There was no set price, no specific date for performance, no hours of work; the terms are uncertain. Often when a statement is an illusory promise, the choice as to whether to perform is completely optional and the offeree does not have ability to enforce the promise. There are not definite or ascertainable terms; this is indicative of a lack of intent to contract.

Example–Offer Demonstrating Intent to Enter into a Contract (Not Gratuitous)

Lapse
when an offer expires due to failure to accept the offer, or failure to exercise the right in the offer, within the stated time frame.

The following proposal fulfills the requirements for an offer because there is an intent to enter into a contract and specific terms that are definite and ascertainable, including price, quantity, and time when the offer will **lapse** or expire. This offer also invites acceptance and is communicated to the offeree.

Mr. Banks needed to relandscape a portion of his property. There are several dead trees requiring replacement as well as a few bare spots in the yard requiring foliage. Banks contacted Midwest Nurseries. Midwest Nurseries visited Banks' property and delivered an offer to do the requested work in the form of a proposal that the Banks could accept or decline.

MIDWEST NURSERIES PROPOSAL

Purchaser and Site for Work
Mr. Edwin Banks
115 Carriage Way
Midwest, Illinois 65432

August 29, 2010

Re: Landscape Improvements for Banks Property

3 Cleveland Select Pear Trees 2.5' at $349.00 each	$1047.00
1 Judd Viburnum 30" at $59.99 each	59.99
1 Endless Summer Hydrangea 18" at $114.99	114.99
20 lb. Yard Garden Soil Mix	20.00
1 Bag 14–14–10 Fertilizer	16.50
1 Bag Yard Hardwood Bark Mulch	42.50
Subtotal	$1310.98

Labor to remove and dispose of debris and plant materials not to be saved, cut and prepare beds, amend soil, install plants, remove debris made by Midwest, and job supervision	$ 650.00
Total	$1960.98

All prices are subject to change if not accepted within thirty (30) days of the above date. No work shall be scheduled until this offer is accepted with the proper signatures and one-half (1/2) of deposit is received.

To accept this offer of proposed work, kindly sign two copies and return them to us for our signature.

■ PRELIMINARY NEGOTIATIONS

Invitation for an Offer—Advertisements

The most common example of a preliminary negotiation is an advertisement. A preliminary negotiation is not an offer when the offeree knows that the offeror does not intend to enter into a contract merely on the basis of the information presented without further indication of assent. The preliminary negotiations do not generally have enough specific terms to constitute an offer.

Example

Retro Heating and Cooling sends out a flyer, by mail, stating: "we have 200 new furnaces that we have to unload before year end. We will install the furnace in your home at our cost. Please call for an appointment."

This is not an offer but an invitation for an offer. It is subject to further negotiation and the establishment of specific terms such as time, price, and furnace model.

CASE ILLUSTRATION

Guided Reading Pointers

This case concerns a newspaper advertisement for a car. The newspaper advertised the incorrect price for the vehicle through no fault of the car seller. The court determined that the ad was not an offer but an invitation for an offer. The court reasoned that there was no meeting of the minds and no details as to terms. The court noted that the ad did not contain any information regarding warranties and equipment. This case provides guidelines to examine to see if an advertisement is an offer.

James L. O'Keefe, Public Administrator of the Estate of Christopher D. O'Brien, Plaintiff-Appellant, O'Keefe v. Lee Calan Imports, Inc., an Illinois Corporation, Defendant-Appellee, Third-Party Plaintiff, v. Field Enterprises, Inc., Third-Party Defendant

Appellate Court of Illinois, First District, Third Division
128 Ill. App. 2d 410; 262 N.E.2d 758

September 3, 1970

Christopher D. O'Brien brought suit against defendant for an alleged breach of contract. . . .

On July 31, 1966, defendant advertised a 1964 Volvo Station Wagon for sale in the Chicago Sun-Times. Defendant had instructed the newspaper to advertise the price of the automobile at $ 1,795. However, through an error of the newspaper and without fault on part of defendant, the newspaper inserted a price of $ 1,095 for said automobile in the advertisement. O'Brien visited defendant's place of business, examined the automobile and stated that he wished to purchase it for $ 1,095. One of defendant's salesmen at first agreed, but then refused to sell the car for the erroneous price listed in the advertisement.

Plaintiff appeals, contending that the advertisement constituted an offer on the part of defendant, which O'Brien duly accepted and thus the parties formed a binding contract. Plaintiff further contends that the advertisement constituted a memorandum in writing which satisfied the requirements of the Statute of Frauds.

It is elementary that in order to form a contract there must be an offer and an acceptance. A contract requires the mutual assent of the parties . . .

The precise issue of whether a newspaper advertisement constitutes an offer which can be accepted to form a contract or whether such an advertisement is merely an invitation to make an offer, has not been determined by the Illinois courts. Most jurisdictions which have dealt with the issue have considered such an advertisement as a mere invitation to make an offer, unless the circumstances indicate otherwise. 157 ALR 744 (1945). As was stated in Corbin on Contracts, § 25 (1963):

"It is quite possible to make a definite and operative offer to buy or to sell goods by advertisement, in a newspaper, by a handbill, or on a placard in a store window. It is not customary to do this, however; and the presumption is the other way. Neither the advertiser nor the reader of his notice understands that the latter is empowered to close the deal without further expression by the former. Such advertisements are understood to be mere requests to consider and examine and negotiate; and no one can reasonably regard them otherwise unless the circumstances are exceptional and the words used are very plain and clear."

In *Craft v. Elder & Johnston Co.*, 38 N.E.2d 416 (Oh. App. 1941), defendant advertised in a local newspaper that a sewing machine was for sale at a stated price. Plaintiff visited the store, attempted to purchase the sewing machine at that price, but defendant refused. In holding that the newspaper advertisement did not constitute a binding offer, the court held that an ordinary newspaper advertisement was merely an offer to negotiate. In *Ehrlich v. Willis Music Co. (Ohio App)*, 113 NE 2d 252 (1952), defendant advertised in a newspaper that a television set was for sale at a mistaken price. The actual price was ten times the advertised price. The court found that no offer had been made, but rather an invitation to patronize defendant's store. The court also held that defendant should have known that the price was a mistake. In *Lovett v. Frederick Loeser & Co.*, 124 Misc 81, 207 NYS 753 (1924), a newspaper advertisement offering radios for sale at 25% to 50% reductions was held to be an invitation to make an offer. Accord, *People v. Gimbel Bros.*, 202 Misc 229, 115 NYS2d 857 (1952).

We find that in the absence of special circumstances, a newspaper advertisement which contains an erroneous purchase price through no fault of the defendant advertiser and which contains no other terms, is not an offer which can be accepted so as to form a contract. We hold that such an advertisement amounts only to an invitation to make an offer. It seems apparent to us in the instant case, that there was no meeting of the minds nor the required mutual assent by the two parties to a precise proposition. There was no reference to several material matters relating to the purchase of an automobile, such as equipment to be furnished or warranties to be offered by defendant. Indeed the terms were so incomplete and so indefinite that they could not be regarded as a valid offer.

In *Lefkowitz v. Great Minneapolis Surplus Store*, 251 Minn 188, 86 NW2d 689 (1957) defendant advertised a fur stole worth $ 139.50 for sale at a price of $ 1.00, but refused to sell it to plaintiff. In affirming the judgment for plaintiff, the court found that the advertisement constituted a valid offer and, upon acceptance by plaintiff, a binding contract. However in that case, unlike the instant case, there was no error in the advertisement, but rather, defendant deliberately used misleading advertising. And in Lefkowitz, the court held that whether an advertisement was an offer or an invitation to make an offer depended upon the intention of the parties and the surrounding circumstances.

In *Johnson v. Capital City Ford Co.* (La App), 85 So2d 75 (1955), defendant advertised that anyone who purchased a 1954 automobile could exchange it for a 1955 model at no additional cost. Plaintiff purchased a 1954 automobile and subsequently attempted to exchange it for a 1955 model, but was refused by defendant. The court held that the advertisement was an offer, the acceptance of which created a contract. However, in that case, the advertisement required the performance of an act by plaintiff, and in purchasing the 1954 automobile, plaintiff performed that act. In the case at bar, the advertisement did not call for any performance by plaintiff, and we conclude that it did not amount to an offer . . .

The judgment of the Circuit Court is affirmed.

Guided Reading Questions

1. What happened in this case? The case detailed that the advertisement was an invitation for an offer. Why? Was there an intent to contract? Why is it significant that the terms were not definite, certain, and identifiable? These are the questions that you must ask when determining if the advertisement is an offer or an invitation for an offer. In this case, the terms were not certain, definite, and identifiable. Additionally, there was no meeting of the minds. There was an erroneous purchase price in the advertisement, which was not the fault of the offeror, the car seller. The newspaper made the mistake concerning the price. The advertisement lacked any additional terms that are essential, such as terms concerning equipment and warranties.

■ TERMS

The terms of the contract must be definite, certain, and identifiable. Regarding certainty in the terms of the offer, the Restatement (Second) of Contracts § 33 states:

(1) *Even though a manifestation of intention is intended to be understood as an offer, it cannot be accepted so as to form a contract unless the terms of the contract are reasonably certain.*

(2) *The terms of a contract are reasonably certain if they provide a basis for determining the existence of a breach and for giving an appropriate remedy.*

(3) *The fact that one or more terms of a proposed bargain are left open or uncertain may show that a manifestation of intention is not intended to be understood as an offer or as an acceptance.*

Subsection (2) is important for the terms let the parties know what they expect to receive under the agreement. If they do not receive what they contracted for, then they can point to the terms to show that the contract was not performed as agreed, was breached, and then the court can attempt to fashion a **remedy** where the nonperforming party must either perform or put the injured party in the position he or she would have been in if the contract had been performed as agreed.

Remedy
way to fix a wrong or to enforce a right.

Additionally, an offer may, but is not required to, stipulate the form of the acceptance that the offer requires. Chapter 3 provides more detail on how a party may accept an offer.

■ SPECIAL TYPES OF OFFERS

Irrevocable Offers

Generally, an offer can be revoked, at any time, by the offeror unless it is an irrevocable offer agreed to in an option contract or when the promisee will be harmed greatly by relying on the offeror's promise. An example of a situation where the party will be greatly harmed when relying on the offer is the Tatum and Brown example that follows.

Example

Mr. Brown offers Mr. Tatum $300 per head of cattle and acceptance is indicated by Tatum driving the cattle 400 miles to the processing plant, and the cattle arrive. Mr. Tatum sells all of his cattle to Mr. Brown to process into steaks with the expectation that Brown will pay $300 per head of cattle. Tatum delivers the cattle to Brown. At this point, Tatum expects to be paid. Tatum drove the cattle 400 miles to the processing plant. Brown knew that Tatum would have to drive the cattle 400 miles when making the offer. At this point Tatum expects to be paid. Tatum and Brown do not have to overtly state that they intend to contract here. Their actions indicate that they intend to contract. Tatum will be greatly harmed if Brown revokes the offer after Tatum drives the cattle to the processing plant.

Option Contracts

The right to exercise an option contract is an irrevocable offer for a certain time period. It is a new and separate contract, formed after the initial contract, in which the parties agree to keep an offer open. An option is an agreement that gives someone the right to do something in the future during a fixed period of time. The offeror does not have the power to revoke the offer during the time period stated in the option agreement.

Example

Michael purchased season tickets for the Cubs baseball team in Chicago to see all of the home games. Under the contract for season tickets Michael paid $1,200 for two seats for all of the home games. The purchase of the season tickets is a contract that Michael entered into with the Cubs. At the end of the season, the Cubs won a great number of games and will be in the playoffs. As a season ticket holder, Michael receives notice that he has the option to purchase two tickets for the playoff games prior to sale to the public. The option to purchase the playoff tickets is for one week. Michael receives a form that he must sign and mail back to the Cubs' ticket office. The form states that Michael must pay the Cubs $15.00 for a one-week option, from October 1–8, for the right to purchase playoff tickets before the tickets are offered for sale to the general public. This means that the Cubs keep open the offer to sell Michael the playoff tickets for one week, but Michael can decide not to exercise the option by not purchasing the playoff tickets. The Cubs can not revoke Michael's right to purchase the playoff tickets during this one week. This is a separate contract from the season tickets.

Example

Mr. Green offers to sell his produce company, Bloom Produce, for $600,000 to Mr. Brown. Mr. Brown is not ready to buy the company right now. Mr. Brown needs to sell his plant nursery first. Mr. Brown pays Mr. Green $1,000 for Green's promise to keep the offer of the sale of the produce company open for one month, or to not revoke the offer for one month. This agreement to keep the offer of the sale of the company, Bloom Produce at $600,000, open for one month, in exchange for $1,000, is the option contract. This is a separate agreement from the offer to sell Bloom Produce for $600,000. Mr. Green cannot revoke the option to let Mr. Brown purchase Bloom Produce for $600,000 during this time period.

An option contract is frequently used in real estate agreements. For example: Mr. Young paid $500 for the seller's promise to not revoke Mr. Young's right of first refusal for the purchase of a specific parcel of real estate. Young purchased the option from the owner of the property, Mr. Zack, to have the right of first refusal for the purchase of a parcel of property in Zion, Illinois. This means that when Mr. Zack lists the property for sale, Mr. Young has the opportunity to purchase the property before any other purchaser is considered. The parties agreed that the option period is one month. Mr. Young is not required to purchase the property; he does not have to exercise his option to purchase the property, but has the option to do so prior to any other party. The offer must be **tendered** to Mr. Young first, during the one-month period, and only after Mr. Young refuses the offer can Mr. Zack tender the offer to other buyers. Since Zack and Young agreed to this option and Young paid Zack $500 in consideration for this option, Zack cannot **rescind** the option and, consequently, Zack cannot revoke the offer to sell the property to Young first.

Tender
to convey in a business transaction

Rescind
to revoke or to invalidate.

■ AUCTIONS

Auctions are an example of an invitation for an offer where an item of real or personal property, or even a service, is offered but the price is subject to bidding. eBay is a popular auction site. There are two types of auctions, even on eBay. "Without reserve" is one type of auction where the bidders set the price by bidding. "With reserve" is when the seller, or auctioneer, sets the minimum price at which the item will be sold. When an item, or a service, is sold with reserve, the auctioneer will not sell the item below a certain price. If the minimum price is not met in an auction with reserve, then the auctioneer is not required to sell the item. The Restatement (Second) of Contracts provides the following regarding auctions:

§ 28 Auctions

(1) *At an auction, unless a contrary intention is manifested,*
    (a) *the auctioneer invites offers from successive bidders which he may accept or reject;*
    (b) *when goods are put up without reserve, the auctioneer makes an offer to sell at any price bid by the highest bidder, and after the auctioneer calls for bids the goods cannot be withdrawn unless no bid is made within a reasonable time;*
    (c) *whether or not the auction is without reserve, a bidder may withdraw his bid until the auctioneer's announcement of completion of the sale, but a bidder's retraction does not revive any previous bid.*
(2) *Unless a contrary intention is manifested, bids at an auction embody terms made known by advertisement, posting or other publication of which bidders are or should be aware, as modified by any announcement made by the auctioneer when the goods are put up.*

■ TERMINATION OF OFFER

Unless otherwise agreed in an option contract where the offer is irrevocable, or when terminating the offer will cause the offeree to suffer great harm (see earlier Tatum/Brown example), an offer may be terminated by the offeror at any time prior to acceptance. Remember that generally the offeror is the master of the offer. Sometimes, an offer will clearly state that the offer remains open until a certain date or time. After the set date or time, as stated in the offer, the offer is said to have lapsed, or no longer exists. After the offer lapses, the offer is no longer available.

Also, an offer no longer exists if it is rejected by the offeree. In addition, when the offeree replies with a different set of terms, a counteroffer is created. An offeree's power of acceptance and when the power of acceptance can be terminated are addressed in Chapter 3.

An offer creates the power in the offeree, by accepting the offer and its terms, to create a contract. The Restatement (Second) of Contracts § 35 indicates that an offer can not be accepted after it is terminated. Once an offer is terminated, a contract cannot be formed. However, an offer is not required to be accepted.

The offer no longer exists when the offer is rejected, or when the offeree replies with new terms (a counteroffer.) Also, the offer ends when the time frame, as stated in the offer, to keep it open expires. This is when the offer lapses. The offer is also terminated when the offeror decides to revoke the offer. The offer may also be terminated upon the offeree's or offeror's death or incapacity to perform. Additionally, an offer can cease to exist if it is based on the occurrence of a condition and that condition no longer exists.

Example

Farmer Murdoch grows crops in most years. Farmer Murdoch offers to hire John Simons to pick crops during the fall of 2010. Farmer Murdoch tells Simons that the offer to pick crops will end, or expire, on October 1, 2010. Simons does not respond to the offer. Farmer Murdoch's offer lapsed on October 2 and is extinguished. If Farmer Murdoch did not plant any crops in 2010 and there is nothing to harvest, the offer is terminated because it was based on the occurrence of a condition (crops to harvest) that did not occur.

■ MISTAKE IN TERMS IN THE OFFER

Generally, a contract cannot be rescinded by either party due to a mistake, particularly if the mistake is not **material**. However, if the mistake is material (meaning that the mistake involves a necessary term or component of the agreement), that is, an essential component of the offer, then there will be no meeting of the minds on the terms of the contract. If there is no meeting of the minds, then a valid contract is not formed. When a party to a contract does not interpret the terms correctly, this mistake does not provide grounds to rescind the contract. However, if there is a mistake as to price in the offer and the contract is made based on the mistaken price, the offeror must show or demonstrate that the agreed upon price is so **detrimental** to his or her business that it would be unfair to require the performance. In the alternative, when a party accepts an offer and fulfills the terms, the offeror cannot withdraw the offer, after acceptance and performance, due to a mistake. This is illustrated in the *Chang* decision in Chapter 1, where the court stated that the bank must communicate the withdrawal of the offer prior to acceptance. The bank failed to inform the Changs that it withdrew the offer, and that the newspaper ad allegedly had a typographical error, until after the bank had used the Changs' $14,000 for over three years. Even though the bank allegedly made a mistake, the offer could not be withdrawn at this point.

Material
very important. Goes to the essence or the subject of the offer. Terms in a contract are material if they concern the essence of the agreement.

Detrimental
causing great harm.

Example

A car dealer presents a contract for the purchase of a Volvo S70, 2007 model, to a customer. The customer knows that the sticker price for the vehicle is roughly $40,000. The customer negotiated the price with the sales manager and arrived, by mutual agreement, at $38,997. The car dealer presents the contract containing the offer to sell the car to the buyer. The typist stated the price for the vehicle as $3899 in the sales contract. The car dealer can demonstrate that this mistake is so detrimental to his business that it would be unfair to require performance.

Checkpoint

1. What are the necessary components of an offer?
2. What is the paralegal's role in the offer?
3. Can an offer be terminated? How?
4. Mrs. Stevens asks Mr. Robinson, of Robinson Appliance Repair, to come to her home on Thursday to provide an estimate to fix her oven. After inspecting the oven at no charge, Mr. Robinson states that he can fix the oven for $94 service call charge, $120 per hour labor for three hours of labor, plus $219 for parts. He can arrive at 10 A.M. the following Monday to make the repairs. Is this an offer? Why or why not?
5. Mrs. Stone says that she will bring brownies to the Ladies' Auxiliary Luncheon in June. The Auxiliary has two luncheons each month. Is this an offer? Why or why not?
6. The local department store mails a flyer that states: "Our Biggest Sale on Furniture Ever! Almost All Furniture is 20% Off!" Is this an offer? Why or why not?

CASE ILLUSTRATION

Guided Reading Pointers

The parties in the case are First Capital, the company that issued the life insurance policy that is being addressed by the court, and Omnicor, the company that Mr. Newell was president of. Since Mr. Newell was company president, Omnicor purchased life insurance for him. The offer here was the life insurance policy. The insurer's letter as to the continuation of coverage indicated that the offer would lapse by a certain date, January 26, 1992. Paying the premiums at a specific time, as stated in the letter, indicated acceptance. Omnicor, on behalf of Mr. Newell, only sent a check for $1,000, which was insufficient to prevent the policy from lapsing. First Capital Insurance sent Omnicor and Mr. Newell a letter stating the insurance reinstatement procedures and returned the check. Paying the premiums is paying for a continuing right to be insured. The terms to comply with the offer were the premiums to be paid by a specific date and were a specific amount of money. The offer of life insurance coverage lapsed (meaning that the coverage is no longer valid) due to nonpayment of the premiums by Omnicor. However, by mistake the life insurance company sent a letter to Omnicor stating that although the premiums were late, Newell was in a grace period and could reinstate the life insurance policy if he paid the premiums by a certain date. Prior to the letter sent in error, there were notices that the premiums were late and that coverage would be suspended. Also, Omnicor and Newell obtained life insurance from another company due to the notice, earlier, that the coverage was forfeited. Then Omnicor and Mr. Newell received a notice that Newell's life insurance policy was in a grace period and they had until August 3. When

Omnicor's insurance agent phoned First Capital, on July 16, to state that they were accepting the offer for maintaining Mr. Newell's coverage, the life insurance company representative realized that there was an error. On July 17, First Capital's representative alerted Omnicor's insurance agent that the policy had lapsed in January and that Mr. Newell would have to be reinstated. First Capital also returned the check received from Omnicor, on July 23, for there was no policy in force. The court supported the holding that the policy was not reinstated by the letter sent in error, for this was a mistake, and due to this mistake, that there was no meeting of the minds.

> *In re First Capital Life Insurance Company in Liquidation. Charles Quackenbush, as Insurance Commissioner, etc., Plaintiff and Respondent, v. Omnicor, Inc., et al., Defendants and Appellants*

Court of Appeal of California, Second Appellate District, Division Seven

34 Cal. App. 4th 1283

May 11, 1995, Decided

This is an appeal from a judgment denying a claim for life insurance benefits from a company under conservatorship. We affirm.

FACTS AND PROCEEDINGS BELOW

In January 1989, First Capital Life Insurance Company (hereafter First Capital) issued a $ 500,000 policy on the life of Howard Newell, the president of Omnicor, Inc. The policy entered a late period November 26, 1991, for nonpayment of the required premium. First Capital sent an initial late notice to Omnicor in November 1991. A second late notice was sent in December 1991 advising Omnicor the policy would lapse on January 26, 1992, if the premium was not paid by that date.

Omnicor responded to the notices by sending a check for $ 1,000 to First Capital. This amount was insufficient to prevent the policy from lapsing. The check was returned by First Capital. On January 7, 1992, First Capital sent a letter to Omnicor and Mr. Newell advising them of the minimum payment required, the reinstatement procedures and the payment deadline of January 26, 1992.

In the meantime, Omnicor and Mr. Newell applied for a replacement policy from Southland Life Insurance Company on January 24, 1992. Two days later, January 26, 1992, the First Capital policy lapsed for nonpayment of premiums. On January 28, 1992, First Capital sent a notice informing Omnicor and Mr. Newell of the lapse.

In April 1992, Mr. Newell was diagnosed with lung cancer.

Omnicor received a late notice dated July 6, 1992, from First Capital stating the policy on Mr. Newell was in a grace period which would end unless the premium stated was received from Omnicor prior to August 3, 1992.

Omnicor telephoned its insurance agent, Jerry Lyke, on July 16, 1992, to inquire about the First Capital policy and inform him it was accepting First Capital's offer to maintain coverage for Mr. Newell. Omnicor also advised

Mr. Lyke it was sending a check in response to the notice. Mr. Lyke telephoned First Capital and questioned a hotline representative about the late notice. Immediately, the representative realized a discrepancy in the notice and ordered the file referred to her supervisor.

The next day, July 17, 1992, First Capital's customer service representative telephoned Mr. Lyke. She informed him the First Capital policy had lapsed in January 1992 and Mr. Newell would have to complete the reinstatement form to obtain coverage by First Capital. Among other things, this would require Mr. Newell to provide proof of insurability. Mr. Lyke advised Mr. Newell and Omnicor of the reinstatement procedures after obtaining this information from First Capital.

First Capital received Omnicor's premium payment on July 23, 1992. Within a week, First Capital returned the payment to Omnicor and advised it the late notice was sent in error, there was no policy in force and the policy could only be reinstated through normal reinstatement procedures previously explained.

Mr. Newell died on July 31, 1992. First Capital was informed of Mr. Newell's death by a letter dated August 7, 1992, which also resubmitted the premium initially sent July 16, 1992. On August 25, 1992, First Capital again informed Omnicor and Mrs. Newell the premium would not be accepted for the reasons previously given.

On May 14, 1991, the Insurance Commissioner of the State of California (hereafter Commissioner) was appointed as conservator of First Capital. In December 1992, Omnicor and Mrs. Newell submitted official forms for death benefits with supporting documentation to the Commissioner pursuant to the claim procedures established by the Los Angeles County Superior Court.

The Commissioner rejected the claim on October 8, 1993. The trial court affirmed the Commissioner's rejection of the claim on June 23, 1994.

DISCUSSION

. . . The issue is whether Mr. Newell's life insurance policy with First Capital was in force when he died July 31, 1992. This is a factual question. Thus, great deference will be given to both the Commissioner's and the trial court's findings.

II. *The Late Notice Sent July 6, 1992, Was an Offer.*

Omnicor argues the late notice sent July 6, 1992, by its terms constitutes an offer to enter into a contract for life insurance. An offer is a " 'manifestation of willingness to enter into a bargain, so made as to justify another person in understanding that his assent to that bargain is invited and will conclude it.' " (*Leaseway Distribution v. Admin. Services* (1988) 49 Ohio App.3d 99 [550 N.E.2d 955, 961], citing Rest.2d Contracts, § 24.) n2

The trier of fact must determine "whether a reasonable person would necessarily assume . . . a willingness to enter into contract." (*Leaseway Distribution v. Admin. Services, supra,* 550 N.E.2d at p. 961.) It could appear to a reasonable person First Capital was offering continued insurance coverage if the premium was paid by the specified lapse date. The notice contains a manifestation of willingness to continue coverage if Omnicor sent the required payment. It informs the reader of the notice of the offer and the amount needed to accept. Furthermore, it expresses the mode of acceptance. Thus, the late notice sent July 6, 1992, may be viewed as an offer to continue a contract with First Capital for life insurance.

III. *Omnicor Accepted the Offer to Enter Into a Life Insurance Contract With First Capital.*

Acceptance is the "manifestation of assent to the terms thereof made by the offeree in a manner invited or required by the offer." (Rest.2d Contracts, § 50.) Omnicor contends sending the premium on July 16, 1992, in response to the offer in the July 6, 1992, late notice constituted acceptance of the First Capital offer for continued life insurance coverage.

Omnicor accepted the offer in the manner invited. It sent the amount required by the late notice by the date required. Thus, there was acceptance of the offer.

IV. *Despite the Offer and Acceptance, There Was No Enforceable Contract Because There Was No Meeting of the Minds Between Omnicor and First Capital.*

(2) A meeting of the minds is essential to the formation of a valid contract. (1 Corbin on Contracts (1963 ed.) § 107, p. 478.) If there is no meeting of the minds due to the offeror's mistake, a court will not find a contract was formed unless the offeror's conduct was such that the other party would not be misled by the mistake. If the proponent of the contract had reason to know of the mistake, the mistaken party can avoid the contract. (Rest.2d Contracts, § 153, com. e.) **(3)** As we explain below, although Omnicor accepted the offer in the manner invited, given the knowledge Omnicor possessed it could not reasonably have believed First Capital intended an offer.

As previously noted, a late notice was sent by First Capital July 6, 1992. From the terms of the notice, it appeared as if the policy was still in force and would remain in force until the end of the grace period, August 3, 1992. However, Omnicor received notice of the pending lapse of the policy twice in late 1991 and again in January 1992. Those notices informed Omnicor the policy would lapse for nonpayment January 26, 1992. First Capital also informed Omnicor and Mr. Newell of the procedures required for reinstatement after the policy lapsed. A final lapse notice was sent January 28, 1992, after the policy was forfeited for nonpayment of the premium. At no time did Omnicor rely on the First Capital coverage. In fact, Omnicor and Mr. Newell purchased a replacement policy in expectation of the impending lapse of the First Capital coverage.

Omnicor had many reasons to know the July 1992 notice was a mistake. Upon receipt of the July 6th notice Omnicor contacted its agent, Mr. Lyke, to inquire about the notice and inform him of its acceptance. On July 16, 1992, Mr. Lyke made further inquiries regarding the offer to continue the life insurance policy for Mr. Newell.

First Capital responded July 17, 1992, to the inquiries stating the policy had previously lapsed and required reinstatement conforming to the required procedures. This information was relayed to Omnicor. At no time did Omnicor or Mr. Newell attempt to comply with the required reinstatement procedures explained by both the January 26th notice and by Mr. Lyke.

The facts known by Omnicor and Mr. Newell provided them abundant reason to believe the July 6th late notice was sent by error. Thus, the trial court correctly concluded there was no meeting of the minds and no contract formed by the parties.

V. *The Policy Purchased by Omnicor and Mr. Newell in 1989 Was Forfeited for Nonpayment of Premiums in January 1992.*

(4) Omnicor argues First Capital's conduct constituted a waiver of its right to declare a forfeiture of the policy. Courts are liberal in construing transactions in favor of avoidance of a forfeiture. (*Miraldi v. Life Ins. Co. of Va.* (1971) 48 Ohio App.2d 278 [356 N.E.2d 1234, 1236].) Insurance policies are strictly construed against the insurer who wrote the provisions which bind the parties. In the case of a forfeiture clause, the terms must be clear and unambiguous to be valid. (*Ibid.*)

The policy in the present case states: "If you do not pay, by the end of the grace period, enough premium (or repay enough loan) to cover the monthly deductions for the grace period plus the month following the grace period, this policy will end."

Such language leaves no room for misunderstanding by the insured or the insurer. The insured had the opportunity to read and understand the language in the policy before purchasing the policy. The purchase of the policy indicates the insured agrees to be bound by the terms in the policy, including the forfeiture clause. (See *Miraldi v. Life Ins. Co. of Va.*, *supra*, 365 N.E.2d at p. 1236.)

The First Capital policy lapsed for nonpayment in January 1992. First Capital was under no contractual obligation or legal requirement to accept a premium payment subsequent to the time for payment specified in the policy. (*Gwinn v. John Hancock Mut. Life Ins. Co.* (1944) 142 Ohio St. 510 [53 N.E.2d 515, 520].) Payment after the policy lapsed could not reinstate the policy without compliance with the reinstatement procedures.

The First Capital policy stated it could only be reinstated upon:

"written request within five years after the end of the grace period and before the maturity date;

"satisfactory proof that the insured is insurable at the original underwriting class and rating factor;

"payment of enough premium or repayment of enough loan to meet the monthly deductions for the grace period and for the month during which reinstatement occurs and for one subsequent month, plus, if lapse occurred prior to the end of the policy year 3 and reinstatement is to occur after the end of policy year 3, an additional amount equal to the surrender charge as of the reinstatement date."

Omnicor sent in the required payment to cover the premium, but did not submit the required proof of insurability.

Besides having to pay the interest on the premium past due, Omnicor would have to provide proof of Newell's insurability. In July 1992 Omnicor would have been unable to provide such proof because earlier that year Mr. Newell was diagnosed with lung cancer. It would have been impossible for Omnicor to re-instate the policy without a waiver of the reinstatement requirements.

. . . The facts in the present case show the policy lapsed in January for nonpayment of premiums. Omnicor and Mr. Newell obtained a replacement policy and did not believe the First Capital policy to be in force. The July 6th notice said the policy would lapse and no longer in force if the premium was not received by August 3, 1992. This notice was in conflict with the No-vember, December, and January notices, as well as the policy itself. The pol-icy stated it would lapse 61 days after the monthly processing date if the payment was not received in that time. There is no ambiguity as to when coverage was forfeited. (See *Reddick v. Globe Life Ins. and Acc. Ins. Co.* (Fla. 1992) 596 [*1291] So.2d 435, 437.) Under these facts, there was no waiver of the reinstatement procedures for Mr. Newell's policy . . .

. . .Thus, the court found no policy was in force at the time of the death.

Omnicor and Mr. Newell would have been required to pay both the last premium with the interest, as well as the next amount due in order to rein-state the policy. To permit payment of a smaller sum does not constitute an admission the policy was still in force in the face of the express statement in the policy and in the reinstatement procedure. (*Laustrup v. Bankers Life Co,* *supra*, 196 S.W.2d at p. 264.)

Omnicor and Mrs. Newell contend the July 6th notice was a waiver of for-feiture because the premium was increased . . . However, as we have previously held, the July 6th notice in the present case was not intended and could not be reasonably interpreted by plaintiffs as an offer to continue the existing policy.

Here, the only act Omnicor claims to constitute a waiver of forfeiture is the July 6th late notice. The late notice is essentially the same as a premium notice. Both inform the insured a payment is required to continue the cov-erage provided by the policy in question. However, the mere sending of a no-tice of the next premium due does not constitute such an act to waive forfeiture . . . Thus, without other affirmative action by First Capital, there was no waiver of the forfeiture of Mr. Newell's life insurance policy.

Though Omnicor and Mrs. Newell issued a check for the amount stated in the July 6th notice, First Capital promptly returned the payment and ex-plained again in the July 30th letter the policy was no longer in force and re-quired reinstatement. The communication sent to Omnicor was a routine notice. There was no indication First Capital intended to waive the previous forfeiture for nonpayment. Therefore, there was no waiver of the reinstate-ment procedures and no policy in force at the time of Mr. Newell's death.

DISPOSITION

The judgment is affirmed.

Guided Reading Questions

1. Who is the offeror in the case?
2. What is the offer in dispute?
3. Why did the original offer, the initial life insurance policy, lapse?

What a Paralegal Needs to Know about Offers

An offer requires:

1. An intent to enter into a contract
2. Set terms. The terms should be definite, certain, and identifiable. Remember that the most important terms include: time, price, quantity, duration, and condition.
3. Date when the offer is extinguished, or when the offer lapses or expires.
4. Identification of party from whom acceptance is required, or party to whom offer is directed.

The Paralegal's Role in the Offer

The paralegal must be aware of the specific terms of the offer. This is important when the offeree accepts the offer and the supervising attorney requests that the paralegal check that the offeree accepts the same terms. Also, the paralegal must be vigilant about the date when the offer expires or lapses. The paralegal should remind the attorney about the date that the offer expires. Finally, if the firm represents the offeror and the offer is to be presented to a particular party, then the paralegal must obtain accurate address information so that it may be tendered properly.

■ THE U.C.C. AND OFFERS

When an Offer Is Made by a Merchant to Another Merchant

Course of dealing
in a business transaction, or in a contract between merchants, the parties' prior conduct is used to understand the parties' conduct in the current exchange or transaction.

The Uniform Commercial Code (U.C.C.) permits an offer to be tendered and a contract to be formed even if all of the terms are not absolutely definite as long as the terms are reasonably definite and the parties intended to enter into a contract. Sometimes the merchants' **course of dealing** or custom in their trade or business permits that the terms in the contract are not required to be definite and certain. This applies to contracts between merchants. The terms must be definite enough so that the court can interpret them and fashion a remedy if the contract is breached. This is addressed in U.C.C. 2–204 (3), which states: "Even though one or more terms are left open a contract for sale does not fail for indefiniteness if the parties have intended to make a contract and there is a reasonably certain basis for giving an appropriate remedy." Additionally, the U.C.C. has specific provisions that assist in filling in the gaps created by the missing terms. These provisions are called "gap fillers." The U.C.C. sections provide guidance on fashioning the following types of terms: price, warranties, timing, and place of delivery.

CHAPTER SUMMARY

This chapter provided guidance on identifying a valid offer. A valid offer is definite and certain. The terms must be identifiable. Generally, an offeror's intent to enter into a contract and conveying that intent with specific terms constitutes a valid offer. Examples of specific terms are price, time, quantity, value, and specific goods. Additionally, an offeror must intend to make an offer and to enter into an agreement with another party. Furthermore, an offer can stipulate that the offer may expire at a certain time in the future. An offeror may cancel the offer. The offer may be revoked upon the offeror's or the offeree's death or incapacity.

The Offer

Requirements for an Offer	Intent to enter into a contract; meeting of the minds; definite, certain and identifiable terms
Preliminary Negotiations	Lack of intent to enter into a contract Often lack definite and certain terms Can be in the form of an advertisement
Special Types of Offers	Irrevocable offers Option contracts Auctions, with reserve and without reserve
Termination of an Offeree's Power to Accept the Offer	Rejection Counteroffer Lapse of time Revocation by offeror Incapacity or death of the offeror or the offeree
U.C.C. and Offers	Between merchants, terms need only be reasonably definite, so that the court can create a remedy if necessary. The parties must intend to enter into a contract

REVIEW QUESTIONS

1. Does an offer require the offeror's intent to contract?
2. What terms are necessary for a valid offer?
3. Does a contract between merchants require definite and certain terms?
4. Provide an example of an irrevocable offer.
5. What is an example of a special circumstance regarding an offer?
6. What does a paralegal need to know about offers?
7. List two ways that an offer can lapse.
8. How can an offer be terminated?
9. What is a preliminary negotiation?
10. In general, is an advertisement an offer or an invitation for an offer?

SKILL-BUILDING APPLICATION EXERCISE

Reread the agreement in this chapter between Midwest Nurseries and Mr. Banks.

What are the terms of the offer in the Midwest Nurseries proposal? Are they definite, certain, and identifiable? After reading the offer letter carefully, do you think it indicates an intent to contract?

SIMULATED LAW OFFICE ASSIGNMENT

The attorney you work for received the following form. The firm's client lives in Idaho and has water rights on his property. Water rights are the legal right to use the water, from a natural source such as a stream or river, that is on an individual's property, for another purpose, such as irrigation or generating power, during a specific time frame. The client is wondering if he fills out this form and returns it, is it an offer for the sale of his water rights or is it an invitation for an offer? Do you think further negotiation between the parties must occur before a contract is formed, or not?

Please write a two- or three-paragraph memo to the supervising attorney outlining your reasons and conclusions regarding whether further negotiations are needed to form a contract, your assessment of the form, and any additional information that the client will need to provide.

STATE OF IDAHO DEPARTMENT OF WATER RESOURCES APPLICATION TO SELL OR LEASE A WATER RIGHT TO THE WATER SUPPLY BANK

Name of Seller/Lessor _____ Phone _____

Post office address _____

1. DESCRIPTION OF WATER RIGHT:

Right evidenced by:

a. Decree No. _____ Decreed to _____
(Name)

in case of _____ vs _____

dated _____ in _____ county of _____
(Name of court)

b. License No. _____ issued by the Idaho Department of
Water Resources.

c. Permit No. _____ issued by the Idaho Department of
Water Resources.

2. DESCRIPTION OF PORTION OF RIGHT FOR SALE OR LEASE:
(If the entire right is for sale or lease, show "all" on line a. below and skip the remainder of part 2.)

a. Amount of water under right: _____ cubic feet per second &/or _____ acre-feet per annum

b. Point of diversion: _____ 1/4 of _____ 1/4
of Section _____ Township _____ Range
_____, B.M. in _____ County.

Additional points _____

c. Place of use:

TWP RGE SEC   N E   N W   S W   S E   Totals

NE

NW SW SE NE NW SW SE NE NW SW SE NE NW SW SE

If the right is for irrigation, show the number of acres for the part of the right to be put into the bank.

Total number of acres _____

3. ADDITIONAL INFORMATION ABOUT RIGHT, OR PORTION
   THEREOF, FOR SALE OR LEASE

a. Explain how the seller/lessor acquired the right, or portion thereof, and attach a copy of the deed to the land to which it is appurtenant or other evidence of ownership of the right. If the right is not recorded in the name of the seller/lessor, attach a copy of a change of ownership form as required by Section 42–248 or 42–1409(6), Idaho Code, together with required documentation.

_____

_____

_____

_____

_____

b. Describe the frequency of water use under the right, or portion thereof, during the past five (5) years of use. Attach watermaster records, pumping power bills, or other evidence to demonstrate that the right has not been lost through abandonment or forfeiture. (This information is not required if a partial decree has been issued on the right within the last 5 years).

_____

_____

_____

_____

_____

c. If the right is from a surface water source, describe the period of the year that water is typically available to satisfy the right.

_____

_____

_____

_____

_____

d. Describe any other water rights with the same purpose and place of use as the right, or portion thereof, offered for lease. Will the present place of use continue to receive water from any source? If so, describe.

_____
_____
_____
_____
_____

e. If the water right is a permit, describe the work accomplished toward developing the right.

_____
_____
_____
_____
_____

f. If the right to the use of the water or the use of the diversion works or irrigation system is represented by shares of stock in a company or corporation, or if such works or system is owned or managed by an irrigation district, a written consent of the sale or lease must be attached.

4. SALE/LEASE AGREEMENT
1. The water right, or portion thereof, described above is offered to the Idaho Water Resource Board:
_____ For sale;
_____ For lease for a period from _____ to
_____
(Day, month, year) (Day, month, year)
(The lease period may be shown as "indefinite", if the total duration of lease is unknown); or _____ As a gift to the state of Idaho.
2. Show the minimum payment acceptable to the Seller/Lessor. Include the method of determining the minimum payment. The minimum payment may be shown as the "current rental rate".

_____
_____

 hereby assert that the information contained in this application is true to the best of my knowledge, and that I have the authorities necessary to offer this right for sale or lease to the Idaho Water Resource Board.

The owner/lessor acknowledges the following:

1. Payment to the owner/lessor is contingent upon the sale or rental of the right from the bank.
2. While a right is in the bank, the owner of the right may not use the right even if the right is not rented.

3. A right accepted into the bank stays in the bank until the Board releases it or until the lease term expires.
4. While a water right is in the bank, forfeiture provisions are stayed.
5. Acceptance of a right into the bank does not, in itself, confirm the validity of the right or any elements of the water right.

_____

Date   Signature

DRAFTING EXERCISE

Your firm represents Mr. and Mrs. Hall. The Halls want to purchase a house from Mr. and Mrs. Royce. The parties agreed to the price of $400,000 for the sale of the home. The buyers are willing to provide $10,000 for earnest money. The date of the agreement is January 30, 2009. The buyers request possession of the property on March 30, 2009, and also wish to close on March 30, 2009. The house is located at 555 Main Street, Poughkeepsie, New York 11223.

Read the following offer for the purchase of real estate. The attorney started to fill in the form but did not have time to finish it. The attorney requests that you finish the form and make a list of any outstanding terms that must be provided.

REAL ESTATE OFFER

Dated January 30, 2010

The undersigned buyers, Mr. and Mrs. Hall, hereby make an offer to purchase from sellers, Mr. and Mrs. Royce, the Real Property situated in the County of Dutchess, State of New York including all improvements thereon, and legally described as follows: lot 12 North meridian Gage's addition at 555 Main Street, Poughkeepsie, New York, together with the personal property described below in Paragraph 13.

Covenants

FIRST: The buyers herewith make an earnest money deposit with the sellers in the amount of 10,000 Dollars ($10,000), properly evidenced by a cashier's check to be applied to the full purchase price of Four Hundred Thousand Dollars ($400,000), which including the earnest money deposit, shall be paid as follows:

$10,000 by the above earnest money deposit
$390,000 at the close of escrow.

SECOND: The buyers shall take title of the property on _____
date _____

THIRD: It is hereby agreed that in the event said purchaser(s) fails to pay the balance of said purchase price, or otherwise fails to complete said purchase as herein provided, the seller(s) may either demand specific performance of this contract in the manner provided by law, or cancel this contract in the manner provided by law and retain the amount paid herein as liquidated and agreed damages.

FOURTH: Title to the premises shall be conveyed by Deed, subject to the conditions of this contract, and seller(s) shall furnish buyer(s), at buyer's(s') expense, a Standard Owner's Title Insurance Policy showing good and marketable title.

FIFTH: The purchaser(s) and seller(s) agree that if the title to the above property be defective, seller(s) or his (her) (their) agent, will be given 60 days from the date of this contract to perfect the same. If said title cannot be perfected within said time limit, the earnest money deposit herein receipted shall, upon the demand of the purchaser(s), be returned to the purchaser(s) and this contract cancelled. Purchaser(s) may, however, elect to accept title to said premises subject to any defects which are not so cured.

SIXTH: It is understood and agreed that the buyer(s) is(are) of legal age and that said property has been inspected by the buyer(s) or the buyer's(s') duly authorized agent: that the same is, and has been, purchased by the buyer(s) as the result of said inspection and not upon any representation made by the seller(s), or any selling agent, or any agent for the seller(s), and the buyer(s) hereby expressly waives any and all claims for damages occasioned by any representation made by any person whomsoever other than as contained in this agreement, and the seller(s) or his (her) (their) agent shall not be responsible or liable for any inducement, promise, representation, agreement, condition or stipulation not specifically set forth herein.

SEVENTH: This contract shall become binding only when executed by the purchaser(s) and by the seller(s), and shall be in force and effect from that date of such execution.

EIGHTH: Time is declared to be the essence of this contract.

NINTH: Upon the seller's(s') acceptance of this contract, the earnest money deposit shall be deposited with an Escrow Agent simultaneously with the execution of the Escrow Instructions to fulfill the terms of this contract. The execution of the Escrow Instructions shall not exceed a period of 10 days from the date of acceptance by the parties. Said Escrow Instructions shall not conflict with the terms and conditions hereof, and shall be prepared upon said Escrow Agent's ordinary form.

TENTH: The seller(s) agrees to deliver, or cause to be delivered to Escrow Agent, all instruments necessary and required to carry out and complete the terms of this contract.

ELEVENTH: The proration of Taxes, Insurance, Rents, Assessments, etc. shall be at the close of Escrow.

TWELFTH: Closing of Escrow shall be on or before _____, 20 _____, subject to any extensions set forth in the Escrow Instructions and the cancellation provisions thereof, with possession of the premises to be delivered to buyer(s) on or before _____, 20 _____.

THIRTEENTH: The following personal property is included with the premises _____

FOURTEENTH: The seller(s) acceptance of this contract must be made on or before _____, 20 _____, otherwise the buyer's(s') offer is withdrawn and voided, unless the buyer(s) agrees in writing to extend such acceptance date.
FIFTEENTH: (Other) _____
IN WITNESS WHEREOF, the buyer(s) executes this Contractual Offer to purchase the above described property on the terms and conditions herein stated, and acknowledges receipt of a copy of this contract and the attached addendum.

DEVELOPING CRITICAL THINKING SKILLS

Read the *First Capital Life Insurance* case, earlier in this chapter, carefully.

1. What was the mistake in the case?
2. Who made the mistake?
3. Was the late notice an offer to reinstate the policy?

PORTFOLIO ASSIGNMENT

An attorney at your firm gave you the following assignment. The firm's client is Gee Whiz Auto Dealers. Gee Whiz wants to place the following advertisement in the local paper. The ad is planned to read as follows:

Come one, Come all
3000 new Chevrolets for sale
Lowest Prices Around

Gee Whiz company president, Ron Olsen, wants to be sure that this is not an offer but an invitation to an offer designed to induce further negotiation, resulting in sales.

Base your answer on *O'Keefe v. Lee Calan Imports*, reprinted in this chapter, and your knowledge of the necessary components of an offer as opposed to an invitation for an offer. Please write three paragraphs, in memo form, to support your answer.

Acceptance

CHAPTER **3**

INTRODUCTION—ACCEPTANCE GENERALLY

Acceptance is an essential element in the formation of a contract. Acceptance may be in the form of a return promise or in the form of performance. Sometimes acceptance is indicated by nonperformance, though it is rarer. Examples of acceptance by not acting are: **restrictive covenants,** a type of **covenant** prohibiting particular types of activities or uses, agreements not to compete, and **forbearance agreements** where a lender agrees to **forbearance** from enforcing remedies against a borrower when the debt is not paid when due. In general, "[A]n acceptance must comply with the requirements of the offer as to the promise to be made or the performance to be rendered." Restatement (Second) of Contracts § 58.

According to the Restatement (Second) of Contracts § 17, a **bargain** requires "a manifestation of mutual assent to the exchange and a consideration." The mutual commitment to the exchange is indicated when the offer is tendered by the **offeror** and the **offeree** accepts by responding with a promise, as in a **bilateral** agreement, or by performing, as in a **unilateral** contract. The Restatement (Second) of Contracts § 22 notes that the "(1) The **manifestation** of **mutual assent** to an exchange ordinarily takes the form of an offer or proposal by one party followed by an acceptance by the other party or parties.

LEARNING OBJECTIVES

After studying this chapter, you will be able to:

1. Determine when an acceptance is valid.

2. Determine if the terms of the offer and acceptance correspond.

3. Identify if the contract is between merchants and decide if the Uniform Commercial Code is applicable.

4. Discuss the mirror image rule and the mail box rule.

5. List the terms of an offer so that a supervising attorney can formulate the acceptance to match the terms or so that the attorney can reply with a counteroffer.

Restrictive covenant
language in a deed restricting certain uses for land or language in a contract restricting certain types of activities.

Acceptance
agreeing to the terms offered.

Covenant
an agreement or promise made between two or more parties.

Forbearance agreement
the agreement to not enforce a right or the agreement to not do an act.

Forbearance
not enforcing a right or not doing an act.

Bargain
the agreement reached between the parties.

Offeror
the person or party extending or tendering the offer.

Offeree
the person or party receiving the offer.

Bilateral
both parties are bound where there is a promise for a promise.

Unilateral
generally means one sided. A unilateral contract occurs when there is a promise without a return promise and generally there is a promise for performance.

Manifestation
to be indicated as obvious.

Mutual assent
where both sides have a meeting of the minds, in which they agree on the intent and the terms.

Furthermore, according to the Restatement (Second) of Contracts § 50:

(1) Acceptance of an offer is a manifestation of assent to the terms thereof made by the offeree in a manner invited or required by the offer.
(2) Acceptance by performance requires that at least part of what the offer requests be performed or tendered and includes acceptance by performance which operates as a return promise.
(3) Acceptance by promise requires that the offeree complete every act essential to the making of the promise.

It is essential that the acceptance occur in the manner required by or stated in the offer. This is the crux of accepting an offer. Always remember that the offeror controls the offer. However, an offer can only be accepted by the party invited to enter into the agreement and whom the offeror invites to furnish the consideration. Restatement (Second) of Contracts § 52.

■ MIRROR IMAGE RULE

The acceptance must mirror the terms and bargain proposed in the offer. The return promise, or performance in the case of a unilateral contract, by the offeree must comply directly and exactly with the offer. The Restatement (Second) of Contracts § 58 states: "An acceptance must comply with the requirements of the offer as to the promise to be made or the performance to be rendered The terms which are accepted by the offeree must mirror the offer."

This is particularly true when the offeror prescribes the time, place, and method or manner of acceptance in the offer—the offeree must comply with the terms. If the time, place, and method or manner of acceptance are not included in the offer, then the offeree may substitute another method of acceptance. Restatement (Second) of Contracts § 60. Additionally, since the offeror is the master of the offer, the offeror can state the format for the acceptance. This means that if the offeror wants acceptance by performance, then this should be stated in the offer.

Generally, the terms of the acceptance must mirror the terms of the offer.

Example

ABC Corporation wants to conduct employee education programs on the topic of workplace tolerance. ABC plans on conducting the programs as part of a lunchtime series for employees. The programs will be held on the first Wednesday of the month, from 12:30 P.M. to 1:30 P.M. The first program will be held in January. ABC contacted Chris Spencer to talk about her new book *Race Relations in the Cubicle*. Chris Spencer offered to speak for $3,000 plus travel expenses on the first Wednesday in January, at ABC Corporation, from 12:30 P.M. to 1:30 P.M. Mary Jones, Director of Employee Training, felt that $1,500 would be a fair fee to adequately compensate Spencer and communicated this new fee to Spencer. Since Jones responded with a different price term, the terms of the offer did not mirror the terms of the acceptance. Consequently, a contract was not formed between the parties.

Objective Theory of Mutual Assent

Not only must both parties, the offeror and the offeree, intend to enter into a contract, but they both must agree as to the terms. There must be a meeting of the minds. The mutual assent focuses on the **material** terms of the offer and complying with those terms. For instance, there will not be an issue regarding mutual assent or the meeting of the minds if the acceptance is sent back to the offeror in a smaller envelope or with green ink instead of black ink, for these are not material terms (unless, of course, the offer directly states that a certain envelope size or ink color is required.)

Material
very important. Goes to the essence or the subject of the offer.
Terms in a contract are material if they concern the essence of the agreement.

▓ MAIL BOX RULE

Offers may be accepted by mail and via the Internet. Acceptance occurs when the acceptance is sent by the offeree, as long as the parties agreed that the mail or the Internet would be the means for indicating assent to the offer, and as long as the party accepting the agreement mails the assent in the time **stipulated** in the offer. The offer cannot be withdrawn at this point by the offeror.

Stipulate
to state precisely.

Generally, an offer may be revoked prior to acceptance. However, when an offer is revoked by mail, the revocation does not occur when mailed but if received by the offeree prior to the time the offeree mails his or her acceptance.

The Restatement (Second) of Contracts § 66 indicates that: "An acceptance sent by mail or otherwise from a distance is not operative when dispatched, unless it is properly addressed and such other precautions taken as are ordinarily observed to insure safe transmission of similar messages."

Checkpoint

1. Rich Hall received a requested proposal for new siding for his home. The proposal stated that ALL AROUND SIDING would reside the home with all-aluminum siding for $4,000, with work to commence on April 15, 2010. ALL AROUND SIDING requested that Hall mail back the signed proposal, in the enclosed addressed envelope, to accept the offer. Hall mailed his acceptance on March 29 and ALL AROUND SIDING received the acceptance on March 31. Do the parties have a contract under the mail box rule? Can ALL AROUND SIDING withdraw its offer after Hall has mailed his acceptance? When did Hall's acceptance occur?

2. Julie Vaughan contacted Mark Flowers to make the centerpieces for her firm's dinner dance on December 24. Mark Flowers sent a written proposal, by mail, to Vaughan with details for fifteen (15) arrangements, 12" in diameter, composed of red and white carnations. Mark Flowers requested that Vaughan telephone and indicate assent to the proposal by telephone. Mark Flowers clearly stated in the proposal that the telephone should be the way that Vaughan should indicate her acceptance, because the flowers are very perishable, and that she needed to provide a credit card by phone immediately. Vaughan mailed Mark Flowers a note indicating that she accepted the offer. Does the mail box rule apply here to Vaughan's acceptance?

CASE ILLUSTRATION

Guided Reading Pointers

Diggs v. El Royale Corporation is included in this chapter to show that a party may state in a contract how its termination may be communicated. Diggs accepted this offer on April 15, 1943, when he entered into the option agreement with El Royale. The plaintiff's option to purchase the apartment buildings was revoked on August 6, 1944. The trial court held for the defendant, that the option was cancelled according to the terms of the agreement. The agreement provided that the option could be cancelled by the posting of written notice by El Royale Corporation and that all of the rights of Diggs shall terminate upon the date of posting of that written notice. The plaintiff appealed this decision to have the court determine if the option agreement was terminated by posting written notice. The appellate court affirmed and held for the defendant that the option was revoked according to and in the manner stated in the terms of the agreement.

Jackson Diggs, Appellant, v. El Royale Corporation (a Corporation)
et al., Respondents Civ. No. 14666

Court of Appeal of California, Second Appellate District, Division Two 67 Cal. App. 2d 341

December 19, 1944

From a judgment in favor of defendants . . . plaintiff appeals.
The essential facts are these:

On April 15, 1943, plaintiff and defendant El Royale Corporation entered into an option agreement whereby plaintiff was given the sole and exclusive right and option to purchase upon certain terms the El Royale Apartments owned by defendant corporation. This agreement contained among others the following provision:

"This option may be exercised only by written instrument signed by the Optionee or his heirs, executors, administrators or assigns, and delivered to an officer of El Royale Corporation, or to Martin Goldman, attorney for said Corporation, personally, or deposited in the United States mail by registered letter, postage prepaid, addressed to Martin Goldman, Attorney, 9000 Sunset Boulevard, Los Angeles, California, on or before the 1st day of May, 1944, provided, however, that the Management Agreement under date of 15th April, 1943, entered into between the El Royale Corporation and Jackson Diggs whereby said Jackson Diggs is employed by the El Royale Corporation as exclusive agent to rent and manage the El Royale Apartments, shall not have theretofore been cancelled, it being the understanding of the parties hereto that the within option shall cease and determine upon the posting of written notice of intention to cancel the aforesaid Management Agreement by the El Royale Corporation, and that all rights of said Jackson Diggs, or his assigns, under this option shall cease upon the date of the posting of the aforesaid notice . . . ."

"...The consideration for this option is the exercise by the parties hereto of the Management Agreement herein above referred to."

On the same day they entered into a management agreement concerning El Royale Apartments [which] contained among others this provision:

"This agreement between parties may be cancelled at any time by either party upon thirty days (30 days) written notice of such intention. In event that Owner elects to cancel under this provision, from the time of posting of said notice all authority and powers of the Agent shall be subject to control by Owner and shall be exercised only with the approval of Fred E. Keeler, II, representing the Owner".

"2. The Agent Agrees:

"(A) To accept and does hereby accept the management of the said premises for the period and upon the terms herein provided, and agrees to furnish adequate and competent services necessary for the renting, operating and managing of said premises."

On August 7, 1943, plaintiff received through the mail a letter from defendant corporation reading thus:

"August 6, 1944
"Mr. Jackson Diggs
c/o El Royale Apartments
450 No. Rossmore
Los Angeles, California

"Dear Sir:

"This is to advise you that the El Royale Corporation does hereby notify you that it is their intention to cancel the Management Agreement between yourself and the El Royale Corporation respecting the El Royale Apartments, and you are further notified that in accordance with the terms of the Option Agreement executed in connection with the said Management Agreement, said Option does, by the posting of this notice, cease and determine, and that all of your rights, or the rights of [A]ssigns, under this option do, by the posting of this notice, thereby cease".

"Very truly yours,
EL ROYALE CORPORATION
By: Martin Goldman
Attorney for El Royale Corp."
MG/rb"

This is the sole question necessary for us to determine:

Was the option agreement terminated on August 7, 1943, by the letter from defendant corporation to plaintiff dated August 6, 1943, set forth supra?

This question must be answered in the affirmative. The agreement expressly provided that the "option shall cease and determine upon the posting of written notice of intention to cancel the aforesaid Management Agreement" by defendant corporation "and that all rights of" plaintiff "or his assigns, under this option shall cease upon the date of the posting of the aforesaid notice."

It is conceded that on August 7, 1943, plaintiff received from defendant corporation a letter through the mail reading in part as follows: "that it is" defendant corporation's "intention to cancel the Management Agreement between" plaintiff and defendant corporation respecting the El Royale Apartments, and plaintiff was notified "that in accordance with the terms of the Option Agreement, executed in connection with the said Management Agreement, said Option does, by the posting of this notice, cease and determine, and all of your rights, or the rights of assigns, under this option do, by the posting of this notice, thereby cease."

The foregoing notice meets the exact requirements of the provision of the option contract for its termination. There is not any ambiguity in the contract and there is not any basis for a different and other construction for this provision of the agreement.

"Posting" means to place in the post office or in a letter box.

2 Webster's New International Dictionary, second edition, (1939) page 1927, defines "post" as follows:

"To dispatch by the post or mail; to place in the post office or mail box for transmittal; to mail; as, to *post* a letter."

VII Oxford English Dictionary, (1933) page 1163, III-6b, defines "post" thus:

"To send through the post office; to put (a letter, etc.) into a post office or letter-box for transmission by the post."

Funk & Wagnalls Practical Standard Dictionary, (1938) page 886, gives this definition of "post."

"To place in the post-office or in a letter-box."

Allen's Synonyms and Antonyms, (1938) page 300, defines "post" as "mail."

In view of the foregoing definitions, there can be no question that the word "posting" as used in the option agreement meant to place in the mail. This, it is conceded, defendant corporation did with its letter of August 6, 1943 . . .

. . . For the foregoing reasons the judgment is affirmed.

Guided Reading Questions

1. What did the agreement say regarding how the termination of the option agreement should be communicated?

2. What does the court say that "posting" means?

■ AUTHORIZED MEANS OF ACCEPTANCE

The offer may indicate the means of acceptance. If the contract states that acceptance may occur through mail or via the Internet, then the compliance with the terms may be transmitted in this manner. If the contract does not state the manner for acceptance, then a reasonable method for communicating acceptance is permitted. This is determined by the parties' prior mode of acceptance, their prior course of dealing, and/or the distance between the parties. If there is a great distance, then the mail or the Internet would be a reasonable mode to communicate acceptance.

Who May Accept the Offer?

Generally, only the party, identified in the offer, to whom the offer is made, may accept the offer. Sometimes, an offer may indicate that it may be assigned to another party. For example: Ken Dobbs was on the train and read an offer, for computer services to be **rendered** for Dobbs Company, that he received. The passenger to Ken's left read the offer as well. The passenger to the left could not accept the offer for he was not identified in it.

Render
to state judgment by a court.

■ MISTAKEN ACCEPTANCE—FAILURE TO UNDERSTAND WHAT WAS ACCEPTED

The offeree can fail to inform herself fully about the terms of the offer or the offer's content or meaning. The offeree may accept the offer but afterward realize that she mistakenly accepted because she did not fully understand the terms or conditions. The offeree is still bound to the contract unless the terms were objectively ambiguous and both the offeror and the offeree found the terms ambiguous. A court will always look at the written document to determine the deal that the parties made. Having a court review a contract is expensive and time consuming. It is best for the attorney, or the paralegal with the attorney's guidance, to carefully examine the offer, before signing, to become fully informed as to what is offered and what will be accepted. There are instances when a party does not fully appreciate the offer because he or she cannot legally contract and cannot legally accept an offer; this will render the contract void. Generally, this occurs when a party is not competent to contract due to minor status or mental incompetence.

■ ACCEPTANCE BY CONDUCT

Acceptance by conduct occurs generally in unilateral contracts where there is a promise for performance. Restatement (Second) of Contracts § 55 states: "Acceptance by promise may create a contract in which the offeror's performance is completed when the offeree's promise is made."

Sometimes, conduct indicates the offeree's manifestation to assent to the offer. Written terms, oral statements, or even actions can indicate the acceptance of an offer as long as the party intends to enter into the agreement and the other party can infer assent. Restatement (Second) Contracts § 19. To further clarify, the Restatement (Second) of Contracts § 53 states that an offer may only be accepted by performance if the offer invites this manner of acceptance. Furthermore, § 54 of the Restatement (Second) of Contracts details that:

(1) Where an offer invites an offeree to accept by rendering a performance, no notification is necessary to make such an acceptance effective unless the offer requests such a notification.

(2) If the offeree who accepts by rendering a performance has reason to know that the offeror has no adequate means of learning of the performance with reasonable promptness and certainty, the contractual duty of the offeror is discharged unless

 (a) the offeree exercises reasonable diligence to notify the offeror of acceptance, or

 (b) the offeror learns of the performance within a reasonable time, or

 (c) the offer indicates that notification of acceptance is not required."

Example

Joe Martin was told by Tom Smith that he would receive $50 when he (Martin) cleared the snow from the company drive. Martin removed the snow (conduct or performance) and Smith paid Martin $50 (promise).

Assigning Acceptance to a Third Party

Generally, the offer can only be accepted by the entity, or individual, identified in the offer. There are some exceptions when the offeree can assign the acceptance of the offer, but this is complex because it is a legal decision and requires an attorney.

■ WHEN THE OFFEREE RESPONDS WITH A COUNTEROFFER

According to § 59 of the Restatement (Second) of Contracts, a reply to an offer that adds new or different terms or that modifies the offer in some way, without the offeror inviting the modification, is not an acceptance but is a **counteroffer**.

Counteroffer
an offer made in reply to an offer made earlier.

 Often in negotiations, rather than accepting an offer, the offeree will reply with a counter-offer. This is very common in transactions. Often an offer is negotiated and the reply, rather than an acceptance, is with a different term. The introduction of a different term is a counteroffer.

When an Offer Is Not Accepted

When an offer is tendered to the offeree, the offeree is not required to accept. When the offer is not accepted, there is no assent and consequently a contract will not be formed.

 Sometimes an offer is tendered and the offeree does not accept the offer. At that point, unless the offer states that the offer remains open, the offer no longer exists. An offeree has the right to decline an offer. The original offeror also has the right to decline the counteroffer.

CASE ILLUSTRATION

GUIDED READING POINTERS

This case is interesting because the offer and acceptance are analyzed. The court did not comment on whether there was a contract. However, the opinion will give you insights into the language used in an offer and an acceptance in a contract. You will also see that the intention of the parties is important. The court reversed the trial court's motion for **summary judgment** and **remanded** the case, to the trial court, to determine if there should be **specific performance** of the contract. Specific performance is a **remedy** used when money damages are inadequate to compensate the injured party. The case was remanded, or sent back, to the trial court so that the trial court could evaluate the facts pertaining to the issue.

> *Frederick E. Betlach, III, Appellant, v. Wayzata Condominium and Douglas Peterson, Respondents, Swanson-Abbott Development Co., et al., Defendants*

Supreme Court of Minnesota
281 N.W.2d 328

April 6, 1979

Appeal from District Court, Hennepin County; Hon.

This case is before us on appeal from a summary judgment entered in the district court dismissing plaintiff's suit for specific performance of an alleged contract. We reverse.

The original negotiations between the parties had been initiated by plaintiff, who was interested in establishing a location for his jewelry enterprise. The building which plaintiff found to be most suitable was then owned by Ruth Herrick, who leased the property to Polly Berg, Inc. During conversation with Polly Berg, plaintiff learned that defendant Wayzata Condominium had obtained a first right of refusal on Polly Berg's lease should she decide to relocate her business. The lease was for a renewable 5-year term and included an option to purchase. The lease specified the price and the conditions under which the option could be exercised. Plaintiff also learned from Polly Berg that defendant Swanson-Abbott Development Company was acting as Wayzata's agent in its real estate dealings.

Plaintiff approached Swanson-Abbott regarding the possibility of subleasing the building. Swanson-Abbott encouraged him to submit an offer which he subsequently did by letter dated February 24, 1976. The letter proposed that the sublease commence on May 1, 1976, that the rent, including utilities, insurance and taxes up to $ 2,400 per year would be $ 1,100 per month and that defendants would give plaintiff notice of any intention to destroy the building by January 31, 1977. It additionally provided that if a determination to raze the building were made, the sublease would not

Summary judgment
a party may move for summary judgment, depending on the Rules of Civil Procedure for the court where the case is being heard, if there is no issue of material fact and the party is entitled to judgment as a matter of law. This is a motion that is made prior to the completion of a case.

Remand
when a court, usually an appellate court, sends a case back to a lower court, usually a trial court, to make a further determination.

Specific performance
this is a remedy where the court requires the contract to be performed according to the terms that the parties agreed to.

Remedy
way to fix a wrong or to enforce a right.

expire until January 31, 1978, at which time plaintiff would be permitted to dismantle and move the structure. If it were decided not to raze the building, plaintiff would then have the right to assume Wayzata's lease, including the option to purchase. This first letter also expressed plaintiff's desire to rent only the ground floor of the building.

Appellant was informed by Swanson-Abbott that his offer was not satisfactory and he thereafter amended his proposal in a letter of February 27, 1976. The first change in plaintiff's proposal was that it now encompassed the sublease of the entire building. This letter stated that the rent was to be $ 725 per month, the same as in the present lease plus an amount, not to exceed $ 5,000, sufficient to cover Polly Berg's relocation expenses. In response, plaintiff received a letter from Swanson-Abbott also dated February 27, 1976. The letter provided that it was "based on our various conversations and your letters of February 24 & 27th." It went on to discuss the form of the sublease to be entered into by the parties and "Acknowledge[d] [plaintiff's] check in the amount of $ 1,000.00 as a nonrefundable earnest money deposit to bind this agreement." It also provided that, "we [defendants] will, however, reserve to ourselves the right to purchase the building." The concluding paragraph of this letter read as follows:

"In view of the mutual understandings outlined in your two letters and of the above we hereby accept your offer and bind ourselves to work out the balance of the details in good faith and as quickly as is practical."

The letter was signed by H. R. Swanson for Swanson-Abbott and was acknowledged by plaintiff.

Plaintiff subsequently moved into the building and commenced making monthly rent payments. He also began renovating the premises, incurring expenses of over $ 25,000 in the process. Defendants furnished plaintiff with a sublease which he found unacceptable and which he returned with some corrections and deletions. This amended version was similarly unsatisfactory to defendants, particularly with respect to plaintiff's belief that he was contractually entitled to assume the lease, including the option to purchase, should the respondent decide not to destroy the building. After several further meetings, negotiations broke down and plaintiff filed praying for a decree of specific performance.

The district court granted defendants' motion for summary judgment, finding that no contract was formed by the parties' negotiations and holding that in the absence of a contract plaintiff could be no more than a tenant at will. Because we believe that there are genuine issues of material fact which were unresolved below, we must reverse and remand for an adjudication on the merits.

Plaintiff asserts that taken together, his letters of February 24 and 27 and defendants' response of the 27th which was executed by both parties, constituted a valid offer and acceptance, thus creating, assuming the presence of consideration, a binding and enforceable contract. The trial court, passing on the motion for summary judgment, found that no contract existed. The court's main rationale for such a finding was the reservation of the right to purchase the building expressed in defendants' response of February 27. The trial court held that this reservation altered the initial offer and therefore the purported acceptance could be no more than a rejection or counter offer. *Minar v. Skoog*, 235 Minn. 262, 50 N.W. 2d 300 (1951).

Plaintiff contends that this language merely refers to the position of the parties prior to the time that plaintiff would be entitled to exercise his option as outlined in his first letter. In light of the earlier language in Swanson-Abbott's letter stating that the agreement was "based on our various conversations and your letters of February 24 & 27th," we find plaintiff's interpretation to be quite probable. The resolution of this problem raises genuine issues of fact, making summary judgment inappropriate. See, Rule 56, Rules of Civil Procedure.

Defendant contends, however, that because the parties contemplated a formal sublease, no contract could arise as a matter of law until its execution, citing in support *A. E. Staley Mfg. Co. v. Northern Cooperatives*, 168 F.2d 892 (8 Cir. 1948). This contention somewhat overstates the principle.

The question at issue is the intention of the parties. In cases where the parties have contemplated a later formalization of the agreement, courts look to whether or not the parties intended legal consequences to arise prior to the formal execution of the later instrument. If not, the general rule is that no binding contract has been created. 1 Corbin, Contracts, § 30. Here, however, there is some indication that the parties intended to be bound from the outset. Defendants' concluding statement from the letter of February 27 that, "we hereby accept your offer and bind ourselves," in conjunction with the tender of earnest money seems to support this supposition. This again is a question of fact.

We do not mean to imply by this decision any opinion as to whether a valid agreement exists between the parties. On appeal from a summary judgment it is the function of this court only to determine (1) whether there are any genuine issues of material fact and (2) whether the trial court erred in its application of the law. *Minneapolis, St. P. & S.S.M.R. Co. v. St. Paul Mercury-Ind. Co.*, 268 Minn. 390, 129 N.W. 2d 777 (1964). Therefore in reversing we hold only that there are genuine issues of fact which must be resolved by the trial court after a full evidentiary hearing.

It should be noted on remand that all evidence offered to clarify or explain ambiguous terms in the letters should be admitted, as long as it is not for the purpose of varying terms whose meaning is plain. *Hayle Floor Covering v. First Minnesota Const.*, 253 N.W. 2d 809 (Minn. 1977).

Reversed and remanded.

Guiding Reading Questions

1. What were the terms of the offer?

2. What were the terms of the acceptance?

3. Was there a counteroffer?

Example

Mr. Jones enters Copying World at 2 P.M. and requests 50 copies of a report, 25 pages each, to be copied and collated for the advertised price of 2 cents per page, 25 cents per document for collating and 5 cents per document for stapling. Mr. Jones merely repeated the advertised fee for this service. Additionally, Mr. Jones requests that this service be performed by 5 P.M. The clerk on duty responds with: "We will have the order ready by 5 P.M., which comprises 50 copies of the 25-page report, collated and stapled for the advertised fee.

Note that the terms of the offer correspond directly with the terms of the acceptance.

However, if the clerk tells Mr. Jones that the material, in lieu of being ready at 5 P.M., will not be processed until the following morning at 9 A.M., this represents a counteroffer. At this point, Mr. Jones can either assent to the new term and a newly formed contract would result between Jones and Copying World or Mr. Jones can decide to decline the counteroffer and take his business elsewhere. Note the material terms in this agreement: time, quantity, price, and service. If Mr. Jones accepts the new terms, the copies would mutually be agreed to be ready by 9 A.M.

Checkpoint

1. How can acceptance be communicated?
2. Should the terms of the acceptance mirror the terms of the offer?
3. Who may accept the offer?

■ WHAT DOES A PARALEGAL NEED TO KNOW ABOUT ACCEPTANCE?

1. The offer and acceptance must correspond, meaning that the acceptance should match what is offered. The paralegal must find out if the contract is between merchants. If the contract is between merchants then the Uniform Commercial Code applies and the rules for acceptance are slightly different.
2. The paralegal must note the terms of the offer and note the manner required for acceptance.
3. The paralegal must keep accurate records of the date to accept and the manner of the acceptance and alert the attorney to these requirements.

Being Aware of the Mirror Image Rule

The paralegal must check to be sure that the terms of the offer and the acceptance match. The paralegal can also double check the attorney's acceptance to be sure that it matches the substantive terms of the offer. The substantive terms are the terms that are material to the offer, that are the essence of the offer and are expressed directly in the offer. Material terms include but are not limited to: price, quantity, time, date, condition, location, and duration. Example: an offer for an iced fudge cake, 9″ in diameter, for $18.00 to be delivered on December 20, 2010, is accepted. The icing on the cake on display is about ¼″ thick. The offeror created his offer on the basis of the cake on display. The offeree accepted the offer for the cake based on the image of the display cake. However, when the offeree receives the cake, the icing is ½″ thick. The icing thickness was not stated in the offer and this variation is not material. An example of a material term is quantity, price, or date.

Complying with the Mail Box Rule

The paralegal must obtain accurate address information. Additionally, all correspondence, even if it involves the transmission of a contract's acceptance, must be absolutely professional.

■ THE ROLE OF THE U.C.C. IN ACCEPTANCE

According to the U.C.C. § 2–104(1), a merchant is defined as:

a person that deals in goods of the kind or otherwise holds itself out by occupation as having knowledge or skill peculiar to the practices or goods involved in the transaction or to which the knowledge or skill may be attributed by the person's employment of an agent or broker or other intermediary that holds itself out by occupation as having the knowledge or skill . . .

According to U.C.C. 2–104(3), an offer, acceptance, or a contract between merchants "means in any transaction with respect to which both parties are chargeable with the knowledge or skill of merchants."

Section 2–207 of the Uniform Commercial Code addresses the issue of acceptance between merchants involving the sale of goods. Section 2–207 provides that acceptance between merchants occurs as long as it is expressed or sent as a written confirmation of the offer within a reasonable time even though the acceptance may contain additional or different terms than the offer. This is permissible unless the offer expressly states that this is not allowed. The additional terms are permissible and are viewed as proposals in addition to the contract between merchants unless these terms substantially alter the agreement.

Mirror Image Rule and the U.C.C.

The comments to the U.C.C. shed light on the purpose behind this provision and explain why it differs from the basic mirror image rule in contract law. Section 2–207 allows for minor variations on the terms to permit commercial understanding and not to impede the formation of an agreement due to the addition of minor terms such as "rush" or due to variations of form offers and acknowledgements. Generally, § 2–207 avoids disrupting a bargain due to discrepancies in the forms between the offer and the acceptance. The focus should be on whether the additional terms substantially change the bargain. If the terms of the acceptance do not substantially change the bargain between the parties and the contract involves the sale of goods between merchants, then the contract is valid.

The paralegal's role is to alert the attorney as to the discrepancies between the terms of the offer and the acceptance and permit the attorney to determine if the variation in the terms is material.

CHAPTER SUMMARY

This chapter explored the acceptance of an offer. Acceptance is an integral **component** in the formation of a contract. An acceptance must mirror the terms of the offer. Also, acceptance may be communicated in the way stated in the offer as well as by mail. The date posted or sent by Internet, not the date received, is the date of acceptance according to the mail box rule. Additionally, both parties must assent to the agreement; there must be mutual assent. You have also learned that if the contract is between merchants and the U.C.C. applies, the terms of the offer and of the acceptance do not have to mirror each other exactly as long as the additional or new terms do not substantially change the offer and the parties did not state that this would not be permissible.

Acceptance

General Requirements for Acceptance	Intent to enter into an agreement Complying with the terms of the offer, in the manner invited in the offer and by the party identified in the offer Accepting with a return promise results in a bilateral agreement Acceptance by performing results in a unilateral contract The offeror is the master of the offer
Mirror Image Rule	The acceptance must mirror the terms and bargain stated in the offer
Mail Box Rule	Offers may be accepted by mail and via the Internet Acceptance occurs when it is sent, not received, as long as the parties agreed that this would be the means of acceptance
Authorized Means of Acceptance Who May Accept the Offer	The offer may state precisely who may accept the offer and how the acceptance should be conveyed Generally, only the party identified in the offer may accept it

Acceptance

Mistake—Failure to Fully Understand the Terms	Even if the offeree realizes that after acceptance, he did not to fully understand the terms of the offer, he is still bound unless the terms are found to be objectively ambiguous
Acceptance by Conduct	This occurs in unilateral contracts where there is a promise for performance but only if this form of acceptance is invited in the offer
Counteroffers	A reply to an offer that varies the terms without the offeror's invitation to do so
The U.C.C. and Acceptance	Acceptance between merchants occurs as long as it is expressed or sent as a written confirmation of the offer within a reasonable time even though the acceptance may not mirror the offer

REVIEW QUESTIONS

1. What is the mirror image rule?
2. List one characteristic of the mail box rule.
3. What does U.C.C. § 2-207 concern?
4. Can a contract be accepted by performance? If so, how?
5. What is mutual assent?
6. What happens if a party mistakenly assents to a contract?
7. When is acceptance a counteroffer?

SKILL-BUILDING APPLICATION EXERCISE

Review the case in this chapter, Diggs v. El Royale Corp., to analyze the following situation.

Ms. Jane Benjamin entered into an agreement with New York Properties to manage three apartment buildings. The agreement between Ms. Benjamin and New York Properties also provided that Ms. Benjamin had the option to purchase the properties, not individually, but all three apartment buildings, if she was still engaged to manage the buildings. This contract was entered into on May 5, 2010. The agreement between the parties, to which both New York Properties and Benjamin assented to, was that the management contract and consequently the option to purchase could be terminated by written notice, via post, at any time. On December 1, 2010, New York Properties sent Benjamin a letter, via mail, that it was terminating her management contract and, consequently, her option to purchase the three buildings would terminate as well. Benjamin contacted your firm on December 10 to see if she could still exercise her option to purchase the buildings.

Based on your reading of *Diggs v. El Royale Corp.*, do you think that Ms. Benjamin's option to purchase the properties was terminated? Did New York Properties alert Ms. Benjamin as to the termination of her management contract, and consequently the termination of her option to purchase the buildings, by mail just as El Royale Corporation alerted Mr. Diggs by mail? Diggs's contract with El Royale was cancelled when the letter terminating their agreement was posted. Was Ms. Benjamin's contract with New York Properties cancelled when New York Properties posted the letter?

SIMULATED LAW OFFICE ASSIGNMENT

CONSULTING SERVICES AGREEMENT USED WORDS, LLC FROM BEADS TO BLING

This Consulting Services Agreement (the "Agreement") is dated as of December 19, 2006, by and between Beads to Bling ("Contractor") and Craft Store ("Client") (collectively the "Parties").

The Parties agree as follows:

1. **SERVICES:** Contractor will perform the consulting services described below (the "Services"): Beads to Bling Representative will provide a two-hour workshop from 6:00 P.M. to 8 P.M. on November 1, 2010, at Craft Store instructing workshop participants on the creation of a beaded project. <u>Other services to be arranged as agreed, etc.</u>

2. **TIME OF COMPLETION:** (*mark the applicable provision*)
   The Services shall be commenced on or before November 1, 2010.

3. **EQUIPMENT:** (*mark the applicable provision*)
   Client shall provide the following equipment for Contractor's use when performing the Services: <u>LCD projector and screen for PowerPoint presentation, sound system.</u> Contractor will provide all other equipment necessary to perform the Services.

4. PAYMENT: (mark the applicable provision)
Client shall pay Contractor for the material and labor to be performed under this Agreement the sum of <u>Two thousand five hundred Dollars ($2500.00)</u>.
Full payment is due within thirty (30) days.

5. OTHER EXPENSES/ACCOMMODATIONS: Client shall reimburse Contractor for the following expenses: <u>Travel expenses November 1–2, 2010.</u>

_____

Client shall be responsible for providing only the following accommodations to Contractor in connection with Contractor's performance of the Services: <u>Accommodations November 1, 2010: One nonsmoking room with Internet access.</u>

6. **GENERAL PROVISIONS:**

(a) Contractor is an independent contractor and not an employee of Client.

(b) Any changes to this document must be signed by both Contractor and Client.

(c) This Agreement shall be construed in accordance with the laws of the state of Washington.

IN WITNESS WHEREOF the Parties have executed this Agreement on the date first written above.

CLIENT: **CONTRACTOR:**

_____   _____
Signature   Signature

_____   _____
Name (please print)   Name (please print)

_____   _____
Title (if applicable)   Title (if applicable)

_____   _____
Date   Date

DRAFTING EXERCISE

The following exercise is based on the form used in the Simulated Law Office Assignment concerning Beads to Bling. The firm that you work for represents Craft Store. The attorney just got off of the phone with Beads to Bling and states that the parties negotiated a new fee arrangement and changed the date. Craft Store requested that the workshop be held on December 1. Beads to Bling requested $3,000 for the workshop since it will occur during the busy holiday period. Both parties agreed to the new terms. Please modify the contract to reflect the new terms.

DEVELOPING CRITICAL THINKING SKILLS

1. A contract was entered into between Tee Party T-Shirt Company and the Iowa Stores for 500 white long-sleeved t-shirts, at $7.00 per shirt, to be delivered to Iowa Stores within thirty (30) days of the signing of the contract. If the acceptance stated that the t-shirts should be shipped "RUSH," what would the U.C.C. say about this?
2. Review *Betlach v. Wayzata* in this chapter. What was the difference in the terms of the offer and the terms of the acceptance? Note that the court never ruled that there was a valid acceptance. It just held that there was a sufficient factual issue about whether a contract existed to defeat a motion for summary judgment. This means that the court could not rule that the moving party was entitled to judgment as a matter of law.

PORTFOLIO ASSIGNMENT

Promissory note
a written agreement in which a borrower agrees to pay back a specific amount of money to a lender according to a specific schedule with a stated rate of interest. A promissory note generally contains the total amount of the loan, the interest rate, payment schedule, time frame establishing when payments are late, and possibly collateral securing the loan.

Your firm represents the borrower, James Shingle. Shingle accepted the terms of the **promissory note**. The attorney asked that you create term sheet for the following promissory note. A promissory note is a contract agreeing to repay a debt of a fixed sum, plus interest, according to a specific schedule. The attorney reviewed the document and has no modifications. The attorney wants a list of terms that his client accepted by agreeing to the offer in the note so that the attorney can be sure that the client will comply with the offer.

PROMISSORY NOTE

James Shingle, Borrower
Bank Two, Minnesota, Lender

1. For the $700,000 received, Borrower James Shingle promises to pay Lender, Bank Two, the amount of $700,000 on December 31, 2010 (Due date) at Bank Two 123 Mall Street, Minneapolis, Minnesota, at the rate of 6% per year from the date this note was signed until the date it is paid in full. The borrower, Shingle, will receive credits for prepayments, reducing the total amount of interest to be repaid.

2. Shingle, Borrower, agrees that this note will be paid in installments, which include principal and interest of not less than $20,000 per month, due on the last day of each month until the sum owed is repaid in full.

3. If any monthly payment, prior to the full repayment of the amount owed, is not received by Bank Two within seven (7) days of the last day of the month, within seven (7) days of the due date, the entire amount of the unpaid principal will become immediately due and payable at the option of Bank Two, the Lender, without prior notice to Shingle, the Borrower.

4. If Bank Two, the Lender, prevails in a lawsuit to collect on this note, Shingle, the Borrower, agrees to pay Bank Two's attorney fees.

Consideration

CHAPTER 4

INTRODUCTION

Consideration at first glance is the most elusive contract term. After reading a bit about consideration, the simplicity of the concept becomes apparent. In its most basic form, consideration is the glue that binds two parties to an agreement. When thought about logically, an individual or an entity would not enter into a contract without the expectation of receiving some sort of **benefit** from the agreement. Additionally, most parties to a contract are aware that entering into an agreement will require that they give up, or forsake, something to cement the other party's willingness to perform. Consideration does not always require that a party tender an amount of money, although money is the most common form of consideration, or relinquish a particular good. Sometimes the consideration, for the formation of a contract, is to forsake something of value or to forbear from taking action.

LEARNING OBJECTIVES

After studying this chapter, you will be able to:

1. Understand that consideration is the value that a party derives from entering into a contract.

2. Understand that consideration ties the parties to the agreement.

3. Recognize consideration in an agreement.

4. Understand that it is not the paralegal's role to determine the adequacy of the consideration, for that is a legal decision.

5. Discuss that consideration is bargained for by the parties.

6. Discuss the U.C.C.'s impact on consideration in contracts between merchants.

Consideration
the value sought by the parties to enter into a contract that cements the agreement and binds the parties.

Benefit
gain.

Adequate
sufficient.

Detriment
harm or sacrifice or personal cost.

Forbearance
to not do something or to not act. Agreeing to not sue is an act of forbearance.

Bargain
mutually agreed and negotiated.

■ FEATURES OF CONSIDERATION

The key feature of consideration is that it must have value to the party making the exchange in the contract. Consideration is **adequate** as long as the parties deem it to be, even if a bystander thinks that the consideration is inadequate. Of course, there are exceptions in situations of fraud, unconscionable contracts, and when a party relies on an agreement to his or her **detriment**. Generally, the consideration makes the deal between the parties worthwhile to the promisor and the promisee. Without consideration, a party can choose to act or not to act. For instance, when the promisor makes a promise and the promisee's return promise is completely optional, there is no consideration on the part of the promisee. The promisee's duty, without consideration, is optional, for there is nothing to bind the promisee to perform the agreement.

■ DEFINITION OF CONSIDERATION

Consideration is what induces the offeror and the offeree to enter into a contract, and it could be the value that each party is willing to proffer for the agreement. In a bilateral contract, consideration is received for a promise; in a unilateral contract, consideration is received for performance. Consideration need not be a monetary amount or measurable in dollars. Consideration can be in the form of an act or action, in the form of **forbearance**, or even in the form of a right.

The Restatement (Second) of Contracts § 71 discusses how consideration is part of the contractual agreement.

Consideration is **bargained** for by the parties entering into the agreement. Consideration can take the form of a performance of an act, a return promise, or even promising not to do something. For instance, performance of an act is when Mr. Cox says to painter, "I'll pay you $200 if you paint my fence." Painting the fence is the performance constituting the consideration provided by the painter. Consideration does not need to have a monetary value. Additionally, the performance can be an act or forbearing from acting. A salesman stating that he will not sell goods in a certain territory, that is, forbearing from selling goods in a specific area, is a form of consideration. Stating that you will not sue or foreclose is a form of forbearance, of not doing an act.

Example: Consideration in a unilateral contract where there is a promise for performance. I will pay you $10 when you clean your room. The worth of the deal, the consideration, to the promisee is the $10. The cleaned room, the performance, is the worth, the consideration, that the promisor extracts from the bargain.

Third Parties and Consideration

Although the topic of third parties and contracts is explored in great detail in Chapter 8, it is important to know that consideration can be given, or assigned, to a third party. Under most contracts, consideration is a right that can be assigned and a duty that can be delegated. One of the major exceptions is a personal service contract for a unique act or item, such as painting a portrait by a particular artist, an athlete's performance, or the sale of a unique piece of artwork. If the consideration is bargained for by the parties and the contract permits, then that consideration can be transferred to another. For instance, the need to proffer consideration to purchase a house can be assigned to a third party. For example: Mr. Thomas enters into a contract to buy a house from Mr. Farrell. Mr. Thomas gives Mr. Farrell $1,000 in earnest money. Prior to closing on the purchase of the house, Mr. Thomas sells his right to purchase the house to Mr. Daniel for $2,000, which is the consideration for the assignment. However, Mr. Daniel now must proffer the consideration for the purchase of the house to Mr. Farrell.

DETRIMENT AND BENEFIT

Consideration is, generally, a detriment to the promisee or a benefit to the promisor. The benefit is some sort of value or advantage that a party obtains from the agreement.

Section 79 of the Restatement (Second) of Contracts indicates that "consideration must be bargained for. Consideration is the value in the agreement. Since a contract is designed to benefit one party, if not all of the parties, the parties want to take away value in some format from the bargain that they reach." In essence, consideration is what the agreement is worth to each side and represents the accord that the parties reached when contracting. As long as the consideration is adequate to the parties contracting, there are no additional requirements in terms of benefit to the promisor or detriment to the promisee.

BARGAINED–FOR EXCHANGE

A bargained-for exchange is the negotiated and agreed upon offer, acceptance, and consideration. An example of a bargained-for exchange is the sale of a coat. A. Row has a black wool coat for sale, in size 10, for $100, and has two in stock. The offer is to sell the black wool coat, in size 10, for $100. Mrs. Peet accepts the offer by tendering $100 to A. Row and receives the coat. The contract is for the coat and the consideration is the $100. The consideration is given and received to support the promise here.

Consideration can be the component that drives the agreement. Consideration can be the promise or the promise in exchange. However, the consideration can be separate from the impetus behind the formation of the contract. For example: Mr. Kay owns a boat that he docks in Smithtown Harbor. Mr. Kay wants to sell the boat but Mr. Jones, the purchaser, has no place to dock the boat. The harbor has a twenty-year wait list for dock space. Mr. Kay sells the boat to Mr. Jones and subleases the dock space to Mr. Jones for $1.00 per year for 100 years. Mr. Jones is on the waitlist for dock space so he will get a slip in twenty years anyway. Here the consideration of $1.00 per year to be tendered to Mr. Kay is not the component of the bargain that motivated

Kay to enter in to the agreement. Kay wanted to sell his boat and the sale of the boat is the impetus behind the formation of the contract here, not the receipt of $1.00 per year for the boat slip.

According to § 81 of the Restatement (Second) of Contracts, the consideration, although bargained for, may not be the inducement for making the promise or for entering into the contract. For example, let's revisit Mr. Kay and his contract for the sale of his boat: The consideration here, of $1.00 per year, is bargained for because the parties agreed to it, but the $1.00 does not induce the making of the promise between the parties.

■ ISSUES ARISING WITH CONSIDERATION

Adequacy

Consideration is adequate when there is a benefit to the promisor and a detriment to the promisee in a bilateral contract. In a unilateral contract, an offer to induce performance occurs when the offeree's performance is consideration for the promisor's agreement. As long as the parties reached an agreement as to the consideration, its adequacy or amount is not at issue. Generally, adequacy of consideration occurs when the parties agree that the amount is sufficient.

However, sometimes the amount of consideration cementing an agreement seems far too negligible. For example, Mrs. Young has a new sewing machine. Mrs. Young wants to sell the new, top-of-the-line sewing machine, which costs $3,000, to Kathy for $100. The consideration here, though seeming negligible at $100, is adequate because the parties agreed to it and it benefits one party and burdens the other party.

The Court's Role

Just because the consideration seems inadequate, a court will not step in to void a contract or to order that a contract be performed with fairer terms. There are remedies, in a court of equity, when the court may step in if the agreement will cause a party undue hardship or great loss. This may possibly occur when the terms of the contract are oppressive, fraudulent, or involve misrepresentation.

When There Is No Current Consideration to Support an Agreement

Past Promises

Past promises are not consideration for a current contract. For example: John Jones is a pharmaceutical representative. The division manager tells John that he should work half the day on Saturdays for one year. The manager said that John was sent to Hawaii two years prior and this is the consideration for working the additional half day each week. This is past consideration because when John was sent to Hawaii, he did not know that in two years he would be asked to work on Saturdays.

Pre-existing Duty

Performing a duty that already was agreed to and owed, under a contract that exists, can not be used as consideration for a new contract. For example: Joe was hired to put flyers in all the doors of the homes in the Sheltingham subdivision. Direct Flyer hired Joe to perform this job for $75 for the morning and $75 for the afternoon. Joe accepted the offer to perform the job. At noon, Joe received a call from Direct Flyer stating that it wanted Joe to deliver flyers to the Sheltingham subdivision and to the Kenilworth subdivision for the $75 already agreed to. There is no increase in pay for the additional subdivision. Joe says he will do this. However, Joe is not obligated to keep this promise. Since Direct Flyer was already obligated to pay him $75, there is no new consideration to support this promise. Joe already promised, in his agreement with Direct Flyer, to deliver the flyers in the afternoon to Sheltingham for $75; he has a pre-existing duty. Therefore he cannot use his agreement to deliver the flyers in the afternoon as consideration for delivering to Kenilworth too.

Moral Obligation and Gratuitous Promise

Promises based solely on moral obligations are merely gratuitous promises, and do not represent adequate consideration because there is no legal duty. The promisor is only induced or motivated to act out of sentiment. There is no bargained-for exchange. For example: Mr. Watt promises to take care of Mr. Brown's widow. This promise is not supported by adequate consideration for it is merely based on moral obligations and sentiment.

Illusory Promises

An illusory promise is not really a promise because performance is optional. Generally, in a bilateral contract, if one party is not obligated to perform, there is no consideration to support his or her promise, and there is no legal contract. The party really does not bind him- or herself to any obligation. This is different from the requirement, as set out in the Restatement (Second) of Contracts § 71 comment (b), which states: "In a typical bargain, the consideration and the promise bear a reciprocal relation of motive or inducement: the consideration induces the making of the promise and the promise induces the furnishing of the consideration . . . both elements must be present." Example: Jennifer went to Gimbel's and saw some sweaters. Jennifer said to the clerk: "I'll buy all of the sweaters that I need." Jennifer is not obligated to perform, by buying all the sweaters that she needs, for there is no detriment and no consideration to support her promise.

Future Gifts

In a future gift, the promisor makes a promise to make a gift at a later date but the promisee does not have to do anything. There is no detriment to the promisee, the promisee does not furnish any consideration, and therefore a valid contract does not result. Future gifts lack the requirement of a bargained-for exchange. For example: Mrs. Marsh was planting bulbs in her garden in the fall. Mr. Hack, who lives next door, walked by Mrs. Marsh as she was gardening. Mr. Hack exclaimed: "I certainly love your flowers each spring."

Mrs. Marsh replied: "I will give you two large bouquets of tulips next spring when these bulbs bloom." Mr. Hack furnished no consideration in return for Mrs. Marsh's promise, so there was no bargained-for exchange.

Checkpoint

1. Is there consideration to support the following scenario? Julie Vong used to teach at Bradley School during the 2009–2010 school year. At Bradley, Julie received $35,000 per year. Now Julie Vong teaches at Ace School. Julie receives $40,000 per year to teach first grade for the 2010–2011 school year at Ace. Bradley asked Julie to work in the afterschool program for the 2010–2011 school year without any compensation. Bradley stated that Vong was compensated more than most teachers when she taught there and that this is the consideration for working in the afterschool program now.
2. Is there consideration to support the following scenario? Mary Ann promised to help her friend Adrienne plan the wake for Mary Ann's father.
3. Is there consideration to support the following scenario? Smithy's Landscaping Service is paid $50 per week to mow the Miller's lawn. The Millers ask Smithy's to mow their lawn and their next-door neighbor's lawn for the $50 already agreed to and with no additional payment for the extra lawn.

■ CONSIDERATION IN CONTRACTS BETWEEN MERCHANTS

The Uniform Commercial Code, § 2-302, requires that when consideration is so inadequate, in a contract concerning the sale of goods, that it is unconscionable, the court may refuse to enforce the unconscionable contract or the unconscionable terms. The court may enforce the remainder of the contract that is not unconscionable. The comments in the U.C.C. under § 2-302 indicate the basis for when the court will step in: [the] "basic test is whether, in the light of the general commercial background and the commercial needs of the particular trade or case, the term or contract involved is so one-sided as to be unconscionable under the circumstances existing at the time of the making of the contract." The court may intervene depending on the sophistication of the parties that entered into the agreement.

Example: Rotisserie International, a manufacturer of rotisserie grills to be used in supermarkets, entered into a contract with Heat Enterprises for Heat to supply 3,000 coils for the heating elements for the rotisseries to be manufactured by Rotisserie International. Both companies have been in the business of manufacturing and selling equipment for over a decade. Heat was aware that Rotisserie needed the coils quickly because Rotisserie obtained a huge order for grills from Large Supermarkets. In very tiny print on the reverse side of the contract for the sale of the coils, Heat Enterprises included a provision that stated that Heat only provided a warranty that the coils were free from mechanical defects for ten (10) days after shipment. Although both parties have experience in their respective trades and the power to drive hard bargains, this provision was unconscionable. The remaining terms in the contract were not unconscionable. The court may then be asked to step in and to not enforce the unconscionable term, the warranty, but will be asked to enforce the remainder of the contract. This applies the test, in the comments under U.C.C. § 2-302, that in view of the commercial backgrounds of the parties, the clause under discussion is so one sided as to be unconscionable under the circumstances at the time the contract was made.

■ DETRIMENTAL RELIANCE AND PROMISSORY ESTOPPEL

Detrimental reliance and **promissory estoppel** are related concepts, for promissory estoppel is a remedy for detrimental reliance. However, promissory estoppel is not used in all instances of detrimental reliance. This is a legal decision to be determined by an attorney and by the court.

Detrimental Reliance

Detrimental reliance occurs when the promisee relies to his or her detriment or extreme disadvantage on the promisor's promise. Detrimental reliance usually involves the promisee changing his or her legal position or financial circumstance on the basis of the promisor's promise. The result is that the promisee suffers a legal or financial hardship in reliance on the promisor's offer. The detriment to the promisee, which ordinarily serves as the consideration to support the agreement, is too harmful.

Promissory Estoppel

The Restatement (Second) of Contracts § 90 details promissory estoppel and states the rule as:

Promise Reasonably Inducing Action or Forbearance

1. A promise which the promisor should reasonably expect to induce action or forbearance on the part of the promisee or a third person and which does induce such action or forbearance is binding if injustice can be avoided only by enforcement of the promise. The remedy granted for breach may be limited as justice requires.

Example: Mr. Hill is offered a new job in San Diego with the San Diego Company. The San Diego Company, the promisor, reasonably expects the promise of the job, to Mr. Hill, to induce him to move to San Diego with his family. The promise of the job with the San Diego Company does cause Mr. Hill to sell his home in St. Louis, purchase a home in San Diego, and move his family there. When Mr. Hill arrives in San Diego a telegram awaits stating that the job offer has been rescinded. Mr. Hill has a good argument for estopping, or barring, San Diego Company from reneging on its promise because he relied to his disadvantage, or detriment, on the promise of the

Detrimental reliance
when a promisor makes a promise that leads the promisee to depend, with resulting harm, on that promise.

Promissory estoppel
a court will enforce a promise made, when that promise reasonably led a party to rely on it, if the failure to enforce the promise will cause the promisee great harm. This bars the promisor's ability to reneg on the promise if justice can achieved by enforcing it.

new job and made many sacrifices to his detriment on the basis of that promise. Mr. Hill's attorney will support his argument with the Restatement (Second) of Contracts § 90 (1) by stating that San Diego Company made a promise of a new job that it reasonably expected to induce action on the part of Mr. Hill and that did induce Hill to act, on the basis of the promise, by selling his home and moving his family. Hill's attorney will argue that this promise is binding, for injustice can be avoided only by the enforcement of San Diego Company's promise or by compensating Mr. Hill.

Promissory estoppel is an equitable remedy that bars the party that made the promise, that the promisee relied on to his or her detriment, from not carrying out the promise. If it is not possible to carry out the promise, then the promisor must compensate the injured party.

Example–Promissory Estoppel: Ms. Cecily promises her niece, Ann, $10,000 per year if Ann lives with Ms. Cecily and takes care of her. Ms. Cecily reasonably expects that her promise to Ann would reasonably induce Ann to live with her and to decline any other job offer. Ann receives a job offer that pays $20,000 per year and declines the job offer because of Ms. Cecily's promise. Also, Ann takes a leave of absence from college on the basis of her aunt's promise of $10,000 per year to live with her aunt and to care for her. Ms. Cecily's promise did induce Ann to move to take care of her aunt and also induced Ann to decline another job opportunity. When Ann arrives at her aunt's home, Ms. Cecily states that she does not want to pay Ann $10,000. Ms. Cecily claims that she doesn't want to pay her niece because Ann should perform these services out of love. Ann relied to her detriment on her aunt's promise. Ann's attorney will assert that Ms. Cecily's promise induced Ann's actions and forbearance and this promise should be binding if injustice can be avoided by the enforcement of the promise.

CASE ILLUSTRATION

Guided Reading Pointers

The following case addresses whether the contract was enforceable due to adequacy of consideration. Look at how the court addresses the issue of promissory estoppel and adequacy of consideration.

Sharron Johnson, et al.
v.
Rodney Lockhart

No. M2002-00623-COA-R3-CV

(2003)

Court of Appeals of Tennessee, at Nashville

Sharron Johnson brought suit against her former husband, Rodney Lockhart, alleging breach of an oral contract to pay equal shares of the college expenses for their son, Paul G. Lockhart. The Circuit Court of Sumner County entered judgment for Ms. Johnson, and Mr. Lockhart appeals. We affirm the judgment of the trial court.

After a ten year marriage, Sharron and Rodney Lockhart divorced in 1980. Born to the marriage was one son, Paul G. Lockhart, also known as Greg. The decree of divorce provided that Sharron Lockhart was the primary residential custodian of Greg, and she resided with Greg in Hendersonville, Tennessee. Rodney Lockhart resided in Madison, Tennessee.

Greg completed Hendersonville High School in December of 1996 and then enrolled in Volunteer State Community College in Gallatin where he took freshman courses until May of 1997. His expenses at Volunteer State Community College were paid in equal shares by his parents.

Greg desired to go to a four year college or university that offered an international studies major. He researched institutions that offered this major over the internet and found Stanford, Princeton, the University of Virginia, the University of Miami and New College of South Florida located in Sarasota. Greg and his mother considered the latter two institutions since they were the most reasonably priced. They drove to Sarasota, Florida to tour the campus of the New College of South Florida but, Greg did not like the small size of this school, which had a student population of approximately 500. Greg also applied to the University of Miami and was accepted for admission by letter dated April 23, 1997. He toured the campus with his mother on May 10, 1997, and his mother (now Mrs. Johnson) left a $150 deposit in order to secure his place in the freshman class. However, Mrs. Johnson cautioned that she would have to talk to Mr. Rodney Lockhart about financial arrangements before Greg could commit to attending the University of Miami because of the expense. Greg applied for financial aid from the University of Miami on forms provided by the school . . .

. . . Ms. Johnson hosted a high school graduation party for Greg on May 23, 1997. Family and friends attended including Greg's father, Mr. Lockhart. At this party Ms. Johnson testified that she heard Mr. Lockhart state how proud he was of Greg's acceptance at the University of Miami and how this was a golden opportunity for Greg and how Greg was living out Mr. Lockhart's dream. Ms. Johnson stated that Mr. Lockhart announced during the party that he and Sharon were about to send Greg off to The University of Miami. Ms. Johnson testified that on this occasion and at other times, Mr. Lockhart agreed to split Greg's expenses at The University of Miami with her. In July of 1997, Ms. Johnson said she received a financial aid package from the University. Shortly thereafter Ms. Johnson said she sat down with Mr. Lockhart at her house to go over the total cost, as itemized in the package, of sending Greg to the University outside of available grants, financial aid or subsidized student loans. Ms. Johnson testified that Mr. Lockhart again told her at this meeting that he would pay one-half of these expenses as long as Greg made good grades. Ms. Johnson stated that Mr. Lockhart had suggested that they borrow the money from the bank each year. Mr. Lockhart denied saying this. Ms. Johnson said she told him that it would be more economical to take advantage of the University's nine-month installment plan which had a 3% origination fee. Ms. Johnson stated that the Defendant and she had numerous meetings whenever she received correspondence from The University of Miami during this time and that they agreed to go on the University's payment plan.

In late August of 1997, Ms. Johnson, Mr. Lockhart and Greg set out together on a 14-hour long trip in Greg's small car to move Greg in at the University of Miami. Ms. Johnson and Mr. Lockhart moved Greg into the dormitory on a Saturday and bought supplies for him. Before leaving the campus to return on a flight back to Tennessee, Ms. Johnson and Mr. Lockhart went to the register's office at the University and enrolled in the nine-month college payment plan of $811.50 each month and made Greg's first monthly payment. Ms. Johnson stated that at no time while the parties were on this extended trip or thereafter did Mr. Lockhart tell Greg or her that he only intended to pay his half of Greg's college expenses for Greg's first year of school. She said it was their goal that Greg graduate from the University. She stated that Greg was able to obtain a Pell grant, a University grant and a government loan and that she did not consider having Greg change schools or discontinue his education there after his freshman year.

For nine months after Ms. Johnson and Mr. Lockhart enrolled Greg at the University of Miami, Mr. Lockhart routinely paid his one-half share of Greg's expenses in the amount of $811.50 by check made out to The University of Miami. Mr. Lockhart either personally delivered his checks to Ms. Johnson's house or mailed them. One month Ms. Johnson testified that Mr. Lockhart asked her to go ahead and pay the whole amount and he would reimburse her which he did three days later.

By letters dated May 15, 1998, July 16, 1998, July 31, 1998, August 7, 1998, and September 18, 1998 which were introduced into evidence, Ms. Johnson sent Mr. Lockhart documentation of what Greg's college expenses were. In these letters, Ms. Johnson also stated the amount she had paid and requested to know when she would receive payment of Mr. Lockhart's one-half share. Ms. Johnson stated that Mr. Lockhart neither responded to any of her letters nor did he give any indication at all that he would not be making any future payments as he had in the past. Mr. Lockhart stated that he did not feel obligated to make any future payments. . . .

Greg Lockhart testified that he worked at the university's swimming pool and as a night security guard for extra money while he was a student. He said that had his father not agreed to share the costs of his expenses at The University of Miami, that he would have stayed on at Volunteer State Community College after his high school graduation.

Sarah Johnson, Sharron Johnson's mother who lived with her, testified that she was present in the room at the financial meeting between Mr. Lockhart and her daughter when they were reviewing the costs of sending Greg to The University of Miami and that she told them not to send Greg down there only to have him come back prematurely due to financial reasons, and that they both indicated to her that they would not do that.

Rodney Lockhart testified that Ms. Johnson initiated the discussion about Greg's college expenses at the University of Miami and that he told her that he would do all that he could do. He stated that he did not promise to pay one-half of Greg's expenses and that he never said that he would contribute for four years. Mr. Lockhart testified that he did not remember having a conference with Ms. Johnson about Greg's college expenses before the parties left for

Miami to move Greg in August of 1997 and that he did not know how much the cost would be prior to going to the school's comptroller's office. Mr. Lockhart admitted that he made the monthly $811.50 payments to Ms. Johnson voluntarily without any prompting from her and that he never informed Ms. Johnson that he would not be making any more payments after Greg's first year at the University. Mr. Lockhart testified that he told Greg throughout his freshman year that he needed to try and get scholarships because he could not afford it. Mr. Lockhart said that he last spoke with Greg in May of 1998 and that Greg didn't give him the chance to tell him he would no longer pay for his college expenses. Mr. Lockhart verified the fact that by deed dated August 14, 1998, he sold his home in Davidson County, Tennessee for $146,900 and by deed dated August 17, 1998 he purchased property in Wilson County, Tennessee for $210,000.

After Rodney Lockhart stopped paying one-half of Greg's expenses at the University of Miami, Ms. Johnson carried the entire financial responsibility for his education (beyond scholarship and college loans) by cashing out her mutual fund account and liquidating her retirement portfolio.

The trial court found that Sharron Johnson and Rodney Lockhart had entered into a bi-lateral oral contract under which each would pay one-half of Greg's college expenses until he graduated. The trial court further found that Rodney Lockhart had breached the agreement and entered judgment in favor of Sharron Johnson for $20,427.25, representing one-half of the expenses she had paid for Paul G. Lockhart's college expenses at the University of Miami. The court also awarded pre-judgment interest in the amount of $3,398.18. Mr. Lockhart filed a timely appeal.

Appellant asserts the issues on appeal to be:

 I. The doctrine of promissory estoppel is not applicable.
 II. There was no enforceable contract creating liability between Rodney Lockhart and Sharron Johnson.
 III. If there was an enforceable contract between Rodney Lockhart and Paul G. Lockhart, Paul was in breach of it by the end of his freshman year.
 IV. Defendant had no duty to Plaintiff, Sharron Johnson, to reimburse her for college expenses paid by her on behalf of the parties' adult son.
 V. Plaintiff, Sharron Johnson, failed to mitigate damages.

The real issues on appeal might better be stated as:

1. Does the evidence preponderate against the trial court's finding that a bi-lateral contract existed between Sharron Johnson and Rodney Lockhart whereby each would pay half of Greg's net expenses for four years at the University of Miami?
2. Does part performance take the contract out of the statute of frauds?
3. If the contract is not supported by consideration, does the doctrine of promissory estoppel apply to estop Rodney Lockhart from relying on lack of consideration? . . .

. . . Addressing first the existence of the contract, in the general sessions court warrant issued December 3, 1998, Sharron Johnson alleged: "Breach of

Contract re: College tuition, board and books for Paul Lockhart." After appeal to circuit court, the Complaint was amended on April 30, 1999. Ms. Johnson alleged an oral contract between her and Mr. Lockhart whereby they would share equally the net costs of Greg Lockhart's college expenses at the University of Miami for the entire four year period. She further alleged that, in furtherance of this contract, Mr. Lockhart, in fact, paid one-half of Greg's college expenses at the University of Miami for two semesters. In answer to this Amended Complaint, Mr. Lockhart denied an agreement of any sort but admitted making several payments to the University of Miami during 1997 and 1998 on behalf of Greg.

The case came on for trial, non-jury, on February 6, 2002. After hearing all of the evidence, the trial court found:

1. The parties were divorced October 1980. The mother was the primary residential custodian of the one son. The final divorce decree did not include college expenses. The son graduated from high school December 1996 and enrolled in low cost public junior college in his home town. The son applied and received conditional acceptance at the University of Miami May 10, 1997. The son desired to pursue education in international studies. The mother and son needed the Defendant's agreement to pay one-half of the college expense in order for the son, PAUL G. LOCKHART, to attend the University of Miami. Beginning May 23, 1997 through July 1997 Plaintiff had several financial discussions with the Defendant, where the Defendant agreed to pay one-half of the college expenses for the son to attend the University of Miami. Relying upon the Defendant's agreement, the Plaintiff signed and submitted the final acceptance documents to the University of Miami in August 199[7]. Plaintiff's son then left the low cost public junior college. Plaintiff and Defendant moved the son in at the University of Miami. Plaintiff and Defendant met with the college financial office and established a loan payment plan for payment of the college expenses. The son thereafter attended the University of Miami. The Defendant paid his one-half of the college expenses during the son's first year. The Defendant, in August of 1998, did unilaterally and without explanation or any communication with the Plaintiff, refuse to continue to pay college expenses. Plaintiff immediately brought action in December 1998 against the Defendant. The son graduated May 2001 from the University of Miami in international studies. The mother and son paid out a total of Forty Thousand Eight Hundred Fifty Four and 00/100 ($40,854.00) Dollars in college expenses for the last three (3) years during this pending litigation. Defendant made no payments after August 1998.

2. The Court finds that promissory estoppel exists and the parties had an enforceable contract. *Calabro v. Calabro*, 15 S.W.3d 873 (Tn.Appeals 1999).

3. The Plaintiff, SHARRON JOHNSON, is entitled to a judgment for one-half of the college expenses totaling Twenty Thousand Four Hundred Twenty Seven and 25/100 ($20,427.25) Dollars against the Defendant, RODNEY LOCKHART. The Court further exercises discretion and awards Plaintiff pre-judgment interest from August 1998. The Defendant

was continuously advised of the amounts due but chose not to pay or even communicate. . .

. . . The evidence certainly does not preponderate against the finding of the trial court of a bi-lateral oral contract to pay equally the net expenses of Greg Lockhart at the University of Miami for four years. Inherent in the finding of the court is a determination that the contract was supported by adequate consideration.

The question of what constitutes consideration adequate or sufficient to support a contract has been addressed by a number of Tennessee courts. The court in *University of Chattanooga v. Stansberry*, 9 Tenn. App. 341, 343 (1928) defined consideration as "either a benefit to the maker of the promise or a detriment to, or obligation upon the promise." (citing *Foust v. Board of Education*, 76 Tenn., (8 Lea), 552). Courts have been willing to find a contract based on facts from which a jury could infer the requisite consideration.

For there to be a consideration in a contract between parties to the contract it is not necessary that something concrete and tangible move from one to the other. Any benefit to one and detriment to the other may be a sufficient consideration. The jury may draw any reasonable and natural inference from the proof and if by inference from the proof a benefit to the promisor and detriment to the promisee might be inferred this will constitute a valid consideration.

Palmer v. Dehn, 29 Tenn.App. 597, 599, 198 S.W.2d 827, 828 (1946); *see also Trailer Conditioners, Inc. v. Huddleston*, 897 S.W.2d 728, 731 (Tenn.App.1995); *Robinson v. Kenney*, 526 S.W.2d 115, 118–19 (Tenn.App.1973).

Calabro v. Calabro, 15 S.W.3d 873, 876–77 (Tenn.Ct.App.1999).

Sharron Johnson was under no more of an obligation to pay one-half of Greg Lockhart's net expenses at the University of Miami for four years than Rodney Lockhart. Both wished to help their adult son to get a college education in international studies at the University if Miami rather than to continue at a relatively inexpensive community college. The detriment to Ms. Johnson is that she undertook, on the strength of the promises of Rodney Lockhart, to pay half of Greg's net expenses for four years when she was not otherwise obligated to do so. The contract was supported by adequate consideration . . .

. . . In this case, part performance by both parties is conclusively established, as both of them paid their respective shares of the net expenses for Greg at the University of Miami through the first two semesters. While it is true that such payment would be consistent with a mere voluntary payment by both parties, which could be discontinued at any time, the trial court has made the factual determination that the oral contract was a four year contract. The evidence does not preponderate against that crucial finding of fact, as the payments by both parties are clearly in partial performance of the four year contract . . .

While the doctrine of promissory estoppel is unnecessary in this case since the oral contract was supported by adequate consideration, the trial court applied the doctrine as an alternative basis for holding Mr. Lockhart liable, and the evidence does not preponderate against such holding. . . .

. . . Under the theory of promissory estoppel, [W]hen one . . . by his promise induces another to change his situation, a repudiation of the promise would amount to a fraud. Where one makes a promise which the promisor should reasonably expect to induce action or forbearance of a definite and substantial character on the part of the promisee, and where such promise does in fact induce such action or forbearance, it is binding if injustice can be avoided only by enforcement of the promise.

Foster & Creighton Co. v. Wilson Contracting Co., 579 S.W.2d 422, 427 (Tenn.App.1978) (citing 17 C.J.S. *Contracts* § 74); *see also* Restatement (Second) of Contracts § 90(1) (1979). This theory of recovery is sometimes referred to as "detrimental reliance" because, in addition to showing that the defendant made a promise upon which the plaintiff reasonably relied, the plaintiff must show that this reliance resulted in detriment to the plaintiff. *Foster & Creighton Co.*, 579 S.W.2d at 427; Quake Constr., 152 Ill. Dec. 308, 565 N.E.2d at 1004 . . .

. . . Further, Promissory estoppel has been explained by this Court as:

A promise which the promisor should reasonably expect to induce action or forbearance on the part of the promisee or a third person and which does induce such action or forbearance is binding if injustice can be avoided only by enforcement of the promise. The remedy granted for breach may be limited as justice requires . . .

. . .

The trial court held that the representations and the actions of Mr. Lockhart were adequate to supply the necessary elements of inducement and reliance, and the evidence does not preponderate against such finding.

The judgment of the trial court is in all respects affirmed, and the case is remanded for such further action as may be necessary. . .

Guided Reading Questions

1. What was the promise that induced reliance?

2. Did Ms. Johnson, the promisee, rely on the promise? How?

3. What were Mr. Lockhart's representations and actions that induced Ms. Johnson to rely on his promise?

■ WHAT A PARALEGAL NEEDS TO KNOW ABOUT CONSIDERATION

The paralegal has to be very careful when ascertaining contractual performance so as to not engage in the unauthorized practice of law. Any decision or determination made that involves a legal decision, or legal conclusion, or that requires a party to change his or her legal position, must be made by an attorney. A paralegal cannot ascertain whether the consideration tendered is adequate to support the agreement. The paralegal cannot decide if the consideration is in actuality a benefit to one party and a detriment to another party. This is solely for the attorney to decide.

The Paralegal's Role Regarding Consideration

The paralegal can look at the contract to determine the form and/or amount of consideration to be tendered in the agreement. After ascertaining the amount, the form, and the agreed time of transfer, the paralegal can make sure that consideration is transferred appropriately to the party, or to a third party, as agreed and also that the consideration is of the value agreed. Consideration need not be measurable in dollar figures. Sometimes consideration is forbearing, or not doing something. If consideration is measurable in dollars, the paralegal should check to see if the amount, the dollar figure, is correct.

CASE ILLUSTRATION

Guided Reading Pointers

Read the abridged *Osborne* case that follows. Pay close attention to the consideration for the agreement. Note that the court comments on adequacy of consideration and past consideration to support a current agreement. The form of the consideration in this case involves a service.

Oliver T. Osborne
v.
The Locke Steel Chain Company

Supreme Court of Connecticut
153 Conn. 527 (1966)

This action was brought by the plaintiff to recover damages for breach of contract, alleged to have been caused by the defendant's refusal to make payments to him under a written agreement entered into between the parties under date of November 4, 1960.

The terms of this agreement provided that the defendant pay the plaintiff $20,000 during the year ending September 30, 1961, and thereafter, $15,000 a year for the remainder of the plaintiff's life. The plaintiff agreed to hold himself available for consultation and advice with the company and its officers and not to engage in or be employed by any business enterprise, directly or indirectly, which is engaged in any line of business in competition with the company within the states of Connecticut, New York, Pennsylvania, Ohio, Indiana, Illinois, Michigan, California or Washington, or in any of the areas abroad in which the company does business. The defendant made payments in accordance with the terms of the agreement for approximately two and one-half years, following which, after the plaintiff refused to consent to a modification of the agreement, the defendant discontinued further payments. The plaintiff then initiated the present action to recover payments due under the agreement. The defendant . . . alleged that the agreement was invalid and unenforceable, claiming in effect (1) inadequate consideration because the contract was based on past services, (2) it was manifestly unfair to the defendant, (3) it was procured through undue influence, (4) it was a lifetime employment contract not authorized or ratified by the shareholders, and (5) the board of directors had no authority to enter into it. The issues were tried to the court, which concluded that the agreement was legally unenforceable. Judgment was rendered for the defendant, and the plaintiff took the present appeal.

The facts necessary to a disposition of the question involved are undisputed. The plaintiff was employed by the defendant from 1912 until November of 1961, progressively holding the positions of order clerk, traffic manager, salesman, sales manager president, and chairman of the board. He was president of the company from 1941 to 1958 and a member of the board of directors from 1941 until 1961. From 1958 until his retirement in November, 1961, he served as chairman of the board of directors . . .

The agreement in suit was approved by the board of directors at a special meeting held on November 4, 1960 . . . After its approval by the board, the agreement was signed by the plaintiff and by the company acting through its president. Regular payments were made to the plaintiff until April, 1963, at which time the company repudiated the agreement and discontinued payments.

The trial court concluded that there was no consideration for the agreement on the part of the plaintiff and that the directors did not have authority to enter into the agreement . . .

. . . We first pass to the question of consideration. The doctrine of consideration is of course fundamental in the law of contracts, the general rule being that in the absence of consideration an executory promise is unenforceable. In defining the elements of the rule, we have stated that consideration consists of "a benefit to the party promising, or a loss or detriment to the party to whom the promise is made." *Finlay v. Swirsky*, 103 Conn. 624, 631, 131 A. 420; *Barnum v. Barnum*, 8 Conn. 469, 471. An exchange of promises is sufficient consideration to support a contract. *Taft Realty Corporation v. Yorkhaven Enterprises, Inc.*, 146 Conn. 338, 342, 150 A.2d 597; *Kay Petroleum Corporation v. Piergrossi*, 137 Conn. 620, 622, 79 A.2d 829.

The recited consideration in the present case consists of the plaintiff's promise to hold himself available for consultation with the defendant in connection with the defendant's business and to avoid serving any enterprise in competition with the defendant within a designated area. In essence, what the defendant bargained for, as contained in the terms of the written agreement, was the exclusive right to the plaintiff's knowledge and experience in his chosen field for the remainder of his life . . .

Absent other infirmities, "bargains . . . moved upon calculated considerations, and, whether provident or improvident, are entitled nevertheless to the sanctions of the law." *United States v. United Shoe Machinery Co.*, 247 U.S. 32, 66, 38 S. Ct. 473, 62 L. Ed. 968. The defendant cannot now be heard to claim, for its own benefit, that the actual undertaking of the parties was other than that which appears in their written agreement. *Lakitsch v. Brand*, 99 Conn. 388, 393, 121 A. 865. Even though it might prefer to have the court decide the plain effect of this agreement to be contrary to the expressed intention set forth in the contract between the parties, it is not within the power of the court to make a new or different contract. *New Orleans v. New Orleans Water Works Co.*, 142 U.S. 79, 91, 12 S. Ct. 142, 35 L. Ed. 943; *Sand Filtration Corporation v. Cowardin*, 213 U.S. 360, 364, 29 S. Ct. 509, 53 L. Ed. 833; 17 Am. Jur. 2d 627, Contracts, § 242; 4 Williston, Contracts (3d Ed.) § 610. The plain implication of the contract must be followed in accordance with the intention of the parties. *Sturtevant v. Sturtevant,* 146 Conn. 644, 647, 648, 153 A.2d 828; *Molyneux v. Twin Falls Canal Co.*, 54 Idaho 619, 626, 35 P.2d 651.

Under the facts of this case, the recited consideration constituted a benefit to the defendant, as well as a detriment to the plaintiff, and was therefore sufficient consideration under the general rule set out in *Finlay v. Swirsky*, supra. An exclusive right to the counseling of the plaintiff, who had had almost fifty years of experience in the defendant's business, including some twenty years in positions of ultimate responsibility, and whose capacities are unchallenged, cannot reasonably be held to be valueless. Exactly what value might be placed on such a right is of course irrelevant to this issue. The doctrine of consideration does not require or imply an equal exchange between the contracting parties. "That which is bargained-for by the promisor and given in exchange for the promise by the promisee is not made insufficient as a consideration by the fact that its value in the market is not equal to that which is promised. Consideration in fact bargained for is not required to be adequate in the sense of equality in value." 1 Corbin, Contracts § 127; see *Clark v. Sigourney*, 17 Conn. 511, 517. The general rule is that, in the absence of fraud or other unconscionable circumstances, a contract will not be rendered unenforceable at the behest of one of the contracting parties merely because of an inadequacy of consideration. 1 Williston, Contracts (3d Ed.) § 115; 17 Am. Jur. 2d, Contracts, § 102. The courts do not unmake bargains unwisely made. The contractual obligation of the defendant in the present case, whether wise or unwise, was supported by consideration, in the form of the plaintiff's promises to give advice and not to compete with the defendant, and that obligation cannot now be avoided on this ground.

One additional aspect of the issue of consideration needs discussion. The defendant has claimed that the agreement was motivated by a desire to compensate the plaintiff during his retirement years for his past services to the company. Judging from certain language in the preamble to the agreement referring to the company's custom of paying pensions to its retired personnel, this was undoubtedly true in part. The general rule is that past services will not constitute a sufficient consideration for an **executory** promise of compensation for those services. *Moore v. Keystone Macaroni Mfg. Co.*, 370 Pa. 172, 177, 87 A.2d 295; see 1A Corbin, Contracts § 235. It is well established, however, that if two considerations are given for a promise, only one of which is legally sufficient, the promise is nonetheless enforceable. 1 Corbin, Contracts § 126; 1 Williston, Contracts (3d Ed.) § 134. Since the agreement contained promises by the plaintiff which we have held to constitute sufficient consideration, the fact that there was additional consideration, not legally sufficient to support the agreement, cannot excuse the defendant from performance . . .

Executory
a contract that has yet to be performed.

. . .

. . . On review of the issues presented, therefore, we hold that the agreement was supported by consideration, was fair to the defendant and was a proper exercise of corporate powers by the board of directors.

There is error, the judgment is set aside and the case is remanded with direction to render judgment for the plaintiff in accordance with this opinion. . .

Guided Reading Questions

1. What was the promise made?

2. What was the consideration given?

3. Was there consideration for the promise to provide consulting services to the company?

4. What does the court say about adequacy of consideration?

CHAPTER SUMMARY

This chapter explored the concept of consideration. Consideration is an essential component of a valid contract. Consideration must be bargained for but is not required to be the motivation for the contract. Additionally, consideration can be in a monetary form but can also be in the form of an act or service. Consideration is deemed adequate when the parties agree to it; consideration can be negligible in value. Consideration can also be in the form of forbearing from acting.

There are instances of when there is no present consideration to support an agreement: when past performance is used as consideration for a current contract; when there is a pre-existing duty; in the instance of a moral obligation; and in illusory promises.

Consideration

Key Features of Consideration	Has value to the parties making the exchange in the contract It is bargained for Can be of negligible value
Consideration Defined	Consideration can induce the offeror and the offeree to enter into the contract It is the value that each party is willing to proffer to support the agreement; it cements the agreement
Benefit to Promisee/Detriment to Promisor	Must be a benefit to the promisee and a detriment to the promisor The benefit and detriment can take the form of money, action, or forbearance
Issues Concerning Consideration	Adequacy: As long as there is a benefit to the promisee and a detriment to the promisor, and the consideration is bargained for and agreed to, consideration is adequate even if negligible

When There Is No Current Consideration	Past promises Pre-existing duty Moral obligations and gratuitous promises Illusory promises Future gifts
The U.C.C. and Consideration	The court will step in, in a contract between merchants for the sale of goods under U.C.C. § 2-302, when the consideration is unconscionable, and refuse to enforce the portion of the contract or the terms that is unconscionable
Promissory Estoppel	When the promisee relies to his or her detriment on the promise, and the promisor knows that the promise induced action or forbearance, a court may, to avoid injustice, bar the promisor from not carrying out the promise
What a Paralegal Needs to Know about Consideration	Do not determine if the consideration is adequate, for that is a legal decision and is the unauthorized practice of law Review the agreement to know the amount and form of the consideration, and the time to tender

REVIEW QUESTIONS

1. Does the consideration have to be of a certain value or worth?
2. What is the paralegal's role regarding determining if the consideration to support the agreement is adequate?
3. How is the nature and amount of the consideration determined?
4. Can forbearing from taking an action, or forbearing from performing an act, constitute consideration?
5. What is detrimental reliance?
6. What is promissory estoppel?
7. What is a benefit to the promisor? Provide an example.
8. What is a detriment to the promisee? Provide an example.
9. Can consideration be assigned to a third party?

SKILL–BUILDING APPLICATION EXERCISES

Please write a paragraph describing the consideration that supported the agreement reached by Sharron Johnson and Rodney Lockhart (case appears earlier in chapter), and explain whether the court determined if the consideration was adequate.

SIMULATED LAW OFFICE ASSIGNMENT

A client of your firm, Youth Education Corporation, wants to expand its operations by offering summer sports camps to children. David Trane is the principal owner of Youth Education Corporation. Your supervising attorney prepared a release for the parents of the child participants to sign. A release is a contract in many respects. Review the language of the release and determine what constitutes the consideration that the parents provide.

Release

In consideration of my child's participation in this camp, I hereby release the Youth Education Corporation staff, officers, employees, and Youth Education Corporation, Inc. for any and all liability arising out of any injury or illness my child incurs while participating in camp activities. I understand the rigorous athletic activity in which he/she will be involved. I understand that participation is voluntary and I choose freely to have my child participate.

Is there a benefit to the promisor here?
Is there a detriment to the promisee?
Is the consideration the inducement for making the contract here? In other words, is the consideration here the inducement for a child's participation in the camp, or is it bargained for but not the inducement for attending the camp?

DRAFTING EXERCISE

Mary Thorne, the firm's client, has an interior design company that she owns and runs called Thorne Designs. From 1989 to 1997, Mary was the chief designer for Town Pillows, a custom pillow manufacturer. Town offered Mary $7,000 per year for fifteen years, starting in 1997 when Mary ceased her employment with Town, to advise Town on pillow trends. Last year, Town requested that Mary modify their agreement to include a limitation on Mary's ability to provide design advice to her own clients in the areas of pillows and soft furnishings. Mary refused to consent to a modification of the agreement. Town discontinued the payments of $7,000 per year.

Reread the *Osborne* case earlier in this chapter. Draft one to two paragraphs, based on the holding in *Osborne*, detailing the bargain that Thorne and Town reached and the consideration supporting that agreement. Address whether Mary Thorne's agreement with Town was supported by adequate consideration and whether Town's request to modify their agreement was supported by consideration.

DEVELOPING CRITICAL THINKING SKILLS

Reread *Johnson v. Lockhart* and *Osborne v. The Locke Steel Chain Co.* reprinted in this chapter. Based on your reading of these opinions, how would you define consideration? What do the cases say about consideration? Any issues regarding timing and adequacy? Please write two paragraphs containing the answers to these questions.

PORTFOLIO ASSIGNMENT

Your supervising attorney recently has met with a client. The attorney has determined that the client relied to her detriment on a promise made by her father. The attorney believes that the *Johnson v. Lockhart* case supports his determination.

Reread *Johnson* carefully before reading the following facts.

Mr. See has a daughter by the name of Mary and Mary has two children, Meg and Greg. Meg and Greg are Mr. See's only grandchildren. Mr. See promised Mary that he would pay for Greg and Meg's college education. Mr. See made this promise on the day that each child was born and has re-iterated his promise at least three times annually. Meg and Greg, twins, were born eighteen years ago and have been accepted to State University. For the past eighteen years, Mr. See has told his daughter not to work because he has set money aside for the children's education. Mary did not take a paying job. In lieu of a paying job, Mr. See asked that Mary be his caretaker and that he would pay for the twins' college education to compensate her for taking care of him. Mary has taken care of her father for the past eighteen years. The twins, enrolled in State University for the current academic year, receive a bill for their tuition. Mary submits the tuition bill to her father for payment. Mr. See does not pay the bill. Mr. See does not tender one penny to State University. Mr. See tells Mary that he decided to keep the money for himself because he is living longer than he anticipated. Instead of paying the tuition bill, Mr. See provides Mary with articles and brochures on how to obtain college loans.

Based on your careful reading of *Johnson*, how has Mary relied to her detriment on Mr. See's promise? Did Mr. See's promise induce forbearance or an action on Mary's part?

Do you think that the *Johnson* case supports Mary's claim of promissory estoppel? Please write a short paragraph explaining why the case supports your supervising attorney's determination.

Formation of Contracts
Issues with Contract Formation

CHAPTER 5

INTRODUCTION

A properly formed contract requires mutuality of obligation, identified parties and subject matter, a clear offer, assent to the terms, and consideration. These foundations, of course, must be laid to form a contract, and there is detailed exploration of these topics in other chapters. Once these foundations are established, additional requirements are necessary for the formation of a contract. Although contracts are not required to be in writing, written agreements are quite common and allow the parties to clearly ascertain their rights if a default or breach should occur. A written contract also has specific requirements. The set requirements for a written contract are: a written agreement embodying the deal that the parties reached, signatures, date, and that it conforms to **public policy** and to the law. Oral contracts are valid and are frequently formed, but may have special rules depending on the subject matter of the agreement and the jurisdiction. Additionally, invalid and unenforceable contracts arise due to failure to adhere to legal parameters in the formative stages.

A contract requires mutuality, or mutual, definite and clear assent (see Chapter 3, Acceptance) of the parties contracting, sufficient consideration to support the promises made (see Chapter 4 for a complete discussion of consideration), and that the parties are competent to contract and the subject matter of the agreement is legal. However, it is not necessary for a contract to be in writing except where required by state statute. Often a state will require

LEARNING OBJECTIVES

After studying this chapter, you will be able to:

1. Discuss specific legal requirements for contract formation.
2. Explain the role of the Statute of Frauds.
3. Discuss the parol evidence rule.
4. Define a contract of adhesion.
5. Discuss void and voidable contracts.

that certain agreements conform to the **Statute of Frauds** requiring that a contract that exceeds $500 in value, a contract for the purchase or sale of real estate, or a contract that requires more than one year to perform be in writing. Certain insurance contracts, according to a particular state statute, must be in writing. Additionally, formal contracts, such as negotiable instruments and letters of credit, must be in writing because they contain very set language and provisions, often controlled by state statutes.

Public policy
legal and societal objectives of the jurisdiction.

Statute of Frauds
almost every state has a Statute of Frauds provision in the state code requiring that certain types of contracts be in writing. Generally, a contract where the value of the agreement exceeds $500, a contract for the sale of real estate, or a contract requiring more than a year to perform must be in writing.

■ SPECIFIC REQUISITES

Writing

When a contract is in writing it need not follow a set format unless it is of a specific subject controlled by statute, such as insurance policies or letters of credit. Additionally, many written contracts are put together from a series of written communications whereby parties, for instance, exchange a series of emails to arrive at an agreement.

Example: Ms. Smith wants Chris Couture to create a custom, unique little black dress for Ms. Smith to wear to the Children's Benevolent Society Benefit this fall. Ms. Smith found Ms. Couture's website while searching the Internet for possible couturiers. On July, 2, Ms. Smith emailed Ms. Couture and detailed her ideas for a dress and the date she needed it. Ms. Couture emailed Ms. Smith some pictures of possible designs with some fabric suggestions on July 9. On July 14, Ms. Smith emailed Couture to state that she liked view B, the dress with the long sleeves. On July 16, Ms. Couture emailed Smith that she would make view B, the black dress with the long sleeves, for $600 and that it would be ready in two weeks. Work on the dress would start immediately when Ms. Smith emailed her assent to the price and terms.

A contract can also be in electronic form and filled in online. Many online lenders, such as CareCredit, which loans money for elective medical procedures, have credit applications on the Internet that potential borrowers can submit and comply with electronically.

■ PARTLY WRITTEN AND PARTLY ORAL AGREEMENTS

A valid contract can also be partly in writing and partly oral. A written contract can be transmitted electronically and still be valid. Always check the state statutes of the appropriate jurisdiction—the attorney can help you determine the applicable state law—to determine if a particular agreement is required to be in writing. For instance, the Statute of Frauds (discussed more fully in the next section) may require that contracts concerning real estate be in writing, or that a life insurance contract be in writing.

STATUTE OF FRAUDS

The applicability of the Statute of Frauds is determined by state law. Generally, regardless of jurisdiction, the Statute of Frauds requires a contract to be in writing when it concerns the sale of real estate, the subject of the agreement is valued at over $500, or if the deal takes a year or longer to perform. Each state has jurisdiction-specific provisions, usually located in the respective state statute, regarding the requirements.

> **Research Tip**   Check the Martindale Hubbell Law Digest, USA Listings, and under each state you can find the state's requirements for the Statute of Frauds.

For example, Georgia's statutes detail the requirements for when a contract is to be in writing and signed by the person obligated under the contract.

Georgia's Statute of Frauds, O.C.G.A. §13–5–30 (2008), provides when a contract should be in writing:

1. promises of an executor regarding his own estate
2. promise to answer for debt of another
3. agreements, such as prenuptial agreements, made in consideration of marriage
4. contracts for the sale of land, or contracts for an interest in real property
5. an agreement that requires more than one year to be performed
6. promise to revive a debt that is barred by the Statute of Limitations
7. promise to lend money

Under §13–5–31, note 3, a contract creating a landlord—tenant relationship that extends over one year must be in writing.

Under §11–2–201, a contract for the sale of goods where the price exceeds $500 also must be in writing.

Formalities Concerning Oral Contracts

Oral contracts are valid. However, certain agreements must be in writing to comply with the Statute of Frauds. The parameters regarding oral contracts are subject to state law. For instance, Georgia requires that insurance contracts be written. Also, the subject matter of an oral agreement may require additional consideration to bind the parties; this too is dependent on state law. Furthermore, contracts that are partly written and partly oral are valid as long as state laws are followed. The Restatement (Second) of Contracts §4 states that a valid contract may be partly in writing and partly oral.

The Role of the U.C.C. and the Statute of Frauds

Under §2–201 of the U.C.C., a contract for the sale of goods in excess of $500 must be in writing and signed by the party who is obligated to perform under the agreement. This writing and signature are required to enforce the terms of the agreement.

■ PAROL EVIDENCE RULE

The parol evidence rule applies to written contracts. Once a contract is written and agreed to, the parties' oral negotiations, prior agreements, and intent are considered to be integrated, or incorporated, into the final written contract. The parol evidence rule underscores the importance of putting the agreement in writing and also that it is essential to include the entire agreement between the parties in the writing prior to finalizing the contract.

The Restatement (Second) of Contracts §209 defines integrated agreements as:

(1) . . . a writing or writings constituting a final expression of one or more terms of an agreement. . . .
(2) "Where the parties reduce an agreement to a writing which in view of its completeness and specificity reasonably appears to be a complete agreement, it is taken to be an integrated agreement unless it is established buy other evidence that the writing did not constitute a final expression."

The Restatement (Second) of Contracts §210 states that an integrated agreement is "adopted by the parties as a complete and exclusive statement of the terms of the agreement."

The written agreement represents the parties' complete bargain. A party, then, cannot go back to the negotiations, to use as evidence, or to establish different intent or terms, if it is not reflected in the written agreement. Additionally, a court will not add additional terms once a contract is in writing for if the terms are not in the written agreement they cannot be added to the contract, or used as evidence, for the written contract is the final expression of the parties' agreement. There is an exception for when the contract is entered into under duress or fraud or when it can be proved that the contract lacks consideration; in such cases the court will permit evidence of agreements and negotiations made in the process of, or prior to, creating the writing.

These exceptions, as stated in the Restatement (Second) of Contracts §214, only permit the admission into evidence of prior and concurrent negotiations, to show:

(a) that the writing is or is not an integrated agreement;
(b) that the integrated agreement, if any, is completely or partially integrated;
(c) the meaning of the writing, whether or not integrated;
(d) illegality, fraud, duress, mistake, lack of consideration, or other invalidating clause;
(e) ground for granting or denying rescission, reformation, specific performance, or their remedy.

In its most general form, the intent of the parol evidence rule allows the court to ascertain the terms and conditions of the agreement from the contract itself and to not have to create terms. The Restatement (Second) of Contracts §213 details the operation of the parol evidence rule as:

(1) A binding integrated agreement discharges prior agreements to the extent that it is inconsistent with them.
(2) A binding completely integrated agreement discharges prior agreements to the extent that they are within its scope.

This does not mean that every detail of the agreement must be stated. However, there are times when a term or condition is vague and the court has to resort to examining the surrounding circumstances and other information to clarify the agreement. The court, however, is hesitant to insert or to construct the essential terms of the contract such as price or timing, for example.

Additionally, an agreement can be partially integrated, where one part of the agreement is reduced to writing.

Example: Mr. Russell hired Sloan Brothers Contractors to build a new front porch on his home. Mr. Russell spoke with the Sloan Brothers at length about the porch design, the rails, and the bead board. The written agreement, signed by both parties, stated that Sloan Brothers would build a $14' \times 6'$ front porch, made from oak. The rails would be spaced at 6″ intervals. The porch would cost $2,000 to construct. Work would start on May 1 and the project would be complete by July 31. The last line of the contract states: "This letter represents the complete agreement between Mr. Russell and Sloan Brothers Contractors."

This is an integrated agreement. The agreement regarding the bead board is discharged since bead board as a component of the porch design is not included in the final, integrated agreement.

The U.C.C. and the Parol Evidence Rule

Under U.C.C. §2–202, concerning the sale of goods, when a written contract is the final expression of the parties' agreement, the terms may be supplemented or explained. These terms may be explained or clarified by terms used in the course of dealing between the parties and by terms used in the particular trade.

Signature

A signature is not required to create a valid contract. Parties are still bound to the terms of the written agreement even if not signed, unless the contract stipulates that accord is indicated by a signature. The Statute of Frauds, in certain jurisdictions, may require an agreement to be signed. Always check the requirements in the jurisdiction by consulting the state statutes or the Martindale Hubbell Law Digest US.

When signing a contract, parties may sign in any manner that indicates assent. A party may sign with an "X" or use a crayon as long as the party intends to sign it.

An electronic signature is valid under federal law, 15 U.S.C. §7001 et seq., as long as it does not conflict with other contractual and statutory requirements. Contracts with electronic signatures are legal and binding even if the entire agreement is in electronic form. The federal statutes require that agreements concerning interstate commerce shall be upheld when in an electronic format. Although the use of electronic signatures is not widespread, companies such as Microsoft use e-signatures for their online contracts, as do many mortgage companies.

Date

The date on a contract is very important because it indicates the date the agreement was executed unless there is a specific provision stating that the agreement becomes effective on a certain date. The date provision permits assessing the timing of the breach, if one should arise. Also, a date permits the tolling (to stop the time from ticking away to bring an action) of the Statute of Limitations. The Statute of Limitations, sometimes called Limitation of Action, is a set time permitted under statute to bring a legal action. The Statute of Limitations for breach of contract differs from state to state. Consult your attorney for the time frame, the appropriate state statute, or the Martindale Hubbell Law Digest.

Against Public Policy

Contracts must comply with the law to be valid. This is discussed in Chapter 6 in greater detail. A contract that is against public policy is basically a contract for an illegal activity, an illegal substance, or that violates the law in the state where the contract is formed. Examples of contracts that are against public policy are contracts for the sale of heroin, contracts to commit murder, agreements for tax evasion, and contracts for the loan of funds at excessive interest rates.

■ VOID AND VOIDABLE AGREEMENTS

A void contract does not have any legal force or effect; it cannot be enforced. For instance, the contract can no longer exist due to illegality of the subject matter. For example, if you draft a contract to commit murder and even though both parties agree to the terms, due to the fact that the subject matter is against public policy, the contract will be void and the agreement will cease to exist. The promise is void of legal effect and there is no remedy for breach nor duty of performance.

A voidable contract differs from a void contract, according to the Restatement (Second) of Contracts §7, for a voidable agreement can be affirmed or rejected at the option of one of the parties.

In a voidable contract, a provision or a portion is unenforceable, so the remaining provisions of the agreement can be in effect or the entire agreement can be voided at the election of the wronged party. Instances of when a contract, or a contract provision, may be voidable include: when a party is a minor; the contract is induced by misrepresentation, fraud, or duress; or breach of warranty.

The Restatement (Second) of Contracts, §4 states that:

> The legal relations that exist after avoidance vary with the circumstances. In some cases the party who avoids the contract is entitled to be restored to a position as good as that which he occupied immediately before the formation of the contract; in other cases the parties may be left in the same condition as at the time of the avoidance. In many cases the power of avoidance exists only if the original situation of the parties can be and is restored at least substantially; but this is not necessarily the case.

A minor can generally avoid his or her obligations under the agreement. However, where fraud occurs, the party defrauded can sometimes choose to void the entire agreement or a particular provision. The Restatement (Second) of Contracts §7 stipulates that a voidable contract creates the right in one of the parties to avoid the obligations under the agreement. Generally the party wronged is empowered to avoid the obligations under the contract.

Instance of When a Contract Is Voidable

When one of the following circumstances arises, the contract can be voidable by the party affected by the action of duress, undue influence, **unconscionable** agreements, fraud, or misrepresentation. The existence of a mistake in the terms, except for a **material** mistake, will not make the contract voidable. Important terms include the following:

Duress—the use of threats to force another to act.

Undue influence—unfair and extreme pressure that motivates a person's acts.

Unconscionable contracts or provisions—an agreement or provision that a reasonable person would not make (discussed more fully in Chapter 6).

Fraud—the intent to deceive. A contract is voidable when fraud can be proved because a party did not consent freely to the agreement and was induced to comply due to an untruth.

Misrepresentation—making a statement or representation that is not factual or the fact is not accurate. This is very similar to fraud. The contract or the particular provision is voidable when misrepresentation is proved.

Mistake—occurs when there is an error or omission. When the mistake is so great and concerns a material term in the contract, there is no meeting of the minds, and no contract will form. A material term is a term that is at the essence of the agreement, such as price, quantity, timing, or condition. A contract can become void if there is mutual mistake because this shows that there was no meeting of the minds. Often, a contract still stands although there is a mistake in a minor provision as long as the parties intended to agree on the particular provision and signed the contract. The Uniform Commercial Code §1–103 discusses the code's rules concerning mistake and states that the existence of a mistake in an agreement should be evaluated first, before other issues.

Unconscionable
an unconscionable contract is even more one sided than a contract of adhesion. A contract is unconscionable when it is oppressively one sided.

Material
essential or important to the agreement. The material terms usually concern price, quantity, timing, and condition. An immaterial term may concern how the shipping labels are placed on a package, for example.

Unenforceable Contracts

Unenforceable contracts are contracts that a court will not enforce. Contracts that concern illegal activities, such as to sell banned substances or to commit murder, are void. However, a court will still enforce an agreement even when the terms are unfair, overreaching, or even onerous as long as the parties consent without duress and are of sound mind. Unenforceable contracts are discussed more fully in Chapter 6.

Special Clauses and Situations

Contracts of Adhesion

Contracts of adhesion are frequently used, and the paralegal must be aware of them. These are sometimes called "take it or leave it" agreements. Contracts of adhesion arise when one party has no leverage or ability to negotiate. Sometimes a contract of adhesion exists when the bargain is onerous to one side. An example of a contract of adhesion is a car rental agreement. The renter must generally comply with the rental agency's terms or not rent the car. Another example is a residential lease whereby the tenant must comply with the landlord's terms or not be able to rent the apartment. On a more egregious level, payday loans are a form of a contract of adhesion because the borrower must pay a high interest rate that is not negotiable. State usury laws have been enacted to protect borrowers. Although they may seem obscure, contracts of adhesion are quite common in the commercial sector and in the consumer arena and have an important economic role.

Noncompete Agreements

This is an agreement to not compete with an entity within a certain geographic area or within a certain industry. Medical doctors often sign agreements that if they are to leave a practice, they cannot set up a similar practice within a certain number of miles. Franchises have covenants not to compete in franchise agreements. Individuals in sales often sign noncompete agreements so that when they take a position with a competitor, they cannot sell or solicit sales within a certain territory. The test often used to determine if the covenant not to compete is reasonable is if it furthers a legitimate business interest. (*Piercing Pagoda, Inc. v. Hoffner*, 351 A.2d 207 [Pa. 1976]).

Forbearance Agreements

Forbearance
to forbear is to not do an act.

Forbearance agreements are contracts to not act or to not exercise a legal right. A common forbearance agreement is a lender's agreement to not foreclose if the mortgage debt is repaid. Another forbearance agreement is for a creditor to agree to not sue a debtor for a debt owed.

Contracts Restraining Trade

Contracts formed that restrain trade are against public policy. Generally, agreements to create a monopoly are against public policy because they restrain trade. Restraint of trade is the interference with the free flow of commerce by, for example, price fixing or creating monopolies. Airlines have been accused of price fixing by agreeing to set fares, and this is a restraint of trade.

Many states have statutes concerning restraint of trade so that contracts entered into that violate the state statute are against public policy. For instance, the Nevada Unfair Trade Practice Act lists prohibited acts that restrain trade:

598A.060. Prohibited acts.

1. Every activity enumerated in this subsection constitutes a contract, combination or conspiracy in restraint of trade, and it is unlawful to conduct any part of any such activity in this state:

(a) Price fixing, which consists of raising, depressing, fixing, pegging or stabilizing the price of any commodity or service, and which includes, but is not limited to:

(1) Agreements among competitors to depress prices at which they will buy essential raw material for the end product.

(2) Agreements to establish prices for commodities or services.

(3) Agreements to establish uniform discounts, or to eliminate discounts.

(4) Agreements between manufacturers to price a premium commodity a specified amount above inferior commodities.

(5) Agreements not to sell below cost.

(6) Agreements to establish uniform trade-in allowances.

(7) Establishment of uniform cost surveys.

(8) Establishment of minimum markup percentages.

(9) Establishment of single or multiple basing point systems for determining the delivered price of commodities.

(10) Agreements not to advertise prices.

(11) Agreements among competitors to fix uniform list prices as a place to start bargaining.

(12) Bid rigging, including the misuse of bid depositories, foreclosures of competitive activity for a period of time, rotation of jobs among competitors, submission of identical bids, and submission of complementary bids not intended to secure acceptance by the customer.

(13) Agreements to discontinue a product, or agreements with anyone engaged in the manufacture of competitive lines to limit size, styles or quantities of items comprising the lines.

(14) Agreements to restrict volume of production.

(b) Division of markets, consisting of agreements between competitors to divide territories and to refrain from soliciting or selling in certain areas.

(c) Allocation of customers, consisting of agreements not to sell to specified customers of a competitor.

(d) Tying arrangements, consisting of contracts in which the seller or lessor conditions the sale or lease of commodities or services on the purchase or leasing of another commodity or service.

(e) Monopolization of trade or commerce in this state, including, without limitation, attempting to monopolize or otherwise combining or conspiring to monopolize trade or commerce in this state.

Nev. Rev. Stat. §598A.060

■ WHAT A PARALEGAL NEEDS TO KNOW

A paralegal should be aware of when a contract must be in writing in the jurisdiction of practice. Familiarity with the Statute of Frauds requirements or being able to locate the state's Statute of Frauds provisions is essential to determine when an agreement must be in writing. Aside from the particular state's requirements, a contract should be in writing when it involves the sale of real estate, when it is valued at over $500, and/or when it will take a year or longer to perform. Additionally, most insurance contracts must be in writing. Furthermore, a paralegal should be aware that if the agreement is in writing, it should contain the entire agreement reached by the parties. However, oral and combination oral/written agreements are legal. The writing can be in electronic format or in pencil or pen. The signature can be in any form, including an electronic signature. The date is also to be included in the agreement. Finally, although a contract may appear to be harsh whereby the promisee can basically take it or leave it (contracts of adhesion), these agreements have a role and enable parties to do business effectively.

The Paralegal's Role

Always ask the attorney supervising, if you are uncertain, which state's law applies to the agreement. Be able to locate the appropriate Statute of Frauds provisions for the state. Ascertain whether the agreement falls within the Statute of Frauds and should be in writing. Check your conclusions with the supervising attorney. Review any written agreement to assess whether it has been signed and dated. Note any instance of when you think that a contract is against public policy or is voidable due to **incapacity**, such as a contract signed by a minor. Ask the attorney about these issues. Do not make a decision as to whether a contract is against public policy, is void, or is voidable, because these are legal decisions only to be made by a licensed attorney.

Incapacity
lacking the mental ability to understand the ramifications of a particular situation. Usually determined by age, for if the individual is a minor, he or she does not have the capacity to contract, nor do the mentally impaired.

CASE ILLUSTRATION

Guided Reading Pointers

This case was brought originally by five orphaned brothers. The brothers sued for breach of contract for being portrayed in a false light and for exploitation. The appellate court held that the **arbitration** clause in the contract was not in bold, was not in a separately initialed paragraph, and was at the end of a lengthy document printed in a small font. Additionally, the brothers only had a little time to review the agreement prior to signing. The appellate court stated that the arbitration clause was unconscionable and unenforceable. Note that this opinion provides an example of a contract of adhesion because the brothers had no bargaining power in regard to the provision at issue. Think about how this is a "take it or leave it" scenario.

Arbitration
the resolution of a dispute by a third party, usually a mediator rather than in a courtroom by a judge.

Charles Higgins II et al., Petitioners,

v.

The Superior Court of Los Angeles County, Respondent; Disney/ABC International Television, Inc., et al., Real Parties in Interest

B187818

Court of Appeal of California, Second Appellate District, Division Eight

140 Cal. App. 4th 1238 (2006)

. . .

In this . . . proceeding, five siblings who appeared in an episode of the television program *Extreme Makeover: Home Edition* (*Extreme Makeover*) challenge an order compelling them to arbitrate most of their claims against various entities involved with the production and broadcast of the program. Petitioners claim the arbitration clause contained in a written agreement they executed before the program was broadcast is unconscionable. We agree . . .

FACTUAL AND PROCEDURAL BACKGROUND

Petitioners Charles, Michael, Charis, Joshua, and Jeremiah Higgins are siblings. In February 2005, when they executed the agreement whose arbitration provision is at issue, they were 21, 19, 17, 16, and 14 years old, respectively.

Real parties in interest, to whom we refer collectively as the television defendants, are (1) American Broadcasting Companies, Inc., the network that broadcasts *Extreme Makeover*; (2) Disney/ABC International Television, Inc., which asserts it had no involvement with the *Extreme Makeover* program in which petitioners appeared; (3) Lock and Key Productions, the show's producer; (4) Endemol USA, Inc., which is also involved in producing the program; and (5) Pardee Homes, which constructed the home featured in the *Extreme Makeover* episode in which petitioners appeared.

Petitioners' parents died in 2004. The eldest sibling, Charles, became the guardian for the then three minor children. (To avoid confusion with his siblings, we refer to Charles Higgins by his first name.) Shortly thereafter, petitioners moved in with church acquaintances, Firipeli and Lokilani Leomiti, a couple with three children of their own . . .

According to Charles, after moving in with the Leomitis, he was advised by members of his church that producers of *Extreme Makeover* had contacted the church and had asked to speak to him about the production of a show based on the loss of petitioners' parents and that petitioners were now living with the Leomitis. In July or August 2004, Charles called and spoke with an associate producer of Lock and Key about the program and petitioners' living situation.

Over the next several months, there were additional contacts between petitioners and persons affiliated with the production of the program, including in-person interviews and the filming of a casting tape. By early 2005, petitioners and the Leomitis were chosen to participate in the program in which the Leomitis' home would be completely renovated.

On February 1, 2005, a Lock and Key producer sent by Federal Express to each of the petitioners and to the Leomitis an "Agreement and Release" for their signatures. The Agreement and Release contains 24 single-spaced pages and 72 numbered paragraphs. Attached to it were several pages of exhibits, including an authorization for release of medical information, an emergency medical release, and, as exhibit C, a one-page document entitled "Release." To avoid confusion with the one-page exhibit C Release, we refer to the 24-page Agreement and Release simply as the "Agreement," and to exhibit C as the "Release."

At the top of the first page of the Agreement, the following appears in large and underlined print: "NOTE: DO NOT SIGN THIS UNTIL YOU HAVE READ IT COMPLETELY." The second-to-last numbered paragraph also states in pertinent part: "I have been given ample opportunity to read, and I have carefully read, this entire agreement. . . . I certify that I have made such an investigation of the facts pertinent to this Agreement and of all the matters pertaining thereto as I have deemed necessary. . . . I represent and warrant that I have reviewed this document with my own legal counsel prior to signing (or, IN THE ALTERNATIVE, although I have been given a reasonable opportunity to discuss this Agreement with counsel of my choice, I have voluntarily declined such opportunity)."

The last section of the Agreement, which includes 12 numbered paragraphs, is entitled "MISCELLANEOUS." None of the paragraphs in that section contains a heading or title. Paragraph 69 contains the following arbitration provision: "69. I agree that any and all disputes or controversies arising under this Agreement or any of its terms, any effort by any party to enforce, interpret, construe, rescind, terminate or annul this Agreement, or any provision thereof, and any and all disputes or controversies relating to my appearance or participation in the Program, shall be resolved by binding arbitration in accordance with the following procedure. . . . All arbitration proceedings shall be conducted under the auspices of the American Arbitration Association. . . . I agree that the arbitrator's ruling, or arbitrators' ruling, as applicable, shall be final and binding and not subject to appeal or challenge. . . . The parties hereto agree that, notwithstanding the provisions of this paragraph, Producer shall have a right to injunctive or other equitable relief as provided for in California Code of Civil Procedure [section] 1281.8 or other relevant laws."

There is nothing in the Agreement that brings the reader's attention to the arbitration provision. Although a different font is used occasionally to highlight certain terms in the Agreement, that is not the case with the paragraph containing the arbitration provision. Six paragraphs in the Agreement contain a box for the petitioners to initial; initialing is not required for the arbitration provision.

The Agreement also contains a provision limiting petitioners' remedies for breach of the Agreement to money damages.

The one-page Release is typed in a smaller font than the Agreement. It consists of four, single-spaced paragraphs, the middle of which contains the following arbitration clause: "I agree that any and all disputes or controversies arising under this Release or any of its terms, any effort by any party to enforce, interpret, construe, rescind, terminate or annul this Release, or any provision thereof, shall be resolved exclusively by binding arbitration before a single, neutral arbitrator, who shall be a retired judge of a state or federal court. All arbitration proceedings shall be conducted under the auspices of the American Arbitration Association, under its Commercial Arbitration Rules, through its Los Angeles, California office. I agree that the arbitration proceedings, testimony, discovery and documents filed in the course of such proceedings, including the fact that the arbitration is being conducted, will be treated as confidential. . . ."

There is no evidence that any discussions took place between petitioners and any representative of the television defendants regarding either the Agreement or the Release, or that any of the television defendants directly imposed any deadline by which petitioners were required to execute the documents.

On February 5, 2005, a field producer from Lock and Key and a location manager for the program went to the Leomitis' home and met with the Leomitis. Although physically present at the house, petitioners did not participate in the meeting. During the meeting, one of the Leomitis asked about the documents they had received, and the producer and location manager advised the Leomitis that they should read the documents carefully, call if they had questions, and then execute and return the documents.

According to Charles, after this meeting, the Leomitis emerged with a packet of documents, which they handed to petitioners. Mrs. Leomiti instructed petitioners to "flip through the pages and sign and initial the document where it contained a signature line or box." Charles stated that from the time Mrs. Leomiti "handed the document to us and the time we signed it, approximately five to ten minutes passed." The document contained complex legal terms that he did not understand. He did not know what an arbitration agreement was and did not understand its significance or the legal consequences that could flow from signing it. He did not specifically state whether or not he saw the arbitration provisions contained either in paragraph 69 or the Release before he signed the documents.

Each of the petitioners executed the Agreement and signed all exhibits, including the Release.

On February 16, 2005, representatives from the show appeared and started to reconstruct the Leomitis' home. When the new home was completed, it had nine bedrooms, including one for each of the five petitioners. The existing mortgage was also paid off.

The program featuring petitioners and the Leomitis was broadcast on Easter Sunday, 2005.

Petitioners allege that, after the show was first broadcast, the Leomitis informed petitioners that the home was theirs (the Leomitis'), and the Leomitis ultimately forced petitioners to leave. Charles contacted Lock and Key's field producer and asked for help. The producer responded that he could not assist petitioners. Sometime thereafter, the *Extreme Makeover* episode was rebroadcast.

In August 2005, petitioners filed this action against the television defendants and the Leomitis. According to the record before us, the complaint includes claims for, among other things, intentional and negligent misrepresentation, breach of contract, unfair competition (Bus. & Prof. Code, §17200 et seq.), and false advertising (Bus. & Prof. Code, §17500 et seq.). With respect to the television defendants, the complaint appears to allege that those defendants breached promises to provide petitioners with a home, exploited petitioners, and portrayed petitioners in a false light (by rebroadcasting the episode when they knew the episode no longer reflected petitioners' living situation) . . .

The television defendants maintained that all claims against both of them and the Leomitis should be arbitrated . . .

Petitioners opposed the petition, claiming, among other things, that the arbitration provision was unconscionable. They claimed it was procedurally unconscionable because the parties had unequal bargaining power, the arbitration provision was "buried" in the Agreement, petitioners were given only five to 10 minutes before they were asked to sign the Agreement, none of the television defendants explained the Agreement to them, and copies of the executed documents were "withheld" from them.

Petitioners also argued the Agreement was substantively unconscionable because its terms were so one-sided as to shock the conscience . . .

Petitioners then filed this writ petition challenging the trial court's ruling . . .

DISCUSSION

. . . under both the FAA and California law, "arbitration agreements are valid, irrevocable, and enforceable, save upon such grounds as exist at law or in equity for the revocation of any contract." (*Armendariz, supra*, 24 Cal.4th at p. 98, fn. omitted.)

(3) One ground is unconscionability, the basis asserted by petitioners below and in this writ proceeding. (See *Flores v. Transamerica HomeFirst, Inc.* (2001) 93 Cal.App.4th 846, 856 [113 Cal. Rptr. 2d 376].) "The '"strong public policy of this state in favor of resolving disputes by arbitration"' does not extend to an arbitration agreement permeated by unconscionability." (*Ibid.*) As is frequently the case with inquiries into unconscionability, our analysis begins—although it does not end—with whether the Agreement and Release are contracts of adhesion. (See *Armendariz, supra*, 24 Cal.4th at p. 113.) Petitioners contend that they are and that the arbitration provisions are unconscionable. A contract of adhesion is a standardized contract that is imposed and drafted by the party of superior bargaining strength and relegates to the other party '"only the opportunity to adhere to the contract or reject it."' (*Ibid.*, quoting *Neal v. State Farm Ins. Cos.* (1961) 188 Cal. App. 2d 690, 694 [10 Cal. Rptr. 781].)

Adhesion contract
a contract that does not permit the promisee to negotiate the terms. Basically, it requires the promisee to "take it or leave it."

Adhesion contracts are routine in modern day commerce, and at least one commentator has suggested they are worthy of neither praise nor condemnation, only analysis. (1 Corbin on Contracts (1993) §1.4, p. 14.) If a court finds a contract to be adhesive, it must then determine whether '"other factors are present which, under established legal rules—legislative or judicial—operate to render it'" unenforceable. (*Armendariz*, at p. 113, citing *Graham v. Scissor-Tail, Inc.* (1981) 28 Cal.3d 807, 820 [171 Cal. Rptr. 604, 623 P.2d 165] (*Graham*).)

One "established rule" is that a court need not enforce an adhesion contract that is unconscionable . . .

. . . Unconscionability has both a procedural and a substantive element, the former focusing on "oppression" or "surprise" due to unequal bargaining power, the latter on "overly harsh" or "one-sided" results. (*Armendariz, supra*, 24 Cal.4th at p. 114.) " 'The prevailing view is that [procedural and substantive unconscionability] must *both* be present in order for a court to exercise its discretion to refuse to enforce a contract or clause under the doctrine of unconscionability.' [Citation.] But they need not be present in the same degree. 'Essentially a sliding scale is invoked which disregards the regularity of the procedural process of the contract formation, that creates the terms, in proportion to the greater harshness or unreasonableness of the substantive terms themselves.' [Citations.] In other words, the more substantively oppressive the contract term, the less evidence of procedural unconscionability is required to come to the conclusion that the term is unenforceable, and vice versa." (*Ibid.*) . . .

. . . Given the limited scope of the trial court's ruling, we could remand to permit it to decide whether the arbitration provision is unconscionable. Instead, because the case is before us on uncontested facts and our review is de novo, we decide the legal issues in the first instance. (*Rayyis v. Superior Court* (2005) 133 Cal.App.4th 138, 150 [35 Cal. Rptr. 3d 12].)

D. The Arbitration Provision Is Unconscionable

The Adhesive Nature of the Parties' Agreement

We begin with whether the parties' agreement was adhesive. (See *Armendariz, supra*, 24 Cal.4th at p. 113.) As discussed above, " '[t]he term [contract of adhesion] signifies a standardized contract, which, imposed and drafted by the party of superior bargaining strength, relegates to the subscribing party only the opportunity to adhere to the contract or reject it.' " (*Ibid.*)

In this case, it is undisputed that the lengthy Agreement was drafted by the television defendants. It is a standardized contract; none of the petitioners' names or other identifying information is included in the body of the document. There is no serious doubt that the television defendants had far more bargaining power than petitioners.

The remaining question is whether petitioners were relegated only to signing or rejecting the Agreement. The television defendants note that there is no evidence petitioners were told they could not negotiate any terms of the Agreement or that petitioners made any attempt to do so. Although literally correct, the uncontested evidence was that on the day petitioners signed the Agreement the television defendants initially met with the Leomitis alone. Inferentially, at the television defendants' urging, immediately after the meeting concluded, the Leomitis gave the Agreement and exhibits to petitioners with directions to "flip through the pages and sign." The documents were returned in five to 10 minutes. One of the producers testified that he told the Leomitis "that these agreements must be executed as a condition to their further participation in the program."

From these facts, we conclude the Agreement was presented to petitioners on a take-it-or-leave-it basis by the party the superior bargaining position who was not willing to engage in negotiations. Accordingly, we conclude the Agreement and exhibits constitute a contract of adhesion . . .

DISPOSITION

. . . to thereafter enter a new and different order denying the petition to compel arbitration . . .

Guided Reading Questions

1. What was the court's definition of a contract of adhesion?
2. Was the contract, in this case, a contract of adhesion?
3. Why did the court state that this was, or was not, a contract of adhesion?
4. Would the court enforce the arbitration provision? Why or why not?

CHAPTER SUMMARY

This chapter explored the additional requirements, aside from an offer, acceptance, and consideration, that are necessary to form a valid contract. A contract does not have to be written and a written contract does not need a signature. The Statute of Frauds, in each state, details when a contract must be in writing. However, if the contract is written, the parol evidence rule will apply and it is a completely integrated agreement. All prior negotiations are considered to be incorporated into the written agreement and cannot serve as evidence of different term or intent. Contracts also must conform to public policy and the subject matter of the contract cannot be illegal. If the subject matter of the contract is illegal, the contract is void and will have no legal effect. A contract or a provision may be voidable, or capable of being accepted or rejected by one party.

Integration in contracts
the written agreement, adopted by parties to a contract, that represents the complete and final statement of their bargain.

Formation

Written Contract	Not required for a valid contract Contract can be oral, or partly written and partly oral A written agreement embodies the bargain that the parties reached Does not have to be signed, but signature can be an "X" or electronic It must conform to public policy and applicable law
Statute of Frauds	Each state has specific requirements Generally, a contract must be in writing if the subject of the agreement is valued at over $500, it will take longer than one year to perform, or if it concerns the sale of real estate

Formation

Parol Evidence Rule	Applies to written contracts Once the contract is agreed upon and written, the parties' negotiations, prior agreements, and intent are merged into the written contract The writing is integrated for it represents their complete agreement; anything that occurred prior to this point cannot be used as evidence, generally, of varying terms or intent
Void and Voidable Contracts	A void contract has no legal effect and there is no remedy for breach nor duty of performance In a voidable contract, a provision or a portion is unenforceable, so the remaining parts of the agreement can be in effect or the entire agreement can be voided at the election of the wronged party Instances of when a contract, or a contract provision, may be voidable: when a party is a minor; the contract is induced by misrepresentation, fraud, or duress; or breach of warranty
Special Situations	Contracts of adhesion Noncompete agreements Forbearance agreements Restraint of trade
The U.C.C.	Under §2–202, when a written contract is the final expression of the parties' agreement, the terms may be supplemented or explained These terms may be explained or clarified by terms used in the course of dealing between the parties and by terms used in the particular trade

REVIEW QUESTIONS

1. Provide an example of a voidable contract.
2. Does a contract have to be in writing?
3. Are electronic signatures allowed?
4. What subject matter does the Statute of Frauds concern?
5. What is the parol evidence rule?
6. List two examples of contracts that are unenforceable due to violations of public policy.
7. What is a contract of adhesion?
8. Where are adhesion contracts used frequently?
9. Provide an example of a special contractual clause.
10. What issues can arise during the formation of a contract? List two.

SKILL-BUILDING APPLICATION EXERCISE

Read the following abridged case. Did the court state that this is a contract of adhesion?

E. Martyn Griffen, Plaintiff v. Alpha Phi Alpha, Inc., et al., Defendants. Civil Action No. 06–1735 United States District Court for the Eastern District of Pennsylvania (2007)

Plaintiff E. Martyn Griffen filed a complaint against Alpha Phi Alpha, Inc., the Psi Chapter of Alpha Phi Alpha, Inc., and two individual defendants, Kelechi Okereke and Lionel Anderson-Perez, alleging that he was assaulted and battered during fraternal activities by these two fraternity members . . . Defendant Alpha Phi Alpha, Inc. has filed a Motion to Dismiss or in the Alternative Stay Litigation Pending Arbitration. The Court will grant the Motion and stay the litigation pending arbitration.

I. FACTUAL BACKGROUND

Plaintiff E. Martyn Griffen aspired to become a member of the Psi Chapter of Alpha Phi Alpha, Inc. at the beginning of his junior year of college at the University of Pennsylvania. At the time, Mr. Griffen was 20 years old and a resident of the State of Arkansas.

Alpha Phi Alpha, Inc. (the "Fraternity") was formed in 1905 at Cornell University by a group of African-American students who bonded together in order to "survive in the racially hostile environment." . . .

The Fraternity required all aspirants, including Mr. Griffen, to complete an Official Application for Membership in order to become a member of the Fraternity. The present dispute turns on the enforceability and scope of the Application's arbitration clause, and specifically, whether it is applicable to the injuries Mr. Griffen allegedly suffered during Fraternity activities. To become a member of the Fraternity, Mr. Griffen and other hopeful candidates were first required to complete an Official Application for Membership. The Application included instructions on how to complete the form and submit the required materials, a "Membership Process" form, a standard form for basic personal identifying information, several sponsorship forms, and a list of the materials, such as a resume, an essay and a transcript, that Applicants were to submit in support of their candidacy for membership . . .

The Membership Process form (the "Form") is a one-page document, placed prominently in the front of the Application. It contains information for aspirants about the details of the "Intake process" into the Fraternity. The Form consists of four paragraphs: (1) a description of the Intake process; (2) a declaration opposing hazing in any form; (3) a description of the Fraternity's dispute resolution process; and (4) a certification that the aspirant agrees to abide by the conditions of the Intake process.

The first and second paragraphs of the form discuss the Intake process. Paragraph one of the Form describes the steps and milestones that candidates must achieve to proceed through the Intake process. These steps included attending Leadership Weekends and presentations, performing community service, interviewing with the current Chapter members, and meeting certain financial obligations, among other things . . . The second paragraph of the Form states the Fraternity's strict prohibition against illegal activities and hazing, whether physical or mental, as a term or condition of membership. It also requires an agreement from the aspirant not to participate in these activities, and an assurance that the Fraternity's members agree not to require aspirants to engage in any prohibited hazing . . .

The third paragraph of the Form is at the center of the present dispute. It instructs aspirants regarding the procedure and process for membership Intake dispute resolution. The paragraph reads:

Any grievances and disputes regarding membership intake should generally be referred to the National director of Membership Services for Investigation and resolution. Matters that cannot be resolved within the Fraternity will be referred to arbitration. The aspirant specifically agrees to follow all the rules, regulations and guidelines relating to the Intake process. The aspirant further agrees to report in writing any Infractions and Violations of the rules, regulations and guidelines relating to the Intake process to: The National Director of Membership Services . . . The aspirant acknowledges that [the Fraternity] is an International organization with Chapters located throughout the United states of America and foreign countries. The aspirant recognizes that by making this application for membership he agrees to the foregoing matters. The aspirant understands that this agreement has an effect on interstate commerce and is subject to the Federal Arbitration Act. The aspirant, his heirs and assigns, and [the Fraternity], its officers, employees, agents, affiliates, chapters and members, agree that any and all disputes, conflicts, claims and/or causes of action of any kind whatsoever, [i]ncluding by not limited to: contract claims, personal injury claims, bodily injury claims, injury to character claims and property damage claims arising out of or relating in any manner whatsoever to the Intake process and application shall be subject to and resolved by compulsory and binding arbitration under the Federal Arbitration Act, 9 et seq.U.S.C. Section 1, and the commercial rules of the American Arbitration Association . . .

The Fraternity required each aspirant to place his initials at the bottom of each of the above paragraphs, and to sign a certification, in paragraph four, that he read, understood, and agreed to abide by the terms and conditions of the Intake process, as described in the Form . . . The Form also provided space for the supplemental certification of a parent or guardian for applicants under the age of 21. *Id.* Mr. Griffen initialed each of the paragraphs, and signed his name to the Form's certification on September 12, 2005. It appears from the Form that Patricia L. Griffen, Plaintiff's mother, signed the certification on the same date.

Unfortunately for all parties, shortly after completing the Application, Mr. Griffen's Intake into Psi Chapter was interrupted by allegations of physical and verbal abuse . . . Late in the evening of October 12, 2005, Mr. Griffen and other aspirants were summoned to the Fraternity house by members of the Psi Chapter in order to study and prepare for Chapter activities . . . During this visit to the Fraternity house, Mr. Griffen claims that Defendant-Psi Chapter members Lionel Anderson-Perez and Kelechi Okereke punished him, and other aspirants, for the actions of another aspirant, Jamol Pendor, who allegedly broke Fraternity rules by revealing Fraternity secrets to a non-Fraternity audience . . .

According to Mr. Griffen, the punishment was physical, and constituted "underground pledging," in violation of the Fraternity's own rules and the University's anti-hazing policy . . . Mr. Anderson-Perez allegedly punched Mr. Griffen repeatedly in the thighs, and Mr. Okereke snapped a rubber band around Mr. Griffen's upper arm . . . As a result of the physical abuse,

Mr. Griffen claims to have suffered serious and permanent injuries . . . Mr. Griffen claims that the Fraternity either knew of, or should have known of the underground pledging, and negligently failed to prevent the banned activities resulting in his injuries . . .

On April 25, 2006, Mr. Griffen filed a ten-count Complaint against Messrs. Anderson-Perez and Okereke, as well as Psi Chapter and the Fraternity. The Fraternity now moves the Court to order that arbitration, and not a judicial forum, is the proper venue to resolve Mr. Griffen's claims. Because the arbitration clause at issue is enforceable, and binds all parties to this dispute to arbitrate Mr. Griffen's claims arising out of the personal injuries he allegedly incurred during the Intake process, the Court will stay this litigation pending arbitration. . . .

III. DISCUSSION

Section 2 of the FAA provides that "[a] written provision in . . . a contract evidencing a transaction involving commerce to settle by arbitration a controversy arising out of such contract . . . shall be valid, irrevocable, and enforceable, save upon such grounds as exist at law or in equity for revocation of any contract." 9 U.S.C. §2. In determining whether an arbitration is the proper forum for resolution of the dispute, a court must first ask whether the parties entered into a valid arbitration agreement and, if so, whether the dispute between the parties falls within the language of the arbitration agreement . . . To conduct this analysis, the court applies ordinary contract law principles.

A. Validity and Enforceability

This Court may not direct the parties to arbitration unless the agreement to arbitrate is valid, *Alexander v. Anthony Int'l L.P.*, 341 F.3d 256, 264 (3d Cir. 2003). . .

. . . Though questions concerning the interpretation and construction of arbitration agreements are determined by reference to federal substantive law, *Harris*, 183 F.3d at 179, the laws of the states yield "generally applicable contract defenses" to the validity of an agreement to arbitrate . . . As a defense to validity, unconscionability relieves a party from an unfair contract or from an unfair portion of a contract. *Id.* at 13 (*citing Harris, 183 F.3d at 181*). . . . . .

i. Procedural Unconscionability

Mr. Griffen argues that the Application is procedurally unconscionable because it is a contract of adhesion. A contract is procedurally unconscionable when the circumstances surrounding its formation reflect "the absence of meaningful choice on the part of one of the parties." *Witmer v. Exxon Corp.*, 495 Pa. 540, 434 A.2d 1222, 1228 (Pa. 1981). Contracts of adhesion are characterized by this absence of choice; they are "standard form contract[s] prepared by one party, to be signed by the party in a weaker position, [usually] a consumer, who has little choice about the terms." . . .

Commonly, adhesion contracts are accompanied by conditions that prevent a consumer from obtaining a product or services except by acquiescing to the contract. . . . They are prepared by a party with excessive bargaining power and presented to the other party on a "take it or leave it" basis. *Ostroff*, 433 F. Supp. 2d at 543 *(quoting Parilla v. IAP Worldwide Services, VI, Inc., 368 F.3d 269, 276 (3d Cir. 2004))*. For this reason, contracts of adhesion are generally procedurally unconscionable. . . .

Though this Application bears attributes of a contract of adhesion, the Court cannot conclude, without an evidentiary hearing, whether the circumstances attendant to the formation of the contract were unconscionable. While it is clear that the Fraternity, a sizeable international organization, unilaterally prepared the Application, there is no evidence of record that the Fraternity refused to negotiate the terms of the contract, or that Mr. Griffen did not understand the contract, or that he found it unfair at the time he entered it . . .

There is also no evidence of record as to whether Mr. Griffen lacked a meaningful choice of whether or not to enter the membership contract. The Court cannot say whether he did or did not have the opportunity to join another Fraternity if this provision was unacceptable to him . . . Furthermore, it would not be appropriate to characterize the circumstances of Mr. Griffen's decision to join Alpha Phi Alpha as similar or equivalent to the dire economic or subsistence constraints accompanying the situations where courts have found a lack of meaningful choice, and thus, an invalid contract of adhesion. *Compare Ostroff*, 433 F. Supp. 2d at 544 (plaintiff's elderly mother was evicted from her former home and had no place to live but for the defendant's assisted living community); *Trailer Marine Transport Corp. v. Charley's Trucking Inc.*, 20 V.I. 282 (1984) (a small trucking company entered into a contract with a larger trucking company that contained an egregious liability provision because it relied on the contract for its economic livelihood) . . .

. . . However, even if Mr. Griffen had pleaded sufficient facts to warrant an evidentiary hearing to determine procedural unconscionability, or if he had proved procedural unconscionability without the need for a hearing, he has not carried the second-prong of his burden to persuade the Court that the membership contract is substantively unconscionable.

ii. Substantive Unconscionability

Substantive unconscionability looks to the terms of the arbitration clause itself and whether the arbitration clause is unreasonably favorable to the party with greater bargaining power. *Witmer*, 434 A.2d at 1228 . . .

. . . The arbitration clause does not restrict discovery, it has no cost shifting provisions, no limitation of remedies, and no unilateral access to the courts. (Form P 3.) Moreover, the arbitration clause at issue does not "create an arbitration procedure that favors one party over another.". .

Though Mr. Griffen argues that the nature of binding arbitration is in itself so restrictive as to be substantively unconscionable, this Court will not rule, inconsistent with the law in favor of private arbitration, that alternative dispute resolution is unfavorable to Mr. Griffen or in general. . . . .

. . . Moreover, fraternity hazing does not present a novel issue outside the purview of what is appropriate for arbitration . . .

. . . Further, the Court finds no inconsistency between the important . . . . . "arbitration is a matter of contract and a party cannot be required to submit to arbitration any dispute which he has not agreed so to submit." *United Steelworkers of America v. Warrior & Gulf Navigation Co.*, 363 U.S. 574, 582, 80 S. Ct. 1347, 4 L. Ed. 2d 1409 (1960). The arbitration clause states: "The aspirant, his heirs and assigns, and Alpha Phi Alpha Fraternity, Inc., its *officers, employees, agents, affiliates, chapters and members* agree . . . that any and all disputes . . . shall be resolved by compulsory and binding arbitration . . ."(Form P 3)(emphasis added).

The agreement clearly binds the Fraternity and the Psi Chapter to arbitration. (Def.'s Mot. To Set Aside Default, Aff. of Sean Walker, Ex. A)(Psi Chapter agreed to be bound by the rules and conditions of the Intake process.) While the Fraternity would not ordinarily have the authority to bind its individuals members to a contract, by signing separate agreements with the Fraternity, Messres. Okereke and Anderson-Perez actually bound themselves to the same agreement to arbitrate any claims of personal injury as did Mr. Griffen. (Def.'s Supplemental Exhibits, Docket Nos. 29, 30.) Though not executed simultaneously, the intent of all the parties to this litigation to be bound by the compulsory arbitration of the present claims is clear. Moreover, it can be said that the execution of the Application in counterparts and the resulting obligation of the members to adhere to all provisions of the Application, e.g. that "[n]o member of the Fraternity is authorized to require any aspirant to engage in any prohibited membership activities suggest or Impose any term," (Form P 2), certainly was part of the benefit of the bargain entered into by Mr. Griffen.

IV. CONCLUSION

For the reasons stated herein, the Court will stay litigation pending arbitration of Plaintiff Griffen's claims . . .

. . .

ORDER

. . . IT IS HEREBY ORDERED that the Motion to stay the instant litigation is GRANTED, and this action is stayed pending submission and disposition of the underlying dispute to contractual arbitration . . .

SIMULATED LAW OFFICE ASSIGNMENT

Find the Statute of Frauds provision for your state regarding what types of contracts must be in writing.

DRAFTING EXERCISE

You represent the landlord of a 100-unit apartment complex. The landlord wants you to draft a form lease for the prospective tenants. The landlord wants to offer three-year leases for apartments. In your jurisdiction, is this required to be in writing? If so, what type of tenancies require a written lease agreement for a tenancy over one year? Is it required to be signed? Regardless of whether your jurisdiction requires a written agreement, find a form for a simple lease for an apartment.

DEVELOPING CRITICAL THINKING SKILLS

Examine this agreement for equipment rental. Do you think that it is a contract of adhesion? Did the renter have to accept the rental company's terms or not rent equipment?

Home Repair Central
Equipment Rental Agreement
Equipment to be Rented by Home Repair Central
1 Pressure Washer
1 Gun 2,000 psi

I may not sublease the equipment or transfer this agreement or any interest herein or the use or possession of the equipment. If I should do so, I will assume all liability and compensate Home Repair Central ("Home Repair") for any loss it suffers, and I may be declared in default of this agreement. No warranties, express or implied, including without limitation, suitability, durability, fitness for a particular purpose, merchantability, condition, quality, or freedom from claims of any person by way of infringement or the like, have been made by "Home Repair" directly or indirectly in connection with the equipment. I am renting the equipment "as is." "Home Repair" shall not be responsible for any loss, damage, or injury to persons or property caused by the equipment. "Home Repair" shall not be responsible for any direct or indirect damages caused by the equipment or by the use of the equipment.

I agree to indemnify and hold "Home Repair" and its officers, agents, and employees harmless against all liabilities, claims, actions, proceedings, damages, costs, and expenses, including attorneys fees for all injuries and/or the death of any person or damage to any property arising from or connected with the use or rental of the pressure washer and the pressure washer gun 2,000 psi.

I agree to pay "Home Repair" for the rental of the pressure washer and pressure gun a fee of $49.00 per day. The rent for the rental term is due and payable upon the execution of this agreement. I agree to tender a security deposit of $200, returnable at the time the equipment is returned, to "Home Repair" after an inspection of the equipment.

The security deposit may be in the form of cash or a credit card charge.

I acknowledge that at all times the title of the pressure washer and gun remain Home Repair's.

I acknowledge that I have examined the equipment and that it is free from defects. Once the equipment leaves the rental counter, any notice of defect must be asserted as soon as the defect is noticed and all use of the equipment must cease. I am responsible for any resulting defects due to use except for normal wear and tear.

I agree that any of the following shall be an event of default: (1) failure to pay due to invalid or overextended credit card; (2) insolvency; (3) fraudulent or mistaken representation by me or my company of any term in this agreement; (4) any voluntary or involuntary bankruptcy proceeding.

Upon default, I waive any and all rights to a hearing prior to Home Repair taking possession of the equipment rented. In the case of legal action by Home Repair, I agree to pay any and all legal fees that Home Repair incurs.

I agree that I have no right to reject, revoke, or modify this agreement.

I agree that Home Repair is entitled to recover immediately, as liquidated damages, for any unpaid rent, and not as a penalty, a sum equal to the total of all unpaid rent and the security deposit, any expenses and losses incurred by Home Repair, plus the replacement value of the rented equipment. This agreement represents and comprises the total agreement between myself, or my company, and Home Repair and shall not be changed without the consent of Home Repair.

Signed _____

Date_____

PORTFOLIO ASSIGNMENT

Your firm's client, 1000 Horse Power Car Rental, wants to establish rental agencies in the state where the firm practices. 1000 Horse Power Car Rental has a standard car rental agreement to be signed and initialed by the renter. The attorney you work for wants to know if it must be signed in a certain manner using ink and with a complete signature. For instance, what happens if the renter uses pencil or just signs with an "X"? Additionally, if the written rental agreement stipulates that the renter receives and rents a mid-sized car, does the contract have to be changed to reflect an upgrade that the renter will rent a full-sized car? If this contract stipulates that it contains the full agreement between the parties, can oral provisions be included that were arrived at after the agreement was signed? Is the date important to include here? Is the price a necessary term? Finally, would the agreement be void if the renter is a minor or if the renter does not have sound mental capacity?

1000 Horse Power Car Rental Agreement

Renter agrees by Renter's Signature that Renter has read, is aware of, and accepts full responsibility for and is bound by the terms and conditions contained in this Rental Agreement. This Agreement shall not be modified and represents the complete Agreement between 1000 Horse Power Car Rental and the Renter. Renter expressly acknowledges that Renter and 1000 Horse Power are the only parties to this agreement, notwithstanding that a reservation for Vehicle may have been arranged by a third party; that a third party may pay for all or part of Vehicle, length of rental, rental rate, and/or selection of optional products. For matters arising from this agreement, Renter authorizes 1000 Horse Power to verify and/or obtain through credit agencies or other sources Renter's personal, credit, and/or insurance information. This Agreement is the entire agreement between Renter and 1000 Horse Power and cannot be altered by another document or oral agreement unless agreed to in writing and signed by Renter and 1000 Horse Power.

Renter acknowledges that the Vehicle is, by ownership, beneficial interest, or lease, the property of 1000 Horse Power. Renter agrees that Renter received the vehicle in good physical condition. Renter is operating the vehicle "as is."

Renter agrees to pay 1000 Horse Power a daily rental rate of $47.95 plus 3% access fee, plus 9% local tax for a period of the rental term, which shall not exceed six (6) days from the time this agreement is signed.

Renter agrees to not permit any other driver or any other individual to drive the vehicle.

Renter agrees to provide collision insurance and to show proof of collision insurance.

Renter agrees to not drive or transport the vehicle outside of the 48 contiguous states.

Renter agrees that in the event of an accident, the damage to the vehicle shall be reported immediately.

Renter agrees that any damage, theft, or loss of the vehicle or any related costs shall be paid by renter and these costs shall not exceed the fair market value of the vehicle.

Renter agrees to be responsible for all injuries and damages to third parties when operating and renting the vehicle that arise out of the use of the vehicle.

Renter shall indemnify and hold 1000 Horse Power harmless from all loses, liabilities, damages, injuries, claims, demands, costs, attorney fees, and other expenses incurred by 1000 Horse Power in any manner from this rental transaction, or from the use of vehicle by any person, including claims of or liabilities to third parties.

1000 Horse Power does not provide personal injury protection.

1000 Horse Power is not responsible for any damage to, loss, or theft of any personal property, whether the damage or theft occurs during or after the termination of rental regardless of fault or negligence.

Renter agrees that he is of 25 years of age or older and is of sound mind. Renter stipulates that he has a valid driver's license.

Acknowledgment of the Entire Agreement

I have read and agree to the terms and conditions in this agreement and by my signature below I am the Renter under this agreement. By signing below, I am authorizing 1000 Horse Power to process charges on my credit card for advance deposits and charges incurred. I certify that the driver's license presented is currently valid and is not suspended, expired, revoked, cancelled, or surrendered.

Renter: _____ Date _____

1000 Horse Power Representative _____

I will return Vehicle by:

_____

Total Deposit on Credit Card _____ (6 days at 47.95 + 3% + 9%); any excess will be refunded if the car is returned prior to the completion of six (6) days.

Terms and Provisions

CHAPTER 6

INTRODUCTION—TERMS AND PROVISIONS IN GENERAL

Generally, a **valid** contract must have **definite** and **certain** terms. Terms and provisions are the words and clauses used to draft a contract. The terms and provisions are important because they express the deal that the parties made, particularly in a written contract. If a term or provision is ambiguous, that is, capable of having more than one meaning, it is not definite and certain. The term or provision should be clearly defined in the contract. Material terms concern a significant aspect of the agreement and can include: subject matter, quantity, duration, payment, price, quality, or the type of work to be performed. Sometimes these are called variable terms. The most common categories of terms, which vary depending on the particular contract, deal with quantity, time, price, condition of the subject matter, and location. In addition to terms that vary in an individual contract, many contracts have boilerplate provisions or clauses. Provisions are clauses in a contract. Boilerplate provisions use fixed or standardized language regardless of the particular subject matter of the agreement. Boilerplate provisions often concern severability (how a contract can be divided up if the parts are not dependent), choice of law (which state's law controls) and arbitration (how contracts disputes will be decided by a

LEARNING OBJECTIVES

After reading this chapter, you will be able to:

1. Understand the need for definite and certain terms to state the agreement.

2. Know the importance of price, time, and quantity terms.

3. Demonstrate knowledge regarding the specific terms to include in a valid contract.

4. Discuss the court's role in interpreting a contract and its terms.

5. Explain the U.C.C. requirements regarding a contract's terms.

6. Know the meaning of a condition precedent and a condition subsequent.

7. Discuss of the role of boilerplate provisions.

Valid
an agreement that is binding on the parties and follows the legal requirements.

Definite
exact and precise.

Certain
distinct, clear, and free from ambiguity.

Remedy
to fix a wrong or to redress a right that has been deprived.

neutral third party and not necessarily a court). The decision as to which boilerplate provisions to include is determined by negotiation. Sometimes boilerplate provisions are included in form contracts, and blank spaces are for the terms that the parties negotiate. The last category of terms are conditional terms, or conditions. The most common conditions are conditions precedent and conditions subsequent, where something must occur to activate a duty or to discharge a duty.

■ HOW COURTS INTERPRET TERMS

Courts hesitate to construct terms for the parties, but if the terms are not clear the court will attempt to carry out the intention of the parties. This is called the *rules of construction* and concerns how courts will construe or determine the parties' intentions in the contract. Often state common law guides the particular court in this area. Generally, a court will read a contract according to its plain meaning, how the words are interpreted on their face. For instance, in Alabama, the rules of construction are as follows: "[w]hen a court construes a contract, the clear and plain meaning of the terms of the contract are to be given effect, and the parties are presumed to have intended what the terms clearly state" (as quoted in *Kelmor, LLC v. Alabama Dynamics, Inc*. Slip Op. 105047 Supreme Court of Alabama 2009). Courts may construct a **remedy** if the contract, when performed, leaves a party completely without any benefit or if the contract is breached. Ascertaining a breach is much easier if the contract spelled out the terms of the agreement in writing, then the aggrieved party can indicate which terms were not fulfilled.

■ DEFINITENESS AND CERTAINTY

All contract terms should be reasonably definite and certain. This permits the parties contracting to be aware of their respective rights, obligations, and duties under the agreement. Definiteness and certainty permit the offeror to extend a clear offer to the promisee and permit the promisee to accept the precise terms of the offer. Without such clarity, the offer and acceptance will not match. Additionally, courts cannot enforce a contract with indefinite terms. Also, it is very challenging to support a claim for breach of contract without definite and certain terms because it is difficult to pinpoint the specific breach. Sometimes, if the terms are indefinite, the offer will be considered to be in the preliminary stages of negotiation rather than a firm offer.

Certainty

The Restatement (Second) of Contracts §33 outlines the requirement of certainty in the contract's terms. Section 33 states that a contract is only formed if the terms are reasonably certain. The terms are reasonably certain if they permit a party to determine the basis of a breach and to fashion an appropriate remedy if necessary. In a contract that is not between merchants for the sale of goods, when one or more terms are left open, it may call into question whether either or both the parties intended to enter into a contract. However, according to §34 of the Restatement (Second) of Contracts, a term may be determined during the course of performance of the contract if agreed by the parties.

■ SUBJECT MATTER AND LEGALITY

The contract's subject matter should be reasonably ascertainable. The subject matter must be legal. A contract is still a contract, even if the subject matter is illegal, but the contract will not be enforceable.

Example

Mr. Stone enters into an agreement with Mr. Miller to purchase ten kilos of heroin at $10,000 per kilo. The heroin must be of street grade. Delivery is to be on January 1, 2010, at 10 A.M. at the corner of 5th and Main.

At first glance this is a valid contract because the terms are definite and certain—the price, quantity, and location are clearly communicated in the agreement. It contains an offer, acceptance, and consideration. However, it is illegal to sell heroin and it is illegal to possess heroin. Therefore the terms of this contract are not enforceable because it is illegal.

Terms and Contractual Capacity and Contractual Intent

A person cannot assent to the terms of the contract, or have the legal **capacity** to enter into a contract, if he or she does not understand the terms due to status as a minor, sometimes called infancy, or due to diminished mental state due to inebriation or mental infirmity. Legal capacity requires that the person is of sound mind and has reached the age of majority in the jurisdiction. The age of majority to enter into a contract is determined by each state and is included in the respective state's statutes. The Restatement (Second) of Contracts §14 states: "unless a statute provides otherwise, a natural person has the capacity to incur only **voidable** contract duties until the beginning of the day before the person's 18th birthday." In Illinois, for instance, a person has the legal capacity to understand and enter into a contract when he or she has sufficient mental capacity to comprehend the nature of the transaction, to understand its terms, and to protect his or her interests. *Redmon v. Borah*, 48 N.E.2d 355, 359–360 (Ill. 1943).

Capacity
the capability to understand one's obligations.

Voidable
allows for a provision of an agreement or an entire agreement to be avoided or not enforced if the aggrieved party chooses.

Enforceability of Terms—Void and Voidable Contracts

A contract entered into by an individual of provable mental incapacity to fully appreciate the terms will result in a **void** or a voidable contract. This also occurs when a party is a minor and is not capable of appreciating the contractual obligations A void contract results in no contract when the mental incapacity is great or when a child enters into the agreement; this means that the contract is not enforceable and is terminated. Sometimes a voidable contract exists when there is a party with proven diminished mental capacity. A voidable contract allows the aggrieved party to choose to avoid or to not enforce a provision of an agreement or an entire agreement.

Void
the agreement or contract has no effect for it has no legal basis.

■ QUANTITY

A valid offer must state the quantity of the item contracted for and the acceptance must mirror the quantity stated. For instance, a contract will not be formed when a party offers to do some writing for an editor. A contract will be formed when a party states that he will write two chapters on supply side economics for the second edition of the Hughton economics textbook; that the chapters are due on June 1, 2011; and the writer will be paid $2,000 upon receipt of the chapters.

■ TIME

Time is a very important term in a contract. Often a contract must be performed within a certain time frame to be valid. The parties stipulate and agree to the precise time in the contract. Any contract that requires longer than one year to perform must be in writing, according to the Statute of Frauds. Occasionally, a contract must be performed within a set time period, and possibly very quickly. When this need occurs and the parties are aware of it at the time the contract is formed, often a specific clause called a "time of the essence" provision will be included in the agreement. A "time of the essence" clause is important when a breach is claimed due to a delay in the performance of the contract. Small or insignificant delays in performing contractual duties do not generally result in a breach. Where time is not of the essence in a contract, delays result in an immaterial breach and the rights and obligations under the agreement should not be suspended. However, where time of the essence is stipulated in the agreement, the duties of the injured party could be suspended when the contract is breached.

Example

The Marins contracted with Homer's Catering to cater a party for twenty teenagers for their daughter's sweet sixteen. The menu was selected and Homer's requested $400 to cater the party. The Marins and Homer's Catering never selected a date for the party. Without stipulating a time for performance, the Marins and Homer's have omitted an essential contract term. Without setting a time for performance, the contract will be considered to be in the preliminary stage and not a valid contract.

■ PRICE

Price is an essential term, if relevant. The price must be agreed upon and mirrored in the acceptance for a valid contract to be formed. Most contracts have an economic component and the price term reflects this. The price term indicates the intent of the parties as to the value agreed upon.

Example

Mr. Cox owns a house and wants a new fence installed. Mr. Cox contracts with Fencing Incorporated to have 100 feet of a three-foot high wood picket fence installed for $15.00 per foot, totaling $1,500. The parties agreed to $1,500. The price represents the value of the fence and is an essential contract term.

LOCATION AND REAL ESTATE

Since real property is unique, the location of the property generally must be included in the contract. This is called a legal description. Also, remember that any contract for the sale of real estate must be in writing to comply with the Statute of Frauds.

Example

Mr. and Mrs. Hall want to sell their residence. It is a single-family residence of 2,200 square feet with an attached garage. The structure is brick. The house has three bedrooms and two bathrooms, a family room, and an eat-in kitchen. There is also a full basement. The lot is 150' × 200'. If the Hills were to offer the house in a contract using the description just stated, this would be an invalid contract for an essential term is omitted. A contract for the sale of real estate should generally include the location of the property.

CONDITIONS

Another category of terms is conditional terms, or commonly called "conditions," where an event or the passage of time is required to trigger or extinguish the obligation in the contract. There are two types of general conditions to be aware of: conditions precedent and conditions subsequent. Currently, the Restatement (Second) of Contracts §230 states that the term *condition subsequent* should not be used, but you will probably encounter the term in your work as a paralegal.

A condition precedent occurs when an action must transpire before performance of the promise.

Example

Ann Brook interviewed with Vanderbilt Bank for a job after college. Vanderbilt Bank promised to employ Brook as an investment banker under the condition that she obtain her B.A. from the University of Pennsylvania prior to the start of employment in August. Receiving the B.A. from the University of Pennsylvania is a condition precedent, an action that must transpire before Vanderbilt Bank performs the promise of employment.

A condition subsequent permits the party, after the occurrence of an act in the future, to no longer be bound to perform. Example: Mr. and Mrs. Smith divorce. Under the terms of the divorce decree, Mr. Smith must pay Mrs. Smith alimony each month for the rest of Mrs. Smith's life or until Mrs. Smith remarries. When Mrs. Smith does remarry, which occurs four years after the divorce, the occurrence of this condition subsequent permits Mr. Smith to no longer be bound to pay alimony.

Although the term *condition subsequent* is still used, in the Restatement (Second) of Contracts §224, comment 7 (e) *occurrence of event as discharge*, the term is said to not be called a condition, but is really a discharge of obligation. "Parties sometimes provide that the occurrence of an event, such as the failure of one of them to commence an action within a prescribed time, will extinguish a duty after performance has become due, along with any claim for breach. Such an event has often been called a 'condition subsequent,' while an event of the kind defined in this section has been called a 'condition precedent.' This terminology is not followed here. Since a 'condition subsequent,' so-called, is subject to the rules on discharge in §230, and not to the following rules on conditions, it is not called a 'condition' in this Restatement."

■ TERMS UNDER THE U.C.C.

U.C.C. Stop-Gap Provisions

Under the Uniform Commercial Code §2-204 and §2-305, a contract can still exist between merchants for the sale of goods even if one or more of the terms are left open. This differs from the common law requirement that the terms be definite and certain. The Uniform Commercial Code essentially requires that the parties intend to enter into a binding contract for the sale of goods and that the agreement be reasonably certain.

Generally, a common law contract must set forth the price to be paid as one of the material terms of the contract. However, under the U.C.C., where the contract/writing evidences an intent to agree on the price later, a court can employ the "gap-filler" provisions of the UCC to add a price term to the contract if the parties fail to do so. However, unless the contract is an output contract (where one party promises to deliver all that it produces) or a requirements contract (where the buyer agrees to purchase all that it requires for a specific transaction), the courts will not use the gap-filler provisions to supply a missing quantity term. See the following Quantity discussion for an explanation.

For example, crops are considered goods under the Uniform Commercial Code because they are movable, tangible items sold apart from land. A farmer wants to sell 2,000 bushels of corn to a buyer, an owner of a supermarket. The parties do not set a price for the corn because the price is quite volatile due to the demand for corn for ethanol. The parties agree to set the price of the corn at the fair market value at the time of delivery. This is not a certain and definite price at the time of the contract. This price will be determined later by the parties and the market at the time of delivery. Here, the price of the corn under the contract is to be determined mutually by the parties. This expresses an intent to have a binding contract and therefore the contract is enforceable. Under the U.C.C., the court will impose a commercially reasonable price that is fair to both parties. The U.C.C. allows the court to take into account such circumstances as trade custom and course of dealing. Course of dealing will be especially useful if the parties have entered into previous contracts. However, the reasonable price at the time of delivery is the primary test. Additionally, the court can also consider a drought and skyrocketing prices of corn when determining a commercially reasonably price.

Quantity

The U.C.C. requires that a contract, to be valid, must contain a quantity term. However, this does not apply to output contracts. Under U.C.C. §2-306, if the agreement is reasonable and conforms to the expectations of the parties at the time of contracting, a buyer may contract to purchase all of the seller's output even if the precise quantity of the output is not known at the time of contracting. When a buyer contracts to buy all of a seller's "output" (or a seller contacts to sell all of a buyer's requirements), such contracts are not invalid for lack of a quantity term. Instead, the buyer will be required to purchase everything that the seller produces as long as the quantity does not exceed the parties' expectations at the time of contracting by a disproportionate amount, and that this is done in good faith.

Example—U.C.C. exception for required quantity term

Buyer contracted to buy (and Farmer to sell) all of the Vidalia onions that Farmer produced on Hicks Farm during the 2010 growing season. This contract would be deemed an output contract, and the lack of a specified quantity term would not invalidate the contract. Buyer and Farmer do not know, at the time of contracting, how many bushels of onions will be grown. Moreover, Buyer is not being forced to buy an extraordinary, disproportionate amount of onions beyond his expectation at the time of contracting.

Here, the farmer and the buyer have entered into a valid output contract because the buyer agrees to purchase "all the Vidalia onions Farmer produces at his farm." This language creates a valid output contract and meets the quantity requirement of the U.C.C. All that is required of the farmer is that he produce and present his output in good faith. Therefore, because the output contract describes the quantity with sufficient certainty and definiteness, it complies with the U.C.C.

Contracts Between Merchants—Exceptions

Contracts between merchants often allow exceptions for failure to deliver the promised quantity. A party is usually in breach of the contract when he or she fails to deliver all of the goods promised at the time set for delivery. However, the U.C.C. recognizes "commercial impracticability" as a defense to breach of contract for failure to perform. The party seeking to avoid performance must show something beyond mere inconvenience to perform; the cause of the impracticability must be unforeseeable and outside of that party's control. An unexpected drought would be unforseeable and could not be said to have been contemplated by the parties at the time of contracting. There is even a provision in the U.C.C., §2-613, that addresses casualty to identified goods.

Example

An owner of Fruit Stands International, a chain of fruit and vegetable markets, contracted with a farmer from Mason County Georgia for 300 bushels of Vidalia onions grown in Mason County during the 2010 growing season. However, 70 percent of Farmer's onions were destroyed in a severe drought so he could not fulfill his contract with Fruit Stands International. Farmer might also support his failure to perform by saying that the contract specifically called for Vidalia onions to be grown on his farm in Mason County and that destruction of the crop's yield was further evidence of his inability to perform. Farmer could not just supply any onions from anywhere else in Georgia (or the rest of the world) because the contract expressly called for Vidalia onions to be grown on his farm in Mason County. The parties have entered into this identical agreement for the past eleven growing seasons.

A breach of a contract occurs when a party either repudiates before the time set for delivery or fails to discharge his or her duties at the time set for delivery. In this case, the Vidalia onion farmer has the defense of commercial impracticability, which will excuse his performance. Commercial impracticability occurs when (1) a material element of the contract becomes impractical to perform; (2) the impossibility is due to no fault of either party; (3) the impracticability was unforeseeable at the time the parties entered into the contract; (4) the adversely affected party did not assume the risk.

For instance, a drought is a foreseeable event that would impact the Vidalia onion crop. However, a drought so severe that would limit the farmer to only 30 percent or less of production certainly is unforeseeable.

Generally, a court will excuse a party's performance, in a contract between merchants, for the proper defense of impracticability. A proper defense of impracticability applies where the event is not foreseeable at the time of entering into the contract, which excuses the party's performance.

Here, neither the farmer nor the buyer could foresee the "severe and unexpected" drought in Mason County because no one can predict the weather conditions for an entire growing season. The court would likely excuse the farmer's lower yield.

■ BOILERPLATE PROVISIONS

Earlier in this chapter we defined *provisions* as clauses in a contract, and many consider boilerplate provisions to be composed of standardized language that is not negotiated. In actual practice, many provisions that are boilerplate are negotiated in the sense that the parties determine whether to include them in the agreement, although the language of the actual provision is standardized. Boilerplate language exists for arbitration, choice of law, indemnification, severability, **warranties**, and many other clauses. Formbooks have many examples. One commonly negotiated provision is the choice of law provision or clause. Each party would prefer to have any

Warranty
a warranty is a promise or a guarantee that an assertion is true.

dispute or any contract claim be governed by the law of the jurisdiction where he or she resides or does business or the jurisdiction that may have the most favorable laws.

Example—Choice of Law Provision

You agree that the laws of the Commonwealth of Massachusetts govern this contract and any claim or dispute that you may have against us, without regard to Massachusetts' conflict of laws, rules. You further agree that any disputes or claims that you may have against us will be resolved by a court located in the Commonwealth of Massachusetts and you agree and submit to the exercise of personal jurisdiction of such courts for the purpose of litigating any such claim or action.

Example—Indemnification Provision

Upon request by us, you agree to defend, indemnify, and hold harmless us and our parent and other affiliated companies, and our respective employees, contractors, officers, directors, and agents, from all liabilities, claims, and expenses, including attorney's fees that may arise from your use or misuse of _____.

Example—Severability and Integration Provision

This contract and any supplemental terms, policies, rules, and guidelines posted on the website constitute the entire agreement between you and us and supercede all previous written and oral agreements. If any part of these Terms of Use is held invalid or unenforceable, that portion shall be construed in a manner consistent with applicable law to reflect, as nearly as possible, the original intentions of the parties, and the remaining portions shall remain in full force and effect.

■ WHAT A PARALEGAL NEEDS TO KNOW ABOUT TERMS AND PROVISIONS

A paralegal can aide the attorney in determining the precise terms of the contract and how the terms are defined. This will help the attorney create a term sheet if it is needed. For instance, a paralegal can ascertain the precise address of a parcel of real estate, the precise quantity or condition of an item, or the price of goods to be sold. A paralegal can also note the date and time of the performance due. When the contract is complex, the paralegal can take the time to list every contract term that is contained in the agreement. The attorney can then decide if the information should be included. Paralegals should ascertain all details regarding all terms and be sure that this is included in the written agreement. Additionally, a paralegal should note if the contract is between merchants, for then the U.C.C. applies to the terms.

Most important, a paralegal needs to know that it is necessary to include all information relevant to the agreement in the written contract prior to signing. Check with the supervising attorney if you are unsure if a term is relevant or if a term needs to be included. Use forms, approved by the supervising attorney, to provide checklists for terms to be included.

Paralegals should also be conscious of the parties' ability to appreciate the terms and provisions. You should be aware of the age of majority, in the particular state that is controlling, so as to know if a party has the capacity to contract. Additionally, the paralegal should be aware of medical conditions and mental infirmities and how these relate to a party's capacity to contract in that state.

Finally, a paralegal must know that the quantity terms in a contract must be precise and accurate. If the contract concerns the sale of goods, and if the contract falls under the U.C.C., ask the supervising attorney if this is a requirements or an output contract, for this may affect the quantity term. Always ask the supervising attorney if the Uniform Commercial Code is applicable, for it may not be apparent that the contract deals with the sale of goods or that the contracting parties are merchants. For instance, you may not realize that a farmer can be a merchant under the U.C.C.

Although some terms are determined by the contracting parties in the specific transaction (price, quantity, condition, time of performance), some provisions are considered to be boilerplate (arbitration, choice of law, severability), and some provisions are conditions, all of these can be negotiated by the parties. When a term or provision is negotiated, this is a legal decision and has the consequence of changing a party's legal position. Negotiating terms and provisions and determining which to include are tasks that are ultimately performed by the supervising attorney or under the close direction and supervision of a supervising attorney.

Case Illustration

Guided Reading Pointers

Note that the court, in the following decision, determined that the farmer is a merchant and is subject to the U.C.C. The farmer has grown and sold soybeans for many years and knew how grain elevators work. This indicated, to the court, that the farmer was a merchant. An oral contract between merchants is permissible. The quarrel between the buyer and the seller had to do with the quantity of soybeans. Johnson did not deliver the entire amount promised to MFA. Johnson received a written contract from MFA for the delivery of 6,000 bushels of beans and failed to sign the contract and failed to deliver that amount. The sum that MFA withheld represented damages for the shortage of beans. Johnson alleged that the contract was not for a definite quantity of beans. Also Johnson alleged that since the contract was oral and was for more than $500, it could not be proven. MFA asserted that an oral contract was admissible because Johnson was a merchant under the U.C.C. and the U.C.C. was applicable. The court stated that Johnson could not avoid his obligation to MFA because the court determined that Johnson was a merchant and under the U.C.C.

his oral contract was valid. For the court to decide if the parties complied with the terms, the court had to first determine that Johnson was a merchant, and that the U.C.C. applied.

Rush Johnson Farms, Inc.
v.
Missouri Farmers Association, Inc.
555 S.W.2d 61 (Mo. App. 1977)

This case presents for the first time in Missouri the question of whether or not a farmer may be considered a "merchant" under the Uniform Commercial Code, §400.2-201, RSMo 1969.

Rush Johnson Farms, Inc., brought suit against Missouri Farmers Association, Inc., (MFA) for $4,094.60 which Johnson claimed to be the balance due for soybeans sold to MFA. MFA defended on the ground Johnson had entered into a contract for the delivery of 6,000 bushels of beans and had failed to deliver the entire amount and the sum withheld represented damages to MFA for the shortage. Johnson contended the contract was not for a definite quantity of beans. Further, Johnson argued the contract was oral and under §400.2-201 could not be proven because it involved more than $500 and was not in writing signed by him. MFA countered by stating Johnson was a "merchant" within the code definition and under subsection 2 of §400.2-201 the oral contract was admissible.

By the court's instructions the jury was authorized to find an indebtedness from MFA to Johnson if there were not a contract for the sale of 6,000 bushels of beans and if MFA had not paid for all of the beans delivered. The jury returned a verdict in favor of MFA.

On this appeal the only question preserved for review by Johnson is whether or not Johnson can be held to be a merchant under sub-section 2 of §400.2-201 so as to invoke the exception therein contained for the proof of an oral contract. Affirmed.

. . . Johnson testified he owned farms in two Missouri counties. In addition, the proof showed he owned a farm in partnership with Andrew Baer who apparently carried out the actual farming operation on both the partnership land and that belonging to Johnson. Johnson testified he had sold soybeans to elevators for many, many years, although this was the first time he had sold his beans to the MFA elevator in Salisbury.

When Johnson was getting ready to sell his '72 crop in 1973, he stated he had checked with a number of elevators to determine the market price of soybeans. He called the MFA elevator at Salisbury and requested he be notified when beans reached $4.00 a bushel. On January 2, 1973, the secretary at such elevator called Johnson and told him beans had reached $4.02 per bushel. He stated he agreed to sell his crop at the $4.02 figure and estimated he would have from 5,000 to 6,000 bushels. The elevator secretary testified the agreement was to sell the definite quantity of 6,000 bushels and the jury found this to be the fact.

Within a few days after January 2, the secretary mailed Johnson a written contract calling for the sale of 6,000 bushels of soybeans at $4.02 per bushel. Johnson stated he received this and was excited, but he did not contact the elevator. Instead he threw the contract away.

The court, at least by implication, found Johnson came within the meaning of the word "merchant" when it submitted this case to the jury.

Section 400.2-105 defines the word "goods" as used in §400.2-201 to include "the unborn young of animals and growing crops." Section 400.2-104 defines "merchant" as: . . . a person who deals in goods of the kind or otherwise by his occupation holds himself out as having knowledge or skill peculiar to the practices or goods involved in the transaction or to whom such knowledge or skill may be attributed by his employment of an agent or broker or other intermediary who by his occupation holds himself out as having such knowledge or skill.

The UCC comment following §400.2-104 states:

The term "merchant" as defined here roots in the "law merchant" concept of a professional in business. The professional status under the definition may be based upon specialized knowledge as to the goods, specialized knowledge as to business practices, or specialized knowledge as to both and which kind of specialized knowledge may be sufficient to establish the merchant status is indicated by the nature of the provisions.

The special provisions as to merchants appear only in this Article and they are of three kinds. Sections 2-201(2), 2-205, 2-207 and 2-209 dealing with the statute of frauds, firm offers, confirmatory memoranda and modification rest on normal business practices which are or ought to be typical of and familiar to any person in business. For purposes of these sections almost every person in business would, therefore, be deemed to be a "merchant" under the language "who . . . by his occupation holds himself out as having knowledge or skill peculiar to the practices . . . involved in the transaction . . ." since the practices involved in the transaction are non-specialized business practices such as answering mail. In this type of provision, banks, or even universities, for example, well may be "merchants." But even these sections only apply to a merchant in his mercantile capacity; a lawyer or bank president buying fishing tackle for his own use is not a merchant.

The question of whether or not a farmer can be considered a merchant under the provisions of the UCC here considered has been the subject of a number of decisions . . . Johnson concedes with reference to the Illinois Court of Appeals cases that the Supreme Court of Illinois in *Sierens v. Clausen*, 60 Ill.2d 585, 328 N.E.2d 559 (1975) has held a farmer may be a merchant and in effect has overruled the Court of Appeals cases.

. . . A number of states have held a farmer may qualify as a merchant under these sections of the UCC. The case which this court finds to be the better reasoned of all of the cases which has considered the question is *Nelson v. Union Equity Co-op. Exchange*, 548 S.W.2d 352 (Texas 1977). In *Nelson* the Supreme Court of Texas thoroughly considered the section involved and cited most of the cases which have dealt with this question. The Texas court reached the conclusion that the farmer involved in that case fell within the definition of merchant as contained in the UCC. The court pointed out the distinction between the definition of the term merchant as used in the UCC and the dictionary definition which has been relied upon by some courts in deciding this question. In *Nelson* the court held the definition to be applied is that contained in the UCC.

In *Nelson* the court stated: "Under that definition, a person is a 'merchant' if he (1) deals in goods of a kind . . ." The court held Nelson satisfied that requirement because he dealt in wheat. The court pointed out the UCC does not define the word "deal" but quoted from Ballentine's Law Dictionary the definition "to buy or to sell." The court held Nelson qualified under that definition because he raised his own wheat and annually sold that crop himself.

Under the circumstances of this case, Johnson would qualify as a merchant since he is shown to be one who deals in beans because for many, many years he has sold his bean crop. He admitted he was familiar with the operation of elevators and how they conducted business and further showed himself capable of ascertaining the market price of beans. In *Nelson* the court also observed that under the definition of merchant in the UCC it is not necessary that a person actually hold himself out as having some particular knowledge or skill to qualify as a merchant, but rather a person by his occupation holds himself out as having knowledge or skill peculiar to the goods involved in the transaction . . .

. . . This court adopts the reasoning in *Nelson*. This court does not believe that anyone in this day and age looks upon any person or corporation who conducts a farming operation as a simple tiller of the soil. It is well known that the marketing of a crop is certainly as important as the raising of it. Johnson fully revealed in this case his knowledge of the market and his thorough familiarity with marketing practices and procedures in trying to obtain the best price possible for his product. Under the definition of merchant, as contained in the UCC, Johnson fully qualified as such so that the oral contract in this case was not barred under the statute of frauds as contained in §400.2–201.

To hold Johnson meets the definition of merchant does not impose any burden on him or any farmer with similar qualifications. The only requirement the UCC imposed upon Johnson was to notify MFA in writing of his objection to the contract which specified 6,000 bushels. For a person entering into a transaction involving almost $25,000, this does not appear to be unreasonable.

This court further finds the definition of goods, quoted above, which includes growing crops as well as the unborn young of animals, to clearly indicate the framers of the UCC contemplated that farmers could be included within the transaction covered by §400.2–201 . . .

. . . It should be made clear a farmer is not per se included in the definition of "merchant." Whether or not a particular farmer qualifies as a merchant under the sections discussed would depend on the individual experience and activities of the person involved. This court holds Johnson in this case fully came within the definition of "merchant." . . .

. . . Johnson was an experienced farmer who was well conversant with the marketing of his bean crop. He received the written confirmation of his agreement to sell. The only obligation the UCC placed upon him was to write a note to MFA stating he had not agreed to sell 6,000 bushels, if that were the fact. This is not a great burden to place upon anyone who is capable of owning and operating a large farming operation and who knows the marketing procedures for his produce. To hold Johnson did not meet the simple requirement of a "merchant" under the UCC would be an affront to his proven experience and capability. This court is not willing to take a head in the sand approach and close its eyes to the plain facts existent in the farming industry.

For the reasons stated, this court holds Johnson came within the definition of "merchant." The judgment is affirmed . . .

Guided Reading Questions

1. Why did the U.C.C. apply to this contract?

2. How did the U.C.C. impact any terms in Johnson's contract with MFA? Did Johnson have to notify MFA regarding the quantity of beans delivered?

3. Why did MFA argue that Johnson was a merchant within the definition in the U.C.C. and that under the U.C.C., the oral contract was admissible?

CHAPTER SUMMARY

This chapter explored the terms and provisions that can be included in a contract. Three main categories of terms are: terms that are subject to change depending on the agreement reached, boilerplate provisions, and conditions or conditional provisions. When a contract is not between merchants and the Uniform Commercial Code does not apply, the terms must be definite and certain. The U.C.C. has gap-filler provisions in contracts between merchants. Also when the parties, subject to the U.C.C., agree to an output contract or a requirements contract, the quantity term does not have to be specifically stated. Boilerplate provisions have specific, standardized language. Conditions, most commonly conditions precedent and subsequent, require an action or event to trigger duties or to discharge duties. This chapter has shown that terms and provisions must be carefully selected and drafted to accurately represent the agreement that the parties reached. This chapter underscores the need for precise drafting when creating a written contract. Determining which terms and provisions to include is a legal decision to be performed by an attorney or under the supervision and direction of an attorney.

Terms and Provisions

Terms and Provisions Generally	The most common categories of terms that vary are: quantity, time, price, condition of the subject matter, and location Provisions are contract clauses Boilerplate provisions use fixed or standardized language regardless of the particular subject matter of the agreement; they often concern severability, choice of law, and arbitration The most common conditional terms, or conditions, are conditions precedent and conditions subsequent, where something must occur to activate a duty or to discharge a duty
How Courts Interpret Contract Terms	This is called rules of construction Generally, a court will read a contract according to its plain meaning and attempt to carry out the parties' intentions Generally determined by state common law
Requirements for Terms in Contracts Not Subject to the U.C.C.	Definite and certain Subject matter must be legal Contractual capacity to understand terms Specificity required for: time of performance, price, quantity, location of real estate, duration
Conditional Terms	Condition precedent Condition subsequent or discharge of duty
U.C.C. and Terms	Gap-filler provisions Quantity term required unless an output or a requirements contract
Boilerplate Provisions	Clauses with standardized language but the decision to include the specific clause may be subject to negotiation Examples of types of boilerplate clauses: arbitration, choice of law, indemnification, severability, warranties
Paralegal's Role	Ultimately, the decision as to which term or provision to include is a legal decision that must be made by a supervising attorney or under the close direction and supervision of an attorney Consult formbooks to obtain a checklist for terms and provisions to consider for a particular contract

REVIEW QUESTIONS

1. What is an output contract?
2. Why do the terms in a contract have to be definite and certain?
3. Is it necessary that the subject matter of the contract be legal?
4. When is location an essential contract term?
5. What is contractual capacity?
6. Provide an example of when a contract is void?
7. What does a "time of the essence" clause require?

8. In a contract between merchants, does the quantity have to be stated precisely?
9. What is a U.C.C. stop-gap provision?
10. What is the paralegal's role regarding a contract's terms and provisions?

SKILL-BUILDING APPLICATION EXERCISE

Review the following agreement and determine if the contract's terms are definite and certain by examining the following: legality, quantity, time, price, enforceability, and location.

AGREEMENT TO PURCHASE INTEREST IN SPA TO OPERATE NAIL SERVICES

This Agreement is made *on January 15, 2010*, between Mary Lynn of 123 Route ZZ, *Sister Bay, Wisconsin* ("seller"), and *Margaret Joseph of 345 Route 42, Sturgeon, Wisconsin* ("buyer"). This contract represents the entire agreement made between the parties. Any change or modification of this agreement must be included in this writing prior to signing. This contract cannot be assigned to any other party since it involves the personal services of the parties. The laws of the state of Wisconsin shall govern this agreement. This sale of the 25 percent interest in the Door County Spa shall take effect immediately after the contract is signed by both parties.

A. Lynn, the Seller, is the sole owner and operator of the Door County Spa located at 123 Route ZZ, Sister Bay, Wisconsin.

B. Lynn wants to sell a portion of her business to a partner who will solely offer manicure and pedicure services.

C. Margaret Joseph, the Buyer, is licensed to provide manicure and pedicure services in the state of Wisconsin. The Seller desires to sell and the Buyer desires to purchase an interest in the Door County Spa and to become a full partner. This agreement represents the bargain reached between the parties and is supported by consideration.

D. Margaret Joseph will pay Mary Lynn $20,000. In receipt of $20,000 from Margaret Joseph, Mary Lynn will provide Joseph with a 25 percent interest in the Door County Spa with the exclusive and sole right to provide manicure and pedicure services at the Door County Spa. Along with the 25 percent interest in the Door County

Spa, Margaret Joseph will receive the benefit of the goodwill accrued in the business.

A. Division of Duties: Margaret Joseph shall exclusively provide all manicure and pedicure services at the Door County Spa. Mary Lynn shall provide any and all remaining services at the Door County Spa, except for nail and toenail procedures. Both parties must put forth individually and jointly their best efforts at maintaining and furthering the business.

B. If a disagreement occurs between the parties, Mary Lynn has the right to repurchase the 25 percent share from Margaret Joseph at the fair market value on the day of the offer. The fair market value is to be determined by an independent appraiser agreed to by both parties.

C. Each party to the agreement must maintain a life insurance policy on the life of the partner. If one of the partners dies, the proceeds of the life insurance policy should be used to buy the remaining partner's share of the business.

Signed on this day _____ , in Door County, Wisconsin, by Mary Lynn and Margaret Joseph

SIMULATED LAW OFFICE ASSIGNMENT

Read over the following contract for the illustrations for a children's book. Are the terms definite and certain?

This agreement for twelve illustrations for *Worlds of Wizards*, a children's picture book, is made today, August 12, 2010, between Anna Artist and Peter Prince, Publisher and Owner of Prince Publishing, in New York City, New York, and is subject to the laws of New York State.

Prince Publishing intends to publish *Worlds of Wizards* in January 2011.

Anna Artist has read the manuscript and understands the expectations of the publisher for the artwork for the illustrations. Anna Artist will submit the twelve pieces of art, in the medium of watercolor, on 8.50" × 110" paper by December 1, 2010. The book has twelve sections and each section shall have one corresponding watercolor illustration created by Anna Artist.

In consideration for Anna Artist's work, she shall receive a grant of $5,000 upon the signing of this agreement. After the book is published, Anna Artist will receive royalties of 2.5 percent of net sales twice annually, in January and June each year.

Copyright—The publisher shall maintain the copyright for all artwork created for *Worlds of Wizards*. Anna Artist, as illustrator, shall have credit on the cover of the book as illustrator.

Warranties—Anna Artist holds out and promises that the works are her original work product and are created solely for this publication of *Worlds of Wizards*.

DRAFTING EXERCISE

The supervising attorney requests that you draft a contract for Anna Artist. The attorney wants you to use the previous contract concerning Anna Artist's illustrations for the *Worlds of Wizards* as a form for this agreement. Anna Artist was asked to provide the illustrations for a video game concept, poster, and jewel case for the game disc. The game is called *The Princess of the Palace*. Anna Artist must create four original illustrations on 12" × 18" poster board using tempura paint. The company requesting the illustrations is U Game, Inc. of Dover, Colorado. Anna Artist resides in New York City. Colorado law will apply. The illustrations are due on March 15, 2009. U Game will pay Anna Artist a flat fee of $4,000 for the four illustrations. There will be no royalties and Anna Artist will retain no rights in the artwork. U Game will retain all of the rights to the artwork.

DEVELOPING CRITICAL THINKING SKILLS

This exercise is based on the *Johnson* decision, reprinted in this chapter, and information in this chapter regarding the terms in a contract between merchants.

Mr. Richards owns 300 acres of land and grows wheat on the land. Richards has grown wheat for the past twenty years and sells his crop annually. He uses the grain elevator in town when he receives the price he wants for the wheat and sells it. According to *Johnson*, would Richards be considered a merchant? Are crops goods? If Richards contracts with Wholesome Bakeries to sell Wholesome all of his output, as long as the output is commercially reasonable, will the contract fail for indefiniteness since the quantity term is not precise?

PORTFOLIO ASSIGNMENT

You work for a small real estate law firm. Most of the clients are buyers and sellers of residential real estate. The attorney that you work for asked that you interview a seller of a home to obtain the necessary information to include in a contract for the sale of real estate. What information would you seek to obtain to be sure that the contract's terms are definite, certain, and identifiable?

Modifying the Contract | CHAPTER 7

INTRODUCTIONS–MODIFICATION IN GENERAL

A **modification** of a contract occurs after the contract is formed but prior to the performance. A modification differs from a counteroffer in that a counteroffer arises prior to acceptance.

A modification of an **executory** contract introduces new terms and conditions into the agreement. Sometimes the modification is material in that it affects the substance of the contract. Sometimes the modification is immaterial in that it doesn't alter the essence of the agreement and does not change essential terms such as price, condition, time, or quantity.

Example—Immaterial Modification: Bill Jones hired Contino Painting to paint his front steps and porch in white shade 122. The written contract stated that Contino should use white shade 122 to paint the steps and the porch. If Contino Painting states, prior to performance, that it will use white shade 121 instead of white shade 122, both pure white, this would be an immaterial modification because the color difference is barely perceptible. However, if Contino Painting alerts Jones, after the contract is finalized and signed yet prior to performance, that the company can only paint the stairs and not the porch as business is quite busy, this would be a material modification because it alters the essence of the agreement.

Contracts between merchants have special rules regarding modification, as explained in this chapter. Additionally, sometimes when an oral agreement is modified, the modification may then require the agreement to be in writing to conform to the state Statute of Frauds **provisions**. For instance, Mr. Cox contracted to buy a $200 gas-powered push lawn mower from Great Pastures Lawn Care to be delivered in two weeks. After the agreement was reached and Mr. Cox paid for the mower, he

LEARNING OBJECTIVES

After studying this chapter, you will be able to:

1. Discuss ways that a contract can be modified.

2. Know the difference between a modification and a counteroffer.

3. Discuss rescission, termination, and discharge and how they differ from modification.

4. Distinguish a modification from a breach.

Modification
alteration that changes some components of a contract or agreement.

Executory
a contract that has not been performed.

Provision
a point, part, or paragraph in an agreement, contract, or statute.

Statute of Frauds
statutory provisions adopted by each state requiring that certain types of contracts be in writing. The most common types of contracts affected by the Statute of Frauds are: contracts that require a year or longer to complete, contracts for the sale of real estate, and contracts for the sale of goods over $500.

Supersede
when an entirely new agreement comes into existence that replaces a prior agreement, the new agreement is said to supersede the prior contract.

decided, as he was leaving the store, that he wanted to purchase the $600 riding mower to be delivered in thirty days. Aside from a receipt, there was no paperwork for the $200 mower. The purchase agreement for the $200 mower was oral. Since the $600 mower involved the sale of goods over $500, the agreement between Cox and Great Pastures now had to be in writing to comply with the **Statute of Frauds**.

Often, contracts must be modified due to circumstances changing in ways not anticipated when the original agreement was formed. Good drafting anticipates issues that may arise, such as changes in prices and availability of goods and labor concerns, and avoids the need to modify agreements later. Sometimes, a provision is included in a contract permitting a party to modify or even rescind the agreement when a specific circumstance arises.

The determination to modify a contract involves many of the same elements that arise when the initial, or primary, contract was formed. Additional consideration is generally required to support the modification of the contract. The major exception to the requirement for additional consideration arises when the contract concerns the sale of goods between merchants. Aside from contracts between merchants, the components of a modification are: offer, acceptance, and consideration; these components are required if the modification is material and involves replacing the earlier contract. If the changes are quite immaterial or very small, the initial agreement can be altered without additional consideration.

When an entirely new agreement comes into existence that replaces a prior agreement, the new agreement is said to **supersede** the prior contract.

Example

Mrs. Par contracted with CarPros to maintain and repair her car for twelve (12) months. After both sides signed the agreement but before any work was done on the car, Mrs. Par decided to spend six months of the year at a retirement community 1,000 miles south of CarPros. It would not be feasible for CarPros to maintain Mrs. Par's car during the six months spent away. The initial agreement had to be modified, reflecting the new situation. The modified agreement would supersede the prior twelve-month maintenance contract.

Sometimes a contract cannot be modified. Often there is language stating that an agreement cannot be modified in the contract itself. Often residential mortgages, credit card agreements, and student loan agreements cannot be modified, especially by the borrower. Commercial loan agreements can be modified.

■ LANGUAGE THAT MODIFIES THE CONTRACT VERSUS COUNTEROFFER

Modifications differ from counteroffers. Unlike a modification, a counteroffer is communicated during the contract formation stage. For instance, before a contract is formed, when an acceptance contains new terms that change the offer, it is no longer an acceptance but is now a counteroffer. Then the parties must agree to the changed terms for a contract to be formed. Modification occurs after the meeting of the minds, after the agreement is reached and is final, but often prior to the complete performance of the contract.

The modification can be in writing, or it can be oral. However, if the modification is oral, the parties must be alert to the Statute of Frauds requirements for the relevant jurisdiction. If the oral modification alters the agreement in such a way as to require the application of the Statute of Frauds, then the agreement, including the modifications, must be in writing. The Statute of Frauds comes into play when the value of the item contracted for exceeds $500, the contract requires a year or longer to perform, and/or when the contract concerns real estate.

Example

Mr. May contracted initially with Guy Grey to work at his advertising agency for three months to draw cartoons for an advertisement. This was an oral agreement. Mr. May spoke with his client and the client was very enthusiastic about the marketing ideas and requested the development of twelve additional advertisements. Mr. May, an experienced advertising executive, realized that the twelve additional ads would require twelve additional months of work from Mr. Grey. Mr. May wants to modify the employment agreement with Mr. Grey from a three-month agreement to a fifteen-month agreement. Since the agreement now requires more than one year to perform, it must be in writing to conform to the Statute of Frauds requirements. This is an example of when an oral contract is modified and the resulting agreement must be in writing to comply with the Statute of Frauds.

■ NEGOTIATION PRIOR TO PERFORMANCE OF THE CONTRACT (AFTER THE AGREEMENT)

Parties can negotiate to modify a contract in a similar manner to the negotiations that occur when creating the original agreement. The Restatement (Second) of Contracts §89 states that executory contracts (contracts not fully performed) can be modified if the modification arises due to a circumstance that was not foreseen by the parties when contracting initially. The modification must be fair and equitable.

Example

Mr. Jones signed a contract with Yarborough Tires to provide new tires for his car at $100 per tire. Five days after signing the contract, Yarborough Tires president John Yarborough was reading the paper and saw an article discussing unrest in South America. Rubber comes from South America, and the price of rubber could rise due to the unrest. On Monday morning, Yarborough sends Mr. Jones a letter stating that the contract must be modified to reflect an increase in the price of rubber. The new tire price is $125 per tire. This is not a fair and equitable attempt at modifying the agreement because the tires Mr. Jones contracted for are already manufactured and in the warehouse.

Commercial loan contracts are frequently modified to reflect the changing economic climate surrounding the loan.

Example—Loan Modification Agreement

LOAN MODIFICATION AGREEMENT

This Loan Modification Agreement is entered into as of June 22, 2010, by
and between PC Program, Inc. ("Borrower")and Your Bank ("Bank").

1. DESCRIPTION OF EXISTING INDEBTEDNESS: Among other indebtedness that may be owing by Borrower to Bank, Borrower is indebted to Bank pursuant to, among other documents, a Loan
   and **Security** Agreement, dated September 19, 2010, as may be amended from time to time (the
   "Loan Agreement"). The Loan Agreement provided for, among other things, a Committed Line of
   Credit in the original principal amount of One Hundred Thousand Dollars ($100,000). Hereinafter,
   all indebtedness owing by Borrower to Bank shall be referred to as the "Indebtedness."

2. DESCRIPTION OF COLLATERAL AND GUARANTIES.   Repayment of the Indebtedness is secured by the **Collateral** as described in the Loan Agreement dated September 19, 2010, by and
   between Borrower and Bank.

DESCRIPTION OF CHANGE IN TERMS.

Modification(s) to Loan Agreement

1. The following terms stated in the section entitled
   "Definitions" are amended as follows:
   "Committed Line of Credit" means $100,000.
   "Deferred Revenue" is all amounts received in advance of performance and not yet recognized as
   revenue.

2. "Financial Accountings" is amended to read as follows:
   . . . as soon as available, but in any event within one hundred twenty (120) days after the end of Borrower's fiscal year, audited consolidated financial statements of Borrower prepared in accordance with
   the Federal Accounting Standards Board, and with the review of a certified public accountant.

3. The third paragraph of Section c should read as follows:
   Bank shall have the right audit Borrower's collateral annually.
   PC Programs and its officers and representatives agree that by modifying the existing loan agreement,
   the original terms and representations and warranties, that have not been modified, are still in effect.

This Loan Modification Agreement is effective as of June 22, 2010.

BORROWER:	BANK:
PC Program, INC.	Your BANK
By: /s/ Randy Randall	By: /s/ Jim James
_____	_____
Name: Randy Randall	Name: Jim James
_____	_____
Title: President	Title: Senior Loan Officer
_____	_____

■ TIMING—COUNTEROFFER VERSUS MODIFICATION

A counteroffer occurs prior to the formation of the contract. A counteroffer can be made by either party, relates to the original offer, and proposes new terms. The new terms must be accepted to form a contract. Instead of an offer mirrored by the acceptance, the promisee (who usually tenders acceptance) submits new terms to the promisor. A counteroffer basically is a new offer that destroys the original offer. This differs from a modification because a modification occurs after the contract is finalized, but not yet completely performed. Counteroffers can occur when the offeror receives the acceptance and counters with additional terms that also must be accepted, or when the promisee receives the offer and responds with additional or new terms. The Restatement (Second) of Contracts §39 states that, in a counteroffer, the "offeree's power of acceptance is terminated by his making of a counter-offer" unless the offeror manifests the intention to keep the negotiations going.

Additionally, according to the Restatement (Second) of Contracts §59: "A reply to an offer which purports to accept it but is conditional on the offeror's assent to terms additional to or different from those offered is not an acceptance but is a counter-offer."

■ CONSIDERATION WHEN MODIFYING A CONTRACT

Sometimes the only consideration required, when modifying an existing contract, is the agreement to modify the terms. According to the Restatement (Second) of Contracts §71, consideration can consist of a bargained-for performance or of a return promise when modifying an agreement. The subject matter of the modification is bargained for if the promisee or the promisor wants the modification in exchange for a promise. The modification of a contract can constitute the performance of a provision. The logic is as follows: Since modifying an agreement can constitute performance, and bargained-for performance can constitute consideration, then the act of modifying the contract is the consideration. Additionally, a bargained-for modification indicates the parties exchanged value. When the contract is modified, one party induces the other to modify or alter an existing agreement with the promise of value.

■ U.C.C. PROVISIONS REGARDING MODIFICATION OF A CONTRACT BETWEEN MERCHANTS

There are special rules concerning consideration when the contract is between merchants.

Section 2-209 of the Uniform Commercial Code sets out the rules regarding contract modification between merchants. The most important point is that the modification of an agreement between merchants requires

Security
used by a lender in a loan to ensure that the loan is repaid; a security interest permits the lender to have a right to the borrower's property if the loan is not repaid. Also, another term for stock or share.

Collateral
either personal or real property that is used as security for a loan.

no additional consideration to be binding. However, a signed agreement that states that a modification or rescission shall not be permitted cannot later be modified except when the modification is requested in writing and signed by the other party. Additionally, the Statute of Frauds requirements must be complied with when modifying the initial agreement (see earlier discussion).

The U.C.C. states that all modifications must be made in good faith. According to U.C.C. §2-103, the test of "good faith" between merchants is the "observance of reasonable commercial standards of fair dealing in the trade" (§2-103), and may in some situations require an "objectively demonstrable reason for seeking a modification . . ."

■ RESCISSION, TERMINATION, AND DISCHARGE VERSUS MODIFICATION

Modification concerns the offer and acceptance, supported by bargained-for consideration, of new terms to a contract that was already created by the parties, yet not fully performed. Rescission, termination, and discharge occur when one party or both parties are relieved from their obligations under the contract or when the contract no longer binds the parties because it ceases to exist.

A rescinded agreement is when both sides are relieved of their duties and obligations under the agreement. Usually, this decision is mutual. Many times, the decision to rescind the agreement is based on financial reasons, often referred to as commercial or economic impracticality.

An agreement to rescind a contract discharges all parties from their remaining obligations under the agreement.

Example

Wilmington Volleyball League sponsors volleyball teams year round. Wilmington held registration for a summer competitive beach volleyball league. Wilmington hired referees for the games, which were scheduled to be held on Tuesday and Thursday night, 6 P.M. to 7 P.M., during the month of July, at Wilmington Beach. The referees would be paid $27.00 per game. Wilmington had insufficient registration for the league. In fact, only three people registered in total. Consequently, Wilmington had to cancel the league. Wilmington had to rescind the contracts with the referees. The referees were eager to be relieved of their contractual obligations to Wilmington so that they could pursue employment elsewhere. In fact, one potential referee had an offer to work in an ice cream shop and could not accept the employment until his referee contract with Wilmington was rescinded. This would be a mutual decision to relieve both sides from their obligations under the contract.

Termination

Termination is the end of a contract. Termination can be mutual, and also a contract can be terminated by one party before the agreement is completely performed. Termination, when used by one party, is used as a remedy by that party, and this usually occurs because the other party defaulted or is not performing as agreed.

Discharge

To discharge is to conclude the duties under the contract and relieve the parties from the legal power of the contract. For instance, a discharge of obligation ends one's obligations under a contract and the parties are no longer subject to the legal power of the agreement.

■ BREACH VERSUS MODIFICATION

A breach of contract occurs when one of the parties fails to fulfill his or her obligation under the contract. This is different from modifying the terms of a contract with an offer to modify the terms, acceptance of the modified terms, and consideration to support the modification.

Example

Smith Company hires Tom Jones Painters to paint the interior offices of the headquarters. The parties agree that Tom Jones should supply ecru latex paint, all painting supplies, and clean up after the work is complete. Tom Jones toured the site and measured the number of square feet of wall space to be painted. The parties agreed on a price that roughly approximates $300 per 100 square feet. Smith Company tendered a deposit to Tom Jones. Tom Jones was scheduled to start work on the painting on the first Monday in July. Tom Jones never showed up to paint. Tom Jones never contacted Smith Company. Tom Jones and the representatives of Tom Jones cannot be reached. Consequently, it can be assumed that Tom Jones breached the contract because the painters failed to fulfill their obligations under the agreement. Compare with Tom Jones contacting Smith Company with an offer to modify the contract to start work on the first Monday in August instead of the first Monday in July.

Material Breach

A material breach occurs when there is a failure to perform an essential component or term of the contract. Usually, an essential term concerns price, time, quantity, duration of agreement, location, and/or performance. An example of a material breach: Mr. Morris contracted with the Smiths to install twenty (20) windows in their home at $75.00 per window on Saturday, September 12. Mr. Morris only installed five (5) windows and refused to install the remaining windows. This is a material breach because the number of windows to be installed was an essential term of the contract.

Immaterial Breach

An immaterial breach is a breach of an unessential provision in the contract. For instance, if Mr. Morris installed the twenty windows but he needed to install the nineteenth and twentieth windows on Sunday, September 13, because the project took longer than he expected, this would be an immaterial breach.

CASE ILLUSTRATION

Guided Reading Pointers

This abridged case involves the modification of a contract to lease a space to a clothing manufacturer, Kids Wear. A lease is a contract. FRIT is the lessor, the party providing the lease for the space, and Kids Wear is the lessee, the party renting the space. The agreement was modified to omit the requirement of a guarantee by the lessee, the party leasing the space. The modification was written by hand. A paralegal for FRIT crossed out the modification. Because the modification was crossed out, FRIT assumed that the guarantees were not eliminated. When reading the case, pay attention to the court's examination of the agreement to see if the new terms are a counteroffer or a modification of an existing contract.

FEDERAL REALTY INVESTMENT TRUST
v.
KIDS WEAR BOULEVARD INC., ET AL
Civil Action No. 93-6310

(E.D. Pa. 1996)

. . . On January 27, 1988, Kids Wear Boulevard, Inc. ("Kids Wear") entered into a Lease Agreement ("the Lease") with Federal Realty Investment Trust ("FRIT"). . . . Pursuant to the terms of the Lease, Kids Wear leased premises consisting of 8,869 square feet, commonly known as Store #17, located at the Northeast Shopping Center on Roosevelt Boulevard, Philadelphia, Pennsylvania ("Leased Premises") for a term of five (5) years . . . An "Addendum" to the Lease provided Kids Wear an "Option to Renew" for two additional five-year periods ("Option Periods") upon the written notice of Kids Wear one hundred twenty (120) days prior to the expiration of the initial term. Exh. 1.

The obligations of Kids Wear to FRIT were guaranteed by defendants Morris Mizrahi, Steven Betesh, Eli Orfali and Oved Subarri (the "Guarantors") pursuant to the terms of a Guaranty Agreement ("Guaranty") dated January 27, 1988. Exh. 2. The Guarantors were the original stockholders of several Kids Wear corporations operating various store locations. . . .

Negotiations concerning whether Kids Wear would exercise its option to extend the Lease for the First Option Period began in early 1992. Tr. 19 and Exh. 6. Steven Betesh contacted FRIT to renegotiate lower rental amounts for an additional five-year term. Tr. 118. At the time of the negotiations, Mizrahi, Betesh and Orfali each owned one third of the outstanding shares of stock of Kids Wear, were the sole shareholders of Kids Wear, and Orfali was the President and Betesh was Secretary of Kids Wear. . . .

During the negotiations, Betesh advised FRIT that he believed the rent for the Option Period was above market rent. Tr. 19-20; Exh. 7. Mizrahi and Orfali were aware that Kids Wear was requesting a rent reduction for the First Option Period. Tr. 116. On May 22, 1992, Kristine Lopes, a leasing agent for

FRIT, wrote a letter to Betesh denying Kids Wear's request for a lower renewal rental amount. Exh. 7.

Subsequent to the May 22, 1992 letter, however, FRIT agreed to renegotiate lower rental amounts in an attempt to retain Kids Wear as a tenant. Tr. 119. At the time Lopes approached Betesh about renegotiating the rent, Betesh also requested the elimination of personal guaranties. Tr. 119. On July 8, 1992, Betesh wrote a letter to Lopes specifically stating that no personal guaranties would attach during the First Option Period. Exh. 8. On September 2, 1992, Betesh met with Jean Connor, Vice President and Director of FRIT, and Lopes to continue negotiations. Tr. 79. Neither Connor nor Lopes remembers specifically discussing personal guaranties with Betesh at that meeting or at any other time . . .

On September 30, 1992, FRIT drafted a one-page Lease Modification Agreement ("Lease Modification")and mailed it to Kids Wear . . . By mutual mistake, the Lease Modification stated that Kids Wear, Inc. was the tenant under the Lease, and by mistake Kids Wear, Inc. executed the Lease Modification rather than Kids Wear . . . The parties stipulate that Kids Wear Boulevard, Inc., and not Kids Wear, Inc., was supposed to be the tenant under the Lease Modification; and Kids Wear Boulevard, Inc., and not Kids Wear, Inc., actually executed the Lease Modification on November 5, 1992 . . . Defendants Mizrahi, Betesh and Orfali knew that Kids Wear had received the Lease Modification and knew that under the Lease Modification the rent would be reduced . . .

The Lease Modification sent to Kids Wear by FRIT did not contain any language relating to the Personal Guaranties . . . Kids Wear mailed the Lease Modification to its counsel, Frederic Weinberg, Esq., to review it. Weinberg added in handwriting a sentence providing for the elimination of the Personal Guaranties . . . Defendants Mizrahi, Betesh and Orfali approved the insertion of the handwritten provision by Weinberg and approved Betesh's execution of the Lease Modification as Secretary of the Corporation . . . Kids Wear dated the document November 5, 1992. Betesh and Orfali, President of the Corporation, signed it, Orfali initialed the handwritten provision, and Kids Wear mailed it back to FRIT without a cover letter . . .

Upon receipt of the Lease Modification from Kids Wear, Margaret Small, a paralegal of FRIT, crossed off both the handwritten sentence concerning elimination of the Personal Guaranties and the initials next to the sentence and had Catherine R. Mack, Esq. execute and redate the document November 9, 1992 . . . Small took this action after confirming that FRIT had not agreed to eliminate the Personal Guaranties . . . Small mailed the executed copy of the Lease Modification to Kids Wear along with a cover letter dated November 17, 1992 . . . The cover letter stated:

Enclosed is one fully executed copy of the Lease Modification Agreement for the above referenced shopping center.

Should you have any additional questions or comments, please let me know.

. . . Kids Wear received FRIT's execution of the Lease Modification with the cover letter . . . In the cover letter, Small did not inform Kids Wear that she had crossed out Weinberg's language, Exh. 12, and no one from FRIT otherwise advised Kids Wear or called its attention to the fact that the handwritten language regarding the elimination of the Personal Guaranties had been crossed out. Tr. 124-25.

Upon Kids Wear's receipt of the Lease Modification and cover letter, Betesh's secretary filed the document. Tr. 124. Betesh did not read the Lease Modification at this time because based upon the language in the cover letter, he assumed the terms remained the same as when he had sent the Lease Modification to Kids Wear. *Id.* Kids Wear paid the reduced amounts of rent set forth in the Lease Modification from February 1, 1993 to December 31, 1993, Stip. P 20, and acted at all times as though the Lease Modification was in effect. Tr. 137, 142-43. In June or July of 1993, Betesh looked at the Lease Modification and took it to his lawyer, but did not recall raising any issue with plaintiff, and did continue to pay rent. . . .

In October and November of 1993, Kids Wear conducted a "going out of business sale" at the Leased Premises. Stip. P 19. On October 15, 1993, FRIT sent Kids Wear, via certified mail, a Notice of Default ("Notice"). Stip. P 24. Kids Wear vacated the Leased Premises on or about December 30, 1993. Stip. P 25. The assets of Kids Wear were sold as of December 30, 1993. Stip. P 26.

Upon taking legal possession of the Leased Premises, FRIT placed a "Space for Rent" sign in the window of the vacated premises and began contacting a number of prospective tenants that it believed might be interested in leasing the space. Stip. P 28. Following initial discussions with several potential tenants, FRIT prepared a lease brief for a transaction with Old Country Buffet; this proposal was approved by management at FRIT. Stip. P 32. Problems developed regarding the compatibility of this tenant's requirements with an adjoining tenant that resulted in Old Country Buffet not entering into a lease with FRIT for this space. Stip. P 33. Negotiations were then resumed with Party City which led to the execution of a new lease for the Leased Premises with Party City in January 1995; that lease provides for the payment of rent following tenant fitup and renovations commencing on June 1, 1995. Stip. P 34. The rent being paid to Plaintiff by Party City is $12,580 per month as of June 1, 1995 for years 1-3 of the Lease. Stip. P 35 . . .

B. The Lease Modification Agreement

By its terms, the initial Lease Agreement expired on January 27, 1993, the Lease Modification was executed on or about November 5, 1992, and Kids Wear occupied the premises until December 30, 1993. The parties differ in their view as to whether they reached a meeting of the minds in the Lease Modification to renew under the Option or whether Kids Wear was holding over. FRIT argues that by continuing to occupy the premises and paying the agreed Minimum Rent pursuant to the terms of the Lease Modification, Kids Wear indicated its acceptance of the terms of the Lease Modification and should be bound by it. Defendants argue that mere continued possession of the Leased Premises does not constitute a renewal of the Lease. Defendants point out that the Option requires a written notice of intention to exercise the Option 120 days prior to the expiration of the Lease. Defendants conclude that, because they never provided such notice, they cannot have exercised the Option to Renew the Lease.

As indicated above, the parties started negotiating in early 1992 to renew the Lease for the First Option Period. In November 1992, FRIT sent the Lease Modification to Kids Wear containing the agreed reduced rentals for the First Option Period. Weinberg returned the Agreement dated November 5, 1992, having added a handwritten sentence initialed by Eli Orfali providing for the elimination of the Personal Guaranties. Upon receipt, Margaret Small crossed out both the handwritten paragraph and the initials next to the sentence and mailed the executed copy of the Lease Modification to Kids Wear on November 17, 1992. Kids Wear never executed the Agreement as finally proposed.

Thus, on November 17, 1992, the parties had yet to come to terms pursuant to a written contract. . . . A reply to an offer which changes the conditions of the offer is not an acceptance, but a counter offer. *Hedden v. Lupinsky*, 405 Pa. 609, 176 A.2d 406, 408 (Pa. 1962); *Accu-Weather, Inc. v. Thomas Broadcasting Co.*, 425 Pa. Super. 335, 625 A.2d 75, 77 (Pa. Super. Ct. 1993). Thus, Weinberg's change to the Lease Modification created a counter-offer. By crossing out the paragraph and sending the Agreement back, Small made a counter offer as well. Thus, when Betesh's secretary received the Lease Modification, the parties had yet to manifest a meeting of the minds.

Based upon the language in the November 17, 1992 cover letter, Betesh assumed the terms remained the same as when he had sent the Lease Modification to Kids Wear. Kids Wear proceeded to pay the reduced amounts of rent set forth in the Lease Modification from February 1, 1993 to December 31, 1993. FRIT of course believed the Lease Modification had been accepted by Kids Wear because Kids Wear continued to occupy the Leased Premises and pay the reduced rent as set forth in the Lease Modification and otherwise performed in accordance with this agreement. Four or five months into the Option Period, Betesh took the Agreement and gave it to his lawyer. Kids Wear presumably was aware at that time that the provision regarding the Guaranty was crossed out, yet it did not object or advise FRIT that Kids Wear believed that the Lease Modification was not enforceable. Kids Wear continued to pay rent and occupy the premises.

. . . Thus, by continuing negotiations with Kids Wear with regard to the rental amounts, FRIT waived the 120-day notice requirement for renewal under the Lease; thus, compliance with that requirement was not a prerequisite for Kids Wear to have renewed for the First Option Period.

Kids Wear concedes that it paid the rent provided for in the Lease Modification for over eight months, including four or five months after having reviewed the Lease Modification Agreement. These actions belie the assertion that Kids Wear had not agreed to the rental terms set out in the Lease Modification. By paying the reduced rents, Kids Wear clearly indicated its assent to "the same thing" FRIT offered—that is, the reduced rent amounts for the First Option Period. *Hahnemann Medical College & Hosp. of Philadelphia v. Hubbard*, 267 Pa. Super. 436, 406 A.2d 1120, 1122 (Pa. Super. Ct. 1979). The difference between these circumstances and typical holdover by a tenant—including holdover as provided for in the Lease Agreement itself—is that the conduct of the parties here indicates that the Lease Option was renewed upon the terms memorialized in the Lease Modification; Kids Wear was not simply continuing to occupy the premises in the absence of these negotiations. FRIT and Kids Wear thus mutually assented to the rental terms for the First Option Period as set out in the Lease Modification.

C. The Personal Guaranty

FRIT argues that Kids Wear's conduct in paying the rental amounts set forth in the Lease Modification—which includes the crossed-out language 'eliminating' the Guaranty—indicates an agreement that the Guaranty would not be eliminated. Kids Wear sought to 'eliminate' the Guaranty and argues that it thought that it had done so. FRIT's argument, Kids Wear's argument and its use of the word "eliminate" all beg the question: determining whether the parties agreed to "eliminate" the Guaranty is necessary only if the Guaranty would otherwise have backed Kids Wear's obligations to pay rent during the Option Period. The threshold issue, therefore, is whether as a matter of law the parties had originally agreed that the Guaranty applies to rent which could become payable during the lease renewals under the Option to Renew . . .

As indicated above, the language of the Guaranty indicates a guaranty of the "Minimum Rent and all additional Rent as provided for in the foregoing and annexed Lease Agreement." The Lease Agreement is a 45-page document to which exhibits and Addenda are attached, including an Addendum called "Option to Renew." The parties executed a Lease Modification Agreement which states that the parties are modifying the rent under the First Option Period. The threshold issue is whether the Option to Renew and any renewal resulting therefrom [sic] should be viewed as part of the Lease Agreement such that the Guaranty stands for lessee's rent obligations thereunder . . .

. . . Here, FRIT similarly could have employed language in the Option specifically indicating that the renewal term would be considered part of the "Lease Agreement," or language in the Lease itself that Minimum Rent would include rent during any renewal period if the Option were exercised. In the absence of such language, the plain meaning of the words of the Guaranty indicates that it backs Kids Wear's obligations under only the "the Lease Agreement," which under Pennsylvania law constitutes the rent for the initial five-year term. Accordingly, for these reasons, I find the Option and the rent obligation under the First Option Period not to be part of the Lease itself. Thus, the Guaranty does not back Kids Wear's rent obligations under the First Option Period. . . .

II. Calculation of Damages

. . . A lease is a contract, and thus "the usual contract measure of damages applies." *Princeton Sportswear Corp. v. H & M Assoc.*, 510 Pa. 189, 507 A.2d 339, 344 (Pa. 1986) (Hutchinson, J., concurring) (citation omitted), *appeal denied*, 533 A.2d 713 (Pa.) and 536 A.2d 1332 (Pa. 1987). In the case of a tenant's breach of a lease agreement, the landlord is entitled to the rent the tenant was bound to pay under the lease until a new tenant has taken possession. Moreover, "as with all contracts, either party may seek . . . incidental or consequential damages for a breach." *Pugh v. Holmes*, 253 Pa. Super. 76, 384 A.2d 1234, 1242 (Pa. Super. Ct. 1978), *aff'd*, 486 Pa. 272, 405 A.2d 897 (Pa. 1979). . .

Kids Wear paid rent pursuant to the terms of the Lease Modification through December 31, 1993. Thus, from January 1, 1994, until May 31, 1995, when a new tenant began to pay rent for the Leased Premises, Kids Wear failed to pay rent and other costs under the Lease and under the agreed rental terms of the First Option Period. Jean Connor, Vice President of the Leasing Department at FRIT, has calculated the amounts owed to it under the Lease and the First Option Period. See Exh. 17. Kids Wear has not contested the accuracy of these figures. FRIT should have collected a total minimum rent of $164,076.48. In addition pursuant to the terms of the Lease, Kids Wear would have paid its share of real estate taxes of approximately $18,092.76; operating costs of approximately $19.097.97; and merchants association dues of $7,272.43. Thus, the total amount of damages due from Kids Wear to FRIT is $208,539.64. . .

Order

AND NOW, this 28th day of February, 1996, it is hereby ordered and declared that judgment is entered for Federal Realty Investment Trust against Kids Wear Boulevard, Inc., in the amount of $208,539.64.

Guided Reading Questions

1. In the lease, which is the contract here, what was modified?

2. Was the modification negotiated and accepted?

3. What happened to the actual modification in the lease?

4. How did the modification in the lease attempt to change the lease terms?

■ WHAT A PARALEGAL NEEDS TO KNOW

The decision to modify an agreement or to rescind a contract is a legal decision to be made only by a licensed attorney. You can tender the modification or rescission upon direction from the supervising attorney. Additionally, as a paralegal, you should never modify a contract or delete modifications inserted into an agreement without express instruction from the supervising attorney on the matter. Be aware of the time frame for performance under the contract. If the contract is not yet fully performed, but is in final form, it can be modified. However, if a new agreement is being negotiated, additional or new terms are counteroffers, not modifications.

The Paralegal's Role

First, you need to alert the attorney that any change in the agreement exists. When you have more than one version of a contract, run "track changes" to see where the subsequent versions differ from the original. Show these changes to the supervising attorney.

Additionally, when a modification of a contract is negotiated, be aware of when the Statute of Frauds may come into play due to the changes in the agreement. For instance, a contract that requires six months to perform would not fall under the Statute of Frauds, but an agreement that requires eighteen months to perform must comply with the Statute of Frauds because agreements that require a year or longer to perform are within the Statute of Frauds.

CHAPTER SUMMARY

To modify a contract is to offer and accept new terms after a contract is formed. The new terms must be supported by consideration. Modification differs from a counteroffer in that a counteroffer occurs, prior to a contract's formation, when an offer is tendered and instead of the offeree accepting the terms, he or she counters with new terms. The offeree then becomes the offeror and the original offeror, now the offeree, must choose to accept the new terms to form a contract. Modification differs from rescission, discharge, and termination in that modification poses new terms for an existing contract whereas rescission, termination, and discharge are all concerned with ending a contract or relieving one's duties under the contract. The Uniform Commercial Code does not require consideration to support a contract modification between merchants if the contract can be modified. The U.C.C. also requires that all contracts must be modified in good faith.

Modification

Modification in General	Occurs after the contract is formed Modification is an offer and acceptance, supported by consideration, of new terms or conditions Material modification concerns the substance of the contract and its terms Immaterial modification concerns unessential terms Modification can be negotiated
Counteroffer Differs from Modification	A counteroffer occurs prior to the formation of a contract Instead of an acceptance, new terms are communicated in response
U.C.C. and Modification	Section 2–209 states that generally no new consideration is required to support the modification of a contract between merchants All contracts must be modified in good faith
Rescission, Termination, and Discharge	All differ from modification because rescission, termination, and discharge are concerned with ending a contract or relieving one's duties under the contract
Breach versus Modification	Breach is a failure to perform or to fulfill one's obligations under a contract whereas modification poses new terms that are agreed upon and are supported by consideration
What a Paralegal Needs to Know about Modification	The decision to modify an agreement or to rescind a contract is a legal decision to be made only by a licensed attorney

REVIEW QUESTIONS

1. What is a rescission of a contract?
2. What is the main difference between contract modification and a counteroffer?
3. What are contract modifications?
4. Why are contracts rescinded?
5. What is a breach of contract?
6. Can a paralegal modify an agreement?
7. Are there special rules concerning modification for contracts between merchants?
8. In a contract that is not between merchants, is it necessary to have consideration to support the modification of an agreement?
9. How is a counteroffer different from the modification of a contract?
10. What is a discharge of obligation?

SKILL-BUILDING APPLICATION EXERCISE

Henry Miller contracted to be a window washer for Town & City Windows. The parties entered into a contract, yet to be performed, where Miller would wash windows by appointment at a rate of $1.00 per window pane, per side (inside and out). Miller would wash a minimum of thirty windows per appointment. Prior to starting his first job, but after signing the agreement, Town & Country asked Miller to modify their agreement. Town & Country wanted to increase the minimum number of windows that Miller would wash per appointment from thirty to forty.

How is the contract modified?

Is there consideration to support the modified agreement?

Suppose Town & Country contacted Miller and stated that business is very bad. Miller realized that business was slow due to the poor economy. Miller has not had any window washing appointments for the past three weeks. Miller would like to work for Hurry Copy and Delivery but cannot accept the employment due to his commitment to Town & Country.

What can the parties do?

If Miller washed Mrs. Jones's windows, fifty windows total, both sides, he should receive $100 for his work. However, Town & Country told Miller that the company does not have any cash and cannot pay Miller. Town & Country cannot fulfill its obligations under the contract.

What did Town & Country do?

SIMULATED LAW OFFICE ASSIGNMENT

Bikram Yoga Studio, Inc., is a business. Bikram holds yoga classes for a fee and sells yoga equipment and apparel. One of the items that Bikram sells is yoga mats. In fact, Bikram sells as many as twenty-five yoga mats per week.

Bikram purchases the yoga mats from a yoga mat manufacturer called Bend & Flex, Inc. The initial contract between Bikram and Bend & Flex reads as follows:

Bend & Flex, a manufacturer and distributor of yoga mats, will provide Bikram Yoga Studio with eighty (80) Yoga Mats per month, in an assortment of colors, at the wholesale price of $12.00 per mat. Bend & Flex will ship the mats to Bikram on the first business day of each month. Bikram shall pay Bend & Flex, by check, within ten (10) days of receipt of the yoga mats, for the full price of the shipment, not less than $960.00.

    This agreement shall remain in effect for a minimum of twelve (12) months from the date that this contract is signed by both parties.

Date: November 25, 2010

_____

John Wings, President of Bend & Flex, Inc.

_____

Hannah Mills, Owner of Bikram Yoga Studio, Inc.

Two days after the agreement is signed and before the mats have been shipped, Bend & Flex wants to modify the agreement. The agreement has not yet been performed. Bend & Flex realized that the price of the mat material would be increasing dramatically over the course of the year. Bend & Flex wants to increase the cost of each mat from $12 per mat to $14 per mat.

The supervising attorney wants to know what the U.C.C. requirements are for modifying a contract between merchants.

DRAFTING EXERCISE

Review the sample of a loan modification agreement at the beginning of this chapter. Write a modification agreement for the following security agreement based on these additional facts: All of Mr. Maycraft's cattle were destroyed due to an outbreak of mad cow disease on April 30, 2010; Mr. Maycraft needed to borrow an additional $5,000 to purchase two new cows and two new bulls. The bank wants to insert a provision requiring that in the event of Mr. Maycraft's death, his heirs would assume his obligations under this security agreement.

MAYCRAFT FARMS SECURITY AGREEMENT

March 21, 2010

Paul Maycraft, of 345 Stuben Road, White Fish, Wisconsin, for valuable consideration, receipt of which is acknowledged, grants to Third Farm Bank, 5 Main Street, White Fish, Wisconsin, a security interest in the following property and in the proceeds of the collateral:

 (i) Fifty head of cattle located at *Maycraft Farm, 345 Stuben Road, White Fish, Wisconsin;*

(ii) All planted crops at the property and all crops harvested at the property for one year from the date of signing this agreement

The security interest granted is to secure payment of $45,000 as provided in the note of debtor.

1. Except for the security interest granted, Mr. Maycraft warrants that he holds clear title to all property, real and personal, used as collateral for this loan and that there are no debts outstanding in regard to any property except for this note;

2. During the term of this loan, Mr. Maycraft will not sell any property except to pay back this loan. Mr. Maycraft will not use any property as a security for an additional loan;

3. Mr. Maycraft will have and maintain an insurance policy for the replacement value of all property used as security;

4. The debtor must pay all taxes on all property, real and personal, and the proceeds from the property in a timely manner and provide documented proof that the taxes were paid in the form of a cancelled check;

5. Mr. Maycraft must make timely payments on this loan and will be in default when a payment is more than ninety (90) days past due.

6. The bank, the secured party, may declare all obligations secured by this agreement immediately due and payable if the debtor defaults on his loan. All remedies under the laws of Wisconsin are available to the bank, the secured party. Upon default, Mr. Maycraft must pay all legal fees.

This agreement signed this day _____ binds Mr. Maycraft upon signing and notarizing to this obligation.

Debtor By _____

Mr. Maycraft

Creditor/Bank _____

Third Farm Bank

DEVELOPING CRITICAL THINKING SKILLS

Review the modification to the agreement that you drafted for Mr. Maycraft in the Drafting Exercise. Based on your study of this chapter, how does this differ from a rescission?

PORTFOLIO ASSIGNMENT

Your firm represents the McCarthy family. Mrs. McCarthy and her brothers, Mr. James Ruskin, Mr. Paul Ruskin, and Mr. Timothy Ruskin, inherited the family farm. Each child received a 25 percent interest in the farm located in Arkansas. The farm is 520 acres and has many heads of livestock as well as several buildings, including a farm house. The siblings decided to incorporate the farm and to divide the ownership in the form of shares. Each sibling received 129 shares of the farm. Mrs. McCarthy wanted to sell her shares to her brothers. After much discussion with her siblings, Mrs. McCarthy and her siblings decided to rescind the offer to purchase her 129 shares of the stock in the farm. Please read this sample letter to use as a model for a letter you will draft. Draft a letter to the brothers detailing the rescission.

BY FACSIMILE

February 10th, 2010
White Bay Auto Parts
2009 White Bay Road
White Bay, Illinois 60043

ATTENTION: Lisa Colt, President

Dear Ms. Colt:
RE: OFFER TO REPURCHASE 10,000 SHARES OF Auto Parts COMMON STOCK—RESCINDED

By letter of December 6th, 2009 (the "Offer"), Auto Parts offered to repurchase from White Bay Auto Parts 10,000 shares of the common stock of Auto Parts held by White Bay (the "Shares") on terms set out in the Offer. The parties have now concluded that they no longer wish to enter into such arrangement for the sale and repurchase of the Shares, and now

---

mutually wish to have Auto Parts rescind the terms of the Offer. By printing, signing, and returning a copy of this letter to the undersigned, White Bay acknowledges and agrees with the rescission of the Offer by Auto Parts and that the Offer is null and void.

Yours sincerely,
Auto Parts, Inc.

Ann Seal
President, Auto Parts, Inc.
Agreed February 10, 2010
AGREED this 10th day of February, 2010.

Third-Party Contracts

CHAPTER 8

INTRODUCTION—THIRD PARTY CONTRACTS IN GENERAL

Generally, contracts bind the original parties, or their agents or representatives, who enter into the agreement. As you know, a contract is an agreement made between the promisor and the promisee. Very often, though, the promisor will delegate his or her duty under the agreement or the promisee will assign his or her anticipated benefit. The instances when the duties under a contract can be delegated to a **third party** or when the benefits can be assigned to another party, aside from the original, create issues concerning enforcement and consideration. Parties involved in the contract, aside from the initial promisor and promisee, are generally referred to as third parties. There are many cases addressing the rights of a third party under a contract. When two parties enter into a contract that is made for the benefit of an additional entity, this additional entity is called the third party. There are occasions when the rights or duties under a contract cannot be assigned. When the contract is for personal service and the subject of the contract is unique, such as a contract for an artist to paint a portrait, then painting the portrait, the duty under the agreement, cannot generally be assigned. Today, under certain circumstances, the third party, the individual or entity that did not directly enter into the agreement, has a right to enforce the terms of the contract if the agreement was intended to be made for his or her benefit.

LEARNING OBJECTIVES

After studying this chapter, you will be able to:

1. Define the concept of a third party to a contractual agreement.

2. Understand that a third party's benefit from the agreement is either intentional or incidental.

3. Identify the existence of an intentional beneficiary under a contract.

4. Realize that the rights detailed in an agreement can be assigned to a third party.

5. Discuss that the duties under a contract can be delegated to a party that is not the offeror or the offeree.

6. Discuss that the Uniform Commercial Code addresses the existence of third parties in consumer transactions and extends warranties, depending on state law, to others aside from the original purchaser.

Third party
Not an original party to a contract, but a party that is either a beneficiary, intended or incidental, under the contract to whom one of the original parties assigns his or her benefit or delegates his or her duty.

Privity
Rights to the agreement. Used in relation to contracts, where the parties to the contract have rights under the agreement. Under the Uniform Commercial Code §2–318, the rights created under this relationship, privity, are now extended to subsequent purchasers of goods. Each state has laws in the respective state statutes concerning privity between the merchant and original purchaser and to the extent that the warranties for the goods are extended to household members, remote purchasers, and other users of the goods.

Warranty
A promise made in the course of the contractual agreement that can be the basis of the bargain.

Breach
A failure by one or more parties to an agreement to honor the terms of the accord.

■ PRIVITY OF CONTRACT

Privity of contract concerns the relationship between the parties to the agreement. Privity of contract means that the legal rights and obligations flowing from a contractual agreement only concern the parties that enter into the contract. However, modern life and the realities of commerce have altered this, and now many rights, especially in consumer transactions involving the sale of goods, extend beyond the parties to the original contract.

The Uniform Commercial Code and Privity

The Uniform Commercial Code addresses privity in situations concerning the sale of goods. Issues concerning privity often arise in consumer transactions in respect to warranties. A **warranty** is a promise in regard to a good when it is sold. An express warranty is usually made as the basis for the bargain between the buyer and seller.

Example–Express Warranty

A merchant, who has purchased tires from Best Year and is in the business of selling tires to consumers, states: "these tires have all weather tread suitable for snow, ice, rain, and dry conditions." The consumer/purchaser buys the tires on the basis of this promise and this promise forms an express warranty concerning the tires. The tires fail to have traction in a snowstorm. The buyer goes back to the seller and claims a **breach** of express warranty.

Example–Implied Warranty

An implied warranty for fitness for a particular purpose concerning the tires would arise if the buyer told the seller that he or she wanted to use the tires on a vehicle that would be driven on a race course and that the seller knew that the buyer was requesting the goods, the tires, to be used for a particular purpose.

Often, prior to the enactment of legislation, a manufacturer was only obligated to fulfill its express warranties concerning a product if the entity, the buyer or ultimate consumer, claiming the breach of warranty was the person who entered into the contract to purchase the goods from the seller and not someone who obtained the goods as a gift or second hand. Prior to the Uniform Commercial Code provision addressing privity, a manufacturer could use a lack of privity of contract, between the seller and the consumer, as a defense.

The U.C.C. §2–318 contains three alternatives that the states could choose to adopt to address the issue of when a lack of privity arises in a breach of warranty. The U.C.C. articulates protections for the plaintiffs even when there is no privity of contract between the consumer and the seller.

Under §2–318, an "immediate buyer" is a buyer that enters into a contract with a seller whereas a "remote purchaser" is a purchaser that obtains the goods, either by purchase or gift, from the immediate buyer or another individual in the chain of distribution. For instance, in the previous example: Best

Year is the original seller, merchant is the immediate buyer, and if the merchant is in the business of selling Best Year Tires and is authorized by Best Year, he too is the seller and the consumer is the immediate buyer. If the consumer sells those tires to his neighbor, the neighbor becomes the remote purchaser.

There are three versions or alternatives stated in the U.C.C. §2–318 for the states to adopt. Subsection A requires that the seller's warranties, either express or implied, extend to any member of the buyer's household or to his or her guests. Subsection B extends the seller's warranties to "any individual who may be reasonably expected to use, consume, or be affected by the goods and who is injured in person by breach of warranty, remedial promise or obligation." Under Section C, the broadest, the seller's warranty, "extends to any person that can be reasonably expected to use, consume, or be affected by the goods and that is injured by the breach of warranty, remedial promise or obligation."

In each section, whichever section is adopted by the particular state, a seller cannot limit this provision or exclude it. Most states have adopted version A. Of the most populous states, Florida, Illinois, New Jersey, and Pennsylvania have adopted version A. New York has adopted version B. Hawaii, Minnesota, and Utah are among the few states that have adopted version C. California, Massachusetts, and Texas have enacted legislation that differs from the Uniform Commercial Code provisions in §2–318.

■ THIRD-PARTY BENEFICIARIES

A third-party **beneficiary** is a party, other than the promisor or the promisee, who has some expectation of receiving a benefit from the contract. The third party does not automatically have the right to enforce the terms of the agreement unless the parties or one of the parties intended to confer benefits to him or her. Very often this intent is indicated in the contract itself, in the language of the provision. Sometimes, a contract will be made with the intent to benefit a third party. An example of this is: Mr. Jones obtains a mortgage from The Bank and pays the mortgage monthly on a home that he purchased for his daughter, Ann. The title to the home is in the daughter's name. The mortgage was entered into between The Bank and Mr. Jones with the intent to benefit a third party, Ann Jones. This agreement does not require that consideration pass between Ann and the parties to the contract even though Ann is intended to receive the benefit of the agreement.

Beneficiary
One who will obtain the advantage or value from the contract.

Intended Third Parties and Incidental Beneficiaries

Intended Beneficiaries

The Restatement (Second) of Contracts §302 states that an intended beneficiary is created when the promisor and the promisee identify or anticipate that a specific third party is meant to benefit from their promise, to receive the consideration. The third party, then, has the right to performance under the contract. This right to performance is either manifested by the promisor paying money to the third-party beneficiary rather than the promisee, a creditor beneficiary, or the promisee agrees that the beneficiary will receive the performance under the contract, a donee beneficiary. Interestingly, as stated in the Restatement (Second) of Contracts §308, the intended beneficiary's rights are not based on whether he or she is identified when the contract is made. However, the intent of the parties must be examined to determine the existence and rights of the intended beneficiary. Additionally, an intended beneficiary has the right to sue for breach of contract if he or she was to purposefully and directly benefit from the agreement. Some states require that the contract expressly state the party to benefit. Also, some jurisdictions require that the benefit is immediate.

Example

Developer has a parcel of land for sale. Bank 90 wants to purchase the land to build a branch. A condominium building is on the east side of the parcel. The Condo Association does not want a bank branch built on the land but would prefer a park. In the sales contract for the property, Developer and Bank 90 agree that Bank 90 will pay $100,000 for the land to Developer and that Developer will pay the Condo Association $5,000 to plant trees along the property line. Here the Condo Association is the intended beneficiary because the parties intended to confer a legally enforceable benefit on the condo association.

Incidental Beneficiaries

Alternatively, an incidental beneficiary occurs when the beneficiary is not anticipated by the original parties at the time of contracting. Regardless of whether the beneficiary is intended or incidental, he or she reaps value from the performance of the contract. However, an incidental beneficiary cannot sue for breach of contract because the parties never planned that he or she would obtain value from the agreement.

CASE ILLUSTRATION

Guided Reading Pointers

In the abridged case that follows, the student, Leonard Verni, is claiming that he was a third-party beneficiary in the contract between Cleveland Chiropractic College and his professor, Dr. Makarov. The court determined that Verni is not a third-party beneficiary because the terms of the contract did not clearly express or state that the contract was intended to benefit him particularly or to benefit a class of which Verni was a member. Because Verni was not mentioned as a third-party beneficiary or included in the class of third-party beneficiaries, Verni did not have standing to enforce the contract. Verni claimed that the faculty handbook was the contract that provided that Verni, as a student, was an intended third-party beneficiary. The court stated that the handbook was executed only for the benefit of the faculty and the college, the parties to it. The court noted that the students are only incidental beneficiaries of the employment contract between the professors and the college. The court reasoned that since the handbook does not clearly and directly state the intent to benefit Verni and the students of the college, the class that Verni claims to belong to, he has no standing to sue to enforce the contract.

Verni
v.
CLEVELAND CHIROPRACTIC COLLEGE
212 S.W.3d 150 (Mo. 2007)

FACTS

Leonard Verni was a student of chiropractic medicine at Cleveland Chiropractic College. Verni enrolled in a dermatology class at Cleveland that was taught by Dr. Aleksandr Makarov. Prior to the first examination in that class, a student anonymously contacted Cleveland's academic dean and alleged that Verni was selling copies of the forthcoming examination. The dean completed an incident report detailing the allegation. Cleveland conducted an investigation, concluding that Verni committed academic misconduct as detailed in the college's handbook by "[b]uying, selling, otherwise obtaining, possessing or using any copy of any material intended to be used as an instrument of academic evaluation in advance of its initial administration." Cleveland dismissed Verni from the college, notifying him by letter of his right to appeal the decision in accord with the "due process" procedures set forth in the student handbook. After exhausting the appeal procedures, Verni filed the present action against Cleveland and Dr. Makarov.

At trial, the case was submitted under the following four theories: (1) breach of contract against Cleveland, (2) fraudulent misrepresentation against Cleveland, (3) breach of contract against Dr. Makarov, and (4) fraudulent nondisclosure against Cleveland. The jury returned a verdict against Cleveland on Verni's fraudulent misrepresentation claim, awarding Verni $20,000 in damages. The jury returned a verdict against Dr. Makarov on the breach of contract claim, awarding Verni $10,000 in damages. The jury returned a verdict in favor of Cleveland and against Verni on the remaining breach of contract and fraudulent nondisclosure claims. On Cleveland's motion for judgment notwithstanding the verdict, the circuit court set aside the verdict against Cleveland on the fraudulent misrepresentation claim. The circuit court denied Verni's motion for additur or new trial on the issue of damages.

Verni appeals from the circuit court's judgment asserting error relating to the amount of damages in the breach of contract claim. Verni also appeals the trial court's judgment setting aside the verdict on Verni's fraudulent misrepresentation claim. Dr. Makarov cross-appeals, asserting error with regard to the jury's verdict on the breach of contract claim.

Verni is not a third-party beneficiary of the contract . . .

Verni's breach of contract claim asserts that he is a third-party beneficiary of the employment contract between Dr. Makarov and Cleveland. Dr. Makarov argues that Verni was not a party to the contract or a third-party beneficiary of the contract and, thus, did not have standing to raise the claim. . .

. . .Only parties to a contract and any third-party beneficiaries of a contract have standing to enforce that contract. . . . "To be bound as a third-party beneficiary, the terms of the contract must clearly express intent to benefit that party or an identifiable class of which the party is a member." *Nitro Distributing, Inc. v. Dunn,* 194 S.W.3d 339, 345 (Mo. banc 2006). "In cases where the contract lacks an express declaration of that intent, there is a strong presumption that the third party is not a beneficiary and that the parties contracted to benefit only themselves." *Id.* "Furthermore, a mere incidental benefit to the third party is insufficient to bind that party." *Id.*

This matter is resolved by examining the contract's language. *OFW Corp. v. City of Columbia,* 893 S.W.2d 876, 879 (Mo. App. 1995). The contract is a one-page document providing that Dr. Makarov would be a full-time faculty member of Cleveland for one year. The contract required him to be on campus a certain amount of time each week and outlined his teaching duties. In return, the contract provided Dr. Makarov's salary and employment benefits. Although the contract might incidentally provide a benefit to Cleveland students, it does not clearly express any intent that Dr. Makarov was undertaking a duty to benefit Verni or a class of students.

The contract also required Dr. Makarov to comply with the policies and procedures stated in Cleveland's faculty handbook and with any institutional modification thereof. Verni alleges that Dr. Makarov violated the handbook's requirement that faculty members treat students with courtesy, respect, fairness, and professionalism. The handbook also provides that students are entitled to expect such treatment. Assuming, for the sake of argument, that the faculty handbook is a binding part of the employment contract, this language does not overcome the strong presumption that the contract was executed solely for the parties' own benefit.

Undoubtedly, Verni and all of Cleveland's students are incidental beneficiaries of employment contracts between the college and faculty members, but not every person who is benefited by a contract may bring suit to enforce that contract. Rather, only those third-parties who are clearly intended beneficiaries may do so. Verni is not entitled to third-party beneficiary status under the contract between Cleveland and Dr. Makarov because the terms of the contract do not directly and clearly express the intent to benefit Verni or any class of which Verni claims to be a member.

The judgment of the circuit court against Dr. Makarov on Verni's breach of contract claim is reversed. . .

. . .

CONCLUSION

Verni is not a third party beneficiary to the contract between Dr. Makarov and Cleveland. The judgment of the circuit court on the breach of contract claim against Dr. Makarov is reversed.

Because Verni did not make a submissible case of fraudulent misrepresentation against Cleveland, the judgment of the circuit court granting judgment notwithstanding the verdict is affirmed.

The judgment is affirmed in all other respects.

Guided Reading Questions

1. What source did Verni rely on to support his argument that he was an intended third-party beneficiary?

2. Did the parties to the contract intend to create a third-party beneficiary?

3. Is the employee handbook a contract between the faculty and the college here?

4. Who was the employee handbook intended to benefit?

■ ASSIGNMENT

According to the Restatement (Second) of Contracts §317, an **assignment** of a right occurs when the entity or individual who has the right to receive performance under the contract assigns that right to a third party. The promisor in a contract is the **obligor** and the promisee is the **obligee**. A party can indicate the assignment by his or her intent to do so, by language, or by act. A right under a contract can be assigned unless prohibited by statute or public policy. Also, a right cannot be assigned when the contract states that it is not permitted. It is also not allowed when the assignment materially alters the performance or obligations set out in the agreement. Additionally, a party that is not entitled to benefit under an agreement cannot assign a right to that benefit. However, a party assigning a right under the contract, the obligee, does not have to obtain permission from the obligor.

The party assigning the right is called the *assignor*. The party to whom the right is transferred is called the *assignee*. Once the assignment is made, the assignor has no liability under the contract.

Assignment
To transfer the benefits or rights under a contract to another party who is not an original party to the agreement.

Obligor
The party that is obligated to perform under a contract.

Obligee
The recipient of the obligations under a contract.

Example

Grace Smith lives on the third floor of a house at 1515 Osage Lane. Ms. Hill rents an apartment on the first floor of the house. The Sullivans rent the apartment on the second floor. The Morgans own the house. Ms. Smith decides to buy a computer and in lieu of paying for the computer, she agrees with Computer Super Store to assign her right to the rent from the Sullivans' apartment. Since Ms. Smith does not own the house and since the Sullivans pay rent to the Morgans, Ms. Smith is not entitled to the rent money. Ms. Smith cannot assign a benefit that she does not have a right to.

Example–Assignment

Mr. and Mrs. Jewel own a fruit and vegetable market. They purchase apples, peaches, cherries, and plums from Racine Orchard. For the last shipment of fruit, the Jewels owe Racine Orchard $800. Racine Orchard assigns its right to the $800 to Shedd Nurseries to pay for the new plants that it purchased. Racine Orchard's right to receive $800 from the Jewels is extinguished. Shedd Nurseries acquires the right to receive $800 from the Jewels. Racine Orchards, the obligee under the contract, does not have to receive permission to assign its right to payment. Additionally, assignment can be made after the formation of the contract. Racine Orchards can assign the payment to Shedd after the contract was formed with the fruit market.

■ DELEGATION

Delegation of duty
Transferring the duty owed to a party under a contract to another.

A **delegation of a duty** arises when the obligor, the person or party who is obligated to perform under the agreement, transfers this duty to perform to another party. A delegation of a duty is permitted unless the contract states otherwise or when it is against public policy. Even when the duty is delegated, the original obligor's responsibilities under the contract are not discharged until performance is effectively rendered. This differs from assignment because the assignor's duty under the contract is satisfied once the assignment is made.

Example–Delegation of Duty

The Youngs hired Mr. Monk to paint their house. Mr. Monk realized that he is very busy. He delegates the sanding, prepping, and painting to Mr. Maurice. Mr. Monk's obligations to the Youngs under the contract are not discharged until Mr. Maurice's performance is effectively rendered.

There are instances when the duty to perform is for a unique or personal service and cannot be delegated.

Example

Lindsey Height is a famous movie star. Lindsey hired the even more famous artist Van Go to paint her portrait. The contract stated that Van Go will paint the portrait for $5,000. The contract also stated that Van Go could not delegate his duty to paint the portrait due to his unique artistic talent. Van Go decided a week before Ms. Height was to sit for the portrait that he is not in the mood to paint for a while. Van Go wants to delegate his duty to perform under the agreement. Since this is an agreement to perform a unique, personal service, and the contract stated that Van Go could not delegate this duty, Ms. Height will not permit Van Go to delegate his duty.

■ NOVATION

Novation
The act of substituting a new agreement or contract for an existing one. This must be done only when the parties to the original contract agree.

In its most basic form, **novation** is the substitution of a new contract for an existing agreement or the substitution of a new party for an existing party. The parties can be the original parties or new parties, or one new party. The requirements for novation are: (1) there must be a valid contract, (2) the parties must agree to a new contract, (3) the original agreement is voided and (4) the new agreement is valid.

A novation differs from an assignment because a new agreement is formed, whereas in an assignment, a party to an existing contract assigns, to another, the consideration due.

■ WHAT A PARALEGAL NEEDS TO KNOW ABOUT THIRD-PARTY CONTRACTS

One must be careful to follow the language in the contract and not to make any legal determinations as to the existence of a third party-beneficiary and whether benefits can be assigned or duties delegated. These are legal determinations. Any and all legal determinations must be made by an attorney because these are legal decisions that will alter a party's legal position. If the supervising attorney indicates that there are issues regarding third parties in the contract, then as a paralegal, perform the following tasks:

First, after the supervising attorney determines there is a valid contract between the original parties, determine the identity of the original parties.

Second, the paralegal must examine the original agreement for specific language or ask the attorney to determine if there are any restrictions on assigning the rights or delegating the duties under the agreement.

Third, the paralegal must look at the agreement to discern if a party to the contract intends for another party or individual to benefit from the contract. The paralegal then must identify the intended beneficiary and obtain the proper name and address of that party. Identify the specific benefits assigned and/or duties delegated.

Fourth, the paralegal must deduce the time frame for performance.

CASE ILLUSTRATION

Guided Reading Pointers

In the following abridged case, the plaintiff, Miss Revels, appeals summary judgment granted in favor of the defendant. Summary judgment is a motion that is made prior to trial, requesting the judge to rule, prior to trial, if there are no issues as to any material fact and the moving party is entitled to judgment as a matter of law. Miss Revels asserts that the defendant is not entitled to judgment as a matter of law because there was sufficient evidence to support that she was a third-party beneficiary under the contract, which in this instance is a franchise agreement between Miss America Organization ("MAO") and Miss North Carolina Pageant Association ("MNCPA"). The court states that to support a claim for status as a third-party beneficiary, the plaintiff must have evidence to show that there is a contract between MAO and MNCPA; that the contract between MAO and MNCPA is valid and enforceable; and that MAO and MNCPA intended to execute the contract for Miss Revels' direct, and not incidental, benefit. It is essential that when the contract was made MAO and MNCPA intended to benefit Miss Revels directly. The court found that there was insufficient evidence to support that Miss Revels was the intended beneficiary under the franchise agreement, the contract at issue; she was neither designated as a beneficiary nor was the agreement executed for her direct benefit.

Revels
v.
MISS AMERICA ORGANIZATION
641 S.E.2d 721 (N.C. App. 2007)

Rebekah Revels ("plaintiff") appeals the order of the trial court granting summary judgment in favor of Miss America Organization as to all claims.

This Court has previously summarized and set forth the facts pertaining to the case at hand in its opinion issued in *Revels v. Miss Am. Org.*, 165 N.C. App. 181, 599 S.E.2d 54, *disc. review denied*, 359 N.C. 191, 605 S.E.2d 153 (2004). Following the previous appeal in which this Court affirmed the trial court's order denying Miss America Organization's ("MAO") amended motion to compel arbitration on the grounds that no contract existed between MAO and plaintiff, the trial court entered an order granting summary judgment in favor of defendant. It is from that order plaintiff appeals.

Plaintiff contends that the trial court erred in granting summary judgment in favor of defendant where there was a genuine issue of material fact and defendants were not entitled to judgment in their favor as a matter of law.

Specifically, plaintiff contends that summary judgment was improperly granted where there was sufficient evidence that she was a third-party beneficiary under the franchise agreement between defendants MAO and Miss North Carolina Pageant Organization ("MNCPO"); . . .

Summary judgment should be granted "if the pleadings, depositions, answers to interrogatories, and admissions on file, together with the affidavits, if any, show that there is no genuine issue as to any material fact and that any party is entitled to a judgment as a matter of law." N.C. Gen. Stat. §1A–1, Rule 56(c) (2005). A moving party "has the burden of establishing the lack of any triable issue of fact[,]" and its supporting materials are carefully scrutinized, with all inferences resolved against it. *Kidd v. Early*, 289 N.C. 343, 352, 222 S.E.2d 392, 399 (1976).

THIRD-PARTY BENEFICIARY

Plaintiff contends on appeal that there was sufficient evidence that she is a third-party beneficiary under the franchise agreement between MAO and MNCPO to establish that there is a genuine issue of material fact.

In order to assert rights as a third-party beneficiary under the franchise agreement, plaintiff must show she was an intended beneficiary of the contract. This Court has held that in order to establish a claim as a third-party beneficiary, plaintiff must show:

(1) that a contract exists between two persons or entities; (2) that the contract is valid and enforceable; and (3) that the contract was executed for the direct, and not incidental, benefit of the [third party]. A person is a direct beneficiary of the contract if the contracting parties intended to confer a legally enforceable benefit on that person. It is not enough that the contract, in fact, benefits the [third party], if, when the contract was made, the contracting parties did not intend it to benefit the [third party] directly. In determining the intent of the contracting parties, the court "should consider [the] circumstances surrounding the transaction as well as the actual language of the contract." "'When a third person seeks enforcement of a contract made between other parties, the contract must be construed strictly against the party seeking enforcement.'" . . .

There was insufficient evidence before the trial court to support a conclusion that plaintiff was an intended beneficiary under the franchise agreement. Plaintiff was not designated as a beneficiary under the franchise agreement and there is absolutely no evidence that the franchise agreement was executed for her direct benefit. The franchise agreement does provide that MAO will accept the winner of the North Carolina pageant as a contestant in the national finals. However, this evidence is insufficient to establish a showing of intent on the parties to make plaintiff an intended beneficiary. Further, the evidence adduced tended to show that the primary intent of the franchise agreement was to ensure uniformity among all franchisees and it provided the incidental benefit of allowing the winner of MNCPO's contest to compete in the national finals. . .

Accordingly, the order of the trial court is affirmed.

Affirmed.

Guided Reading Questions

1. What must a plaintiff demonstrate, in North Carolina, to establish a claim as a third-party beneficiary under a contract?

2. Was Miss Revels requesting that the court rule that she was a third-party beneficiary, or rule that summary judgment was improper on this issue and that there was a genuine issue of material fact for a trial?

CHAPTER SUMMARY

This chapter explored the issues concerning the legal rights of entities that are not original parties to an agreement. These entities are collectively referred to as third parties. A third party may not be in privity to the original agreement but may have the right to enforce the contract. Sometimes a third party is intended to receive a benefit under a contract either as a creditor or as a donee by virtue of a gift. Other times, the third party is permitted to receive the protections of a warranty that was provided to the original purchaser although he or she is a subsequent purchaser. In additional instances under an agreement, a third party is assigned a right to receive the consideration due or is delegated a duty either to pay a debt, to tender consideration, or to perform.

Third-Party Contracts

Third Parties, in General	Where the benefit is assigned or the duty is delegated by one of the parties to the contract A third-party beneficiary is a party other that the promisor or the promisee who has some expectation of receiving a benefit under the contract
Privity of Contract	The legal relationship between the parties to the contract
The U.C.C. and Third-Party Contracts	In consumer transactions, warranties no longer extend only from the merchant to the immediate buyer but now can extend to members of the buyer's household, his or her guests, a remote purchaser, or even to anyone who can reasonably be expected to use the goods. This is determined by the applicable state law
Intended Beneficiary	Created when the promisor and the promisee identify or anticipate that a specific third party is meant to benefit from the promise and to receive consideration
Incidental Beneficiary	An incidental beneficiary is not anticipated by the original parties at the time that the contract was formed
Assignment	An assignment of a right occurs when an entity or individual who has the right to receive performance under a contract assigns that right to a third party
Delegation	A delegation of duty arises when the party obligated to perform under the contract transfers his or her duty to perform to another party Some contracts, such as personal service contracts, may prohibit the delegation of a duty

Novation	Substitution of a new contract for an existing contract or the substitution of a new party for an existing party
What a Paralegal Needs to Know	The supervising attorney will determine if there is a third-party interest, for this is a legal decision.

REVIEW QUESTIONS

1. Can a warranty extend to a subsequent purchaser?
2. Is privity of contract always required to enforce a party's rights under an agreement?
3. What is the difference between an intended beneficiary and an incidental beneficiary?
4. What is assignment of a right?
5. What is delegation of a duty?
6. Does novation require the consent of the parties?
7. Define *obligor*.
8. Define *obligee*.
9. Is there any instance when a duty cannot be delegated?
10. What is privity of contract?

SKILL-BUILDING APPLICATION EXERCISE

Find, in your state statutes, the particular alternative section of U.C.C. §2–318 that was adopted by your state. Section 2–318 concerns the issue of when a lack of privity arises in a breach of warranty. The U.C.C. has protections for the consumer, in some instances even when there is no privity of contract between the remote purchaser and the seller, when there is a breach of warranty.

SIMULATED LAW OFFICE ASSIGNMENT

The head of the commercial law group, Lisa Michaels, Esq., at the firm asked you to help on the following matter. The firm represents Mays Pretzel Company. Mays entered into a valid, binding contract to be purchased by Rider Foods, a large conglomerate. At the time of the sale to Rider, Mays owed Heavy Equipment Corporation $95,000 stemming from the purchase of new pretzel-making machinery that Mays took possession of six months prior to the sale to Rider. The contract of sale, between Mays and Rider, states that Rider will now pay Heavy Equipment Company the $95,000 for the equipment. Ms. Michaels wants you to write a letter to

Mays, Rider, and Heavy Equipment detailing the agreement that Rider will now pay Heavy Equipment the $95,000. Assume there is a valid contract for the sale and that the parties negotiated and agreed upon the terms. The following questions will have to be answered to write the letter:

1. Who are the original parties to the agreement?
2. Who is the promisee in the original agreement between Mays and Rider?
3. Did the original parties intend that a third party benefit from the agreement?
4. Is a party under an obligation to a third party? Which party?
5. Under the contract, will the promised performance discharge an obligation to a third party?
6. Would Heavy Equipment Company have any rights under the contract between Mays and Rider?

DRAFTING EXERCISE

Ludwig Mist is a famous architect. Mr. Mist was hired by Paul Harness to design and build a house for the Harness family. In the contract, Mr. Harness stipulated that Mist's services are unique and that Mist could not assign his architectural design services. Mr. Mist has a large company and not only designs structures but manages the entire construction process. Mr. Harness knew, when entering into the contract with Mist, that although Mist would design the home, the construction management would be performed by other Mist employees. Two weeks prior to the commencement of the architectural design process, Mr. Mist became gravely ill. Mist Architectural Design contacted Mr. Harness with the news. Sullivan Louis, Mr. Mist's protégé and collaborator, spoke with Mr. Harness about the intended project. Mr. Louis convinced Mr. Harness that Mist's design concept could be executed by him. Since this was a personal service contract and the duties of Ludwig Mist could not be delegated, an amendment to the agreement must be drafted. Please draft an amendment stating that Mist's duties to Harness can be delegated to Louis.

DEVELOPING CRITICAL THINKING SKILLS

Read *Revels v. Miss America Organization* reprinted in this chapter. What are the requirements to prove status as an intentional beneficiary under a contract? Write your answer in one or two paragraphs.

PORTFOLIO ASSIGNMENT

Fact pattern: Our client is Eastmore Country Club.

Eastmore Country Club is a privately owned company that provides catering, event space, dining, golf, tennis, and social programs to its membership. Eastmore has over fifty employees and a paid membership of 300 families. Each family pays an initiation fee of $25,000 and an annual membership fee of $3,000. The annual membership permits access to all of the club's services, but many of the services are charged as separate fees to the members. Additionally, each member family must spend $2,000 on dining and catering annually to maintain the family membership.

The Brown family has maintained a membership at Eastmore for the past fifty years. Mrs. Brown's daughter, Jane, is a high school senior and is seventeen years old. Jane is a member of the Hospital Junior Board and wants the Junior Board Fashion Show to be held at Eastmore on April 29, 2011. The parent advisors for the Junior Board asked Jane to provide information about the expenses and the details of having the Fashion Show at Eastmore. On September 14, 2010, Jane presented a signed contract that required a nonrefundable deposit to the parent advisors. Mrs. Brown signed the contract and provided Eastmore with the nonrefundable deposit. Mrs. Brown promptly called the President of the Hospital Women's Board to obtain reimbursement for the deposit she thought she made on behalf of the Junior Board.

The following are copies of the agreement and the proposal.

Letter establishing agreement:

Eastmore Country Club
2347 East Road
Easton, Illinois 65431

Mrs. Joan Brown
17 Thomas Place
Easton, Illinois 65431
September 14, 2010

Dear Mrs. Brown:

Thank you for hosting the Hospital Junior Auxiliary Fashion Show. We are looking forward to hosting the "Hospital Junior Auxiliary Fashion Show" on April 29, 2011, at Eastmore. The show will be held in our large banquet room. I am confident that our professional and dedicated staff will provide you and your guests with the unsurpassed service and accommodations for which we are noted. Our high quality standards, attention to detail, and commitment to excellence are a few of the reasons that Eastmore Country Club continues to exceed your expectations.

To guarantee this booking, please sign and return one copy of this letter with a nonrefundable deposit of $500.00. Please keep the second copy for your records.

I am very excited to work with you on this afternoon event and welcome any questions or changes you may have. I have a flexible schedule that allows me to set evening and weekend appointments if necessary. Please contact me at any time for more information.

Cordially,

Amanda Green
Joan Brown
9/14/10

INVOICE

Bill to:

Name	Mrs. Joan Brown
Event Date	April 29, 2011
Event Name	Hospital Junior Aux. Bd. Fashion Show

Quantity		Unit Price	TOTAL
30	Cookies-Dozen @15.00/dozen	$15.00	$450.00
	Food Service Charge 20%	$90.00	$90.00
	Tax Exempt		$0.00
	FOOD SUB-TOTAL $540.00		**$540.00**
2	Coffee Station-Gallons @ $35.00/gallon	$35.00	$70.00
4	Iced Tea–Gallons @ $20.00/gallon	$20.00	$80.00
4	Lemonade–Gallons @ $20.00/gallon	$20.00	$80.00
	Beverage Service Charge 20%	$46.00	$46.00
	Tax Exempt		$0.00
	BEVERAGE SUB-TOTAL $276.00		**$276.00**
	Valet @ $3.00/car 100 cars $300		$300.00
	Large Banquet Rm. Rental $300		$300.00
	Grand total $1416.00		
	We enjoyed having you as our guest		
	and we hope that we create a		
	memorable experience.		
		Event Total	$1416.00

Ms. Green, as an agent and employee of Eastmore, entered into this agreement with Mrs. Brown. Mrs. Brown entered into this agreement with the intention that Hospital Junior Board is the beneficiary of the contract. John East, owner and president of Eastmore Country Club, asked our firm to determine if Mrs. Brown can assign the rights under the contract and delegate the duties. Please write a memo with your determinations.

Performance and Discharge of Obligations

INTRODUCTION—PERFORMANCE AND DISCHARGE, IN GENERAL

We learned that a contract requires an offer, acceptance, and consideration to be valid. Once these components are exchanged, it is assumed that the contract is complete. However, the agreement still must be performed according to the terms agreed to by the parties. Of course, many contracts are performed and completed based on the offer accepted and the consideration tendered. Issues can arise during performance. Sometimes impediments interfere with a party's or parties' ability to carry out the terms of the agreement, to execute the contract, due to an occurrence or act outside of a party's control, such as an Act of God, or due to a situation within a party's control, such as failing to order adequate materials in a timely manner. Sometimes, a party's failure to perform as promised creates outstanding obligations. This failure to perform sometimes results in discharging the party's obligations under the contract and sometimes it results in a breach of contract. When a contract is breached, it is important to determine whether the breach is material or whether there is substantial performance. This chapter will explore issues concerning the performance of the obligations under the agreement, particularly **conditions**. Also, you will learn when a party may not be **discharged** from his or her obligations, after a contract is finalized, as doing so would result in a breach. You will be able to identify the specific legal and factual scenarios that permit a party to be discharged from his or her obligations under a contract.

LEARNING OBJECTIVES

After studying this chapter, you will be able to:

1. Understand and contrast material breach and immaterial breach.

2. Discuss substantial performance.

3. Define anticipatory breach.

4. Discuss the concept of conditions generally and know that a condition may impact a duty to perform.

5. Identify circumstances that may permit the discharge of a contractual obligation.

Condition
An event that is to happen or has happened that affects or triggers a legal obligation.

Discharge
Relieving a party's obligations under a contract, either by performance or by other means such as impossibility.

■ PERFORMANCE

Performance occurs when the parties comply with the terms of the contract that they agreed to. We learned that an offeree can reject an offer within the time period set out for acceptance, then the offer is terminated and no contract results. There are instances when the offer is accepted but the offeree requires an act or forbearance that must occur to trigger the fulfillment of the promise. This is a condition. Failing to fulfill a condition differs from breach of contract. A breach of contract is the failure to perform what is promised under the agreement.

Failure to Perform

According to the Restatement (Second) of Contracts §241, to determine if the breach is a material breach, examine:

(a) the extent to which the injured party will be deprived of the benefit which he reasonably expected;

(b) the extent to which the injured party can be adequately compensated for the part of that benefit of which he will be deprived;

(c) the extent to which the party failing to perform or to offer to perform will suffer forfeiture;

(d) the likelihood that the party failing to perform or to offer to perform will cure his failure, taking account of all the circumstances including any reasonable assurances;

(e) the extent to which the behavior of the party failing to perform or to offer to perform comports with standards of good faith and fair dealing.

In a material breach, the injured party is relieved from his or her duties to perform under the agreement, and discharged from his or her obligations under the contract.

Example

Denise Dunn hired Jane Land Copying Service to copy all of Smith Company's Tax Returns from the last five years, and to collate and staple the returns. Dunn agreed to pay Jane Land Copying $1,000 for the work. Jane Land shredded the returns instead of copying them. This is a material breach because Dunn is deprived of the benefit she reasonably expected under the contract. Dunn would be relieved of her duties, to pay Jane Land, under the contract.

In contrast, an immaterial breach would occur if Jane Land used a paper clip on one return instead of stapling it because she ran out of staples. Dunn would not be relieved of her duties under the contract.

Substantial Performance

This occurs when the party to perform under the contract performs a significant portion, a material portion, of his or her obligation. When the injured party receives a substantial portion of the benefit from the agreement, the breach is immaterial and the injured party is not relieved from his or her duty to perform under the contract. A party substantially performs his requirements under the agreement when it is not feasible for him to fully perform but he makes every effort to fulfill the material elements of the contract. The outstanding work or promises, less than full performance, are then compensated for. An honest and good-faith effort to perform, as agreed, must be made.

Example

Robert Rike entered into a contract with Handsome Roofing to reroof his home and to replace all of the gutters. Handsome Roofers arrived on the date promised with a crew of eight workers. The workers completely reroofed Rike's home in two days. On the third day, Handsome replaced 95 percent of the gutters. Handsome could not complete the job because they ran out of copper gutters and did not estimate the amount of copper gutters that would be required. Here, Handsome made a good-faith effort to perform as agreed.

Rike cannot claim breach of contract because Handsome substantially performed the contract. Since Handsome substantially performed, Rike is not relieved of his duty under the agreement, which would be to pay Handsome for labor and materials. However, Rike can adjust the amount to be paid according to the performance provided by Handsome.

■ CONDITIONS TO PERFORMANCE

Parties to the contract must agree that the event or act that must occur is a condition. Conditions are created in one of three ways. A condition that is stated in words and included in the contract is called an express condition. An implied condition is either implied in fact, understood from the conduct of the parties, or implied in law, imposed by the court to prevent unfair gain from the agreement. The timing of the condition also impacts performance. If the fulfillment of the condition must precede performance, it is a condition precedent; if it is simultaneous, it is a condition concurrent; and if the condition requires an act or event to terminate the contract, it is a condition subsequent.

Types of Conditions

Condition Precedent

A condition precedent arises when the event or act must occur for the obligation under the contract to be triggered. Basically, the condition precedes the contractual duties.

Example

Roberta Ray was accepted to the State University. Roberta Ray was concerned about obtaining on-campus housing in a dormitory for the academic year. As a condition precedent to signing the contract for university housing, Roberta must be accepted to State University for that academic year.

Example

Chris Conway was hired to sew a wedding gown for Jane Rust with fabric, lace, and buttons supplied by Jane. Supplying the materials to construct the dress is a condition precedent to the performance of the contract.

Condition Subsequent

A condition subsequent is an act or event that occurs after the contract is formed that changes a party's obligations or extinguishes a party's obligations under a contract. A condition subsequent is not very common. It occurs when the condition is subsequent to the contractual duties.

Example

Mr. Michael Houseman rented an apartment from Urban Property for five years. The lease was an annual lease and each year the rent increased by 10 percent. Each year Mr. Houseman renewed the lease. Mr. Houseman lived alone and was the sole tenant in the unit and on the lease. There was a provision in the lease that the lease would terminate upon the death of the tenant if the tenant was the sole tenant. During the fifth year of Mr. Houseman's tenancy, he died. When Mr. Houseman died, the lease was terminated. The occurrence of the condition subsequent, Houseman's death, terminated the obligations under the lease.

Concurrent Conditions

A concurrent condition requires that each party's performance is contingent upon the other party's fulfillment of a condition. Both parties have a condition precedent to the performance of the contract.

Equitable Issues Concerning Conditions

Sometimes a court will determine that there is a condition in the contract to avoid injustice. This is an instance of a condition implied in law. Sometimes a court will enforce a contract to prevent injustice, as in instances of detrimental reliance where a party relies to his or her detriment on the expectation that a promise will be fulfilled.

■ DISCHARGE OF OBLIGATION

Common Reasons for Discharge, Generally

A discharge of obligation under the contract occurs when a party is excused from performing. There are various ways to discharge the duties under the contract.

The easiest and simplest way to discharge obligations is to perform the agreement according to its terms. The second simplest is to mutually agree to rescind the contract.

Release

A **release** occurs when a party offers to relinquish the other party's claim or right under the contract. Sometimes one party may give the other party a release from the obligation in exchange for cash payment or property. Generally, a release is in writing and is signed.

Release
Agreeing to permit a party to be relieved from his or her obligations under the agreement. Usually a release is in writing.

Example–Sample Release

RELEASE

FOR GOOD AND VALUABLE CONSIDERATION, identified below, TREE CORPORATION, dba ARBORIST ("Arborist") as owner of the materials which include images grants to PLANT NURSERIES, INC, ("PLANT") and its parent companies, affiliates, assigns, licensees, legal representatives, successors-in-interest, advertising, promotion and fulfillment agencies, and their employees and agents ("PLANT"), the irrevocable, unrestricted, absolute, worldwide and perpetual right to use the BRANCH trademark, and a photograph or likeness of the "BRANCH" on a cover of a book entitled "Plant your way to Happiness" ("the BOOK") and in all forms of media including print and websites for purposes of publicity, advertising and sales promotion of the BOOK.

Arborist understands that it shall have no right of approval, no claim to compensation other than stated below, and no claim (including, without limitation, claims based upon right of privacy, defamation, or right of publicity) arising out of any use or any blurring, distortion, alteration, optical illusion, or use in composite form, of the Mark described above.

ARBORIST understands that as compensation for the use of the MARK, PLANT will include the MARK on the cover of the BOOK.

PLANT releases ARBORIST and its parent companies, affiliates, assigns, licensees, legal representatives, successors-in-interest, advertising, promotion and fulfillment agencies, and their employees and agents from any and all existing claims that may subsequently arise, based on the use of the Mark, including any claim for damages for libel, defamation, infringement of the right of publicity, invasion of privacy, portrayal in false light or false endorsement.

This Release and all terms included and contained in this document shall be binding upon the parties, their successors, assigns and executors, administrators, personal representatives and heirs.

I understand that this is a legal document and that I have read this RELEASE and am fully familiar with and agree with its contents. In signing this RELEASE, the representative warrants to 'PLANT that he has the full authority to do so.

By: _____
President of PLANT NURSERIES, INC.

Date: _____
Address:_____

_____

Novation

A novation is the substitution of a new contract for an existing agreement with the consent of the parties. In essence, because a new agreement is formed, the parties are discharged from their obligations under the original contract.

Termination

One party, or both parties by mutual agreement, may decide to end the contract. This occurs after the offer has been accepted. This differs from the rejection of an offer for in that case, the contract has not yet been formed.

Discharge by Agreement

In this situation, both parties concur that the contract is not suited to their respective goals and each party discharges the other's duty under the agreement.

Anticipatory Breach

Anticipatory breach, also called anticipatory repudiation, occurs when a party chooses to not fulfill his or her obligation under the agreement prior to the time when performance is due. Anticipatory breach does not discharge a party's obligation to perform and the other party can treat it as a breach of contract generally. Usually, the breaching party does not have a justification for the breach. Sometimes, anticipatory breach arises when a party realizes that it would be prohibitively expensive to perform and it is less expensive to compensate the aggrieved party. Occasionally, anticipatory breach will motivate the parties to renegotiate the agreement.

Example

Smith Jewelers designs, manufactures, and sells gold jewelry. Smith had a contract with April Department Stores to provide 300 14-carat-gold rings by November 1, 2011, and April Department Stores would pay Smith $90.00 per ring. The parties signed the contract in 2008. In the interim, Smith decided that he no longer wants to be a jeweler and wants to enter the Peace Corps. Smith communicates, on March 1, 2010, to April Department Stores that he will not perform the agreement and will not tender the rings on November 1, 2011. This communication occurs prior to the time that the performance, under the contract, was due. Smith made a statement indicating that he will not perform his obligation under the contract prior to November 1, 2011.

Accord and Satisfaction

Accord
An agreement.

Satisfaction
Performing to satisfy the obligation under the contract or tendering a substituted performance that will fulfill the terms.

An **accord** and **satisfaction** of a contract, in its simplest terms, is the tender of an amount in the settlement of an obligation that is generally for less than the original amount owed. The parties agree that this amount satisfies the debt and replaces the amount originally owed. Sometimes, this can be a novation because it is a substitution of a new agreement. The creation of new terms creates a new contract. Accord and satisfaction is used frequently when a party does not fulfill all of the obligations under an agreement or the quality of the goods or performance is not what one party anticipated. The offeree accepts the limited performance and pays a portion of what was originally agreed; this in essence creates a new agreement, satisfies the parties' obligations, and discharges the claim. Very often a note will accompany the payment stating that the check is in accord and satisfaction of the amount owed.

Example

The Mulroys contracted with Smith Plowing to have their driveway plowed on a monthly basis when the snow accumulated more than four inches. The Mulroys agreed to pay Smith $80 per winter month for this service. During the month of January, accumulated snowfall of four inches occurred four times. However, Smith was very busy and only plowed the Mulroys' driveway three times. The Mulroys send Smith a check for $60.00 and write "acceptance of this check is in accord and satisfaction of our obligation."

Impossibility of Performance

Generally, impossibility of performance will not discharge a party's obligation under an agreement. Good drafting can create provisions where a party can anticipate situations where the obligations can be discharged and when performance will not be excused. There are some situations, discussed next, that illustrate instances when a contract can be discharged due to impossibility of performance. This means that when a party doesn't perform the agreement, under one of these circumstances, performance is excused.

Death

As long as the contract is for a unique, personal service such as painting a portrait, the contract is terminated on the death of the party who was to perform the unique task. If the performance does not require the unique skills of the party to perform and can be performed by another individual, then the contract will not be discharged. Generally, language in the contract states this.

Example

Jet Jeans entered into a contract with Now Stores to supply Now with 100 pairs of jeans at $30.00 per pair wholesale by May 1. The President of Jet Jeans, Joe Jet, died suddenly and unexpectedly on April 15. The agreement between Jet Jeans and Now Stores will not be discharged because performance does not require the unique skills of Mr. Jet and the agreement can be performed by others at the company.

Impossibility and the Personal Service Contract

A personal service contract exists when one of the contracting parties is offering to perform an act or service that is unique and that cannot be assigned to another to perform. Personal service contracts arise when contracting with artists, performers, and designers. When a famous artist is unable to perform as contracted due to health reasons that are unanticipated and are not his or her fault, of course another artist cannot be substituted to perform, there arises impossibility of performance, and the contract can be discharged. Many drafters now anticipate the situations when a personal service contract can be discharged and when it is breached by failure to perform.

Temporary Impossibility

Temporary impossibility arises when there is an impediment to performance that arises due to a third party after the agreement is made. This can occur if there is a strike, for instance, by laborers in the port and goods cannot be shipped, or a writers' strike and new television shows cannot be created. Other examples of temporary impossibility are quarantines and embargos. In these instances, performance is not discharged but is generally delayed.

Commercial Impracticality

Commercial impracticality usually does not discharge obligations under a contract. Parties assume some risk, usually economic, whenever a contract is entered into. Commercial impracticality arises after the contract is formed but prior to complete performance. This occurs frequently when the contract can be performed but it is economically challenging for one of the parties. An example is when the cost of raw materials skyrockets after a contract is finalized. Sometimes a natural disaster will occur, a gas pipeline will be affected, and the cost of natural gas will increase markedly.

A recent example of this is ethanol production increasing the cost of corn. A grocer contracted in September to purchase bushels of corn for $10.00 per bushel, for twenty (20) bushels, for the following July. In May, the farmer realizes that he can sell the corn to an ethanol plant for $25.00 per bushel. The farmer claims it is commercially impractical to sell the corn to the grocer. This is commercial impracticality but does not excuse performance just because the farmer will lose money.

Commercial Impracticability

This is also an event that happens after the contract is formed and is outside the control of the parties. However, performance is not more expensive, it is impossible. Often a contract will have a provision, called a *Force Majeure clause*, that anticipates "acts of God." Parties can also include provisions addressing the possibility of terrorism, war, embargos, quarantines, and detailing whether the party must perform as agreed or if nonperformance is excused, resulting in no breach of the contract. These provisions have become more prevalent since the terrorist attacks of September 11, 2001. If nonperformance due to impossibility or impracticability occurs, and the agreement allows for this, then there is no breach of contact.

The Restatement (Second) of Contracts §261 states: "[W]here, after a contract is made, a party's performance is made impracticable without his fault by the occurrence of an event the non-occurrence of which was a basic assumption on which the contract was made his duty to render that performance is discharged. . ." unless the parties agreed otherwise in the contract.

The following sections provide examples of instances of impracticability.

Frustration of Purpose

Frustration of purpose arises when the underlying reason for the contract no longer exists or a party's circumstances surrounding the contract may render performance of the terms useless.

For instance, New Britain Ship Builders was hired to build four warships for the Second World War. New Britain signed the contract in April of 1945. A peace treaty was entered into and the war ended. The United States no longer needed the warships because there was no longer a war.

Example

ReadyPotato Company contracted with the Department of Defense in 1951 to provide dehydrated potatoes for the troops in Korea. ReadyPotato completed the production of the dehydrated potatoes and they were available to ship at the end of 1952. The war in Korea was ending and the troops no longer needed the potatoes. The obligation under the contract is discharged due to frustration of purpose.

Acts of God or Force Majeure

Sometimes an act of God will prevent performance of the agreement. Examples of acts of God are hurricanes, tornados, floods, and earthquakes. An act of God in recent memory is Hurricane Katrina. Performance is generally excused if there is not provision to the contrary. The act of God must directly interfere with a party's ability to perform. For instance, a publisher in Chicago cannot be excused from performing a book publishing agreement with an author in Chicago due to Hurricane Katrina because the hurricane did not affect the party's ability to perform.

Example

Acme Builders was supposed to complete the Nottingham Subdivision by August 1. On July 25, a category 4 hurricane blew through the subdivision, destroying many of the homes and causing water damage to the remaining homes. Due to the hurricane, an act of God, Acme's obligation to complete the houses may be discharged. Good drafters often include a *force majeure clause* that discharges a party's obligations under a contract when complete performance is prevented due to an act of God. Depending on the situation, the parties, and the particular agreement, more time to perform may be granted or a party may be discharged from his or her obligation.

Destruction of Subject Matter

This occurs when the subject matter contracted for is completely destroyed. For instance, a bridge collapses that is under contract to be painted or a fire destroys a building to be decorated.

Supervening Illegality

A zoning change may discharge an obligation under a contract.

Example

A municipality may permit the sale of alcohol within its borders. After a contract is made to open a bar with a national franchise, but before the bar

Supervening

Arising after the initial terms. For instance, a supervening illegality arises, after the initial terms of the contract are agreed upon based on existing law, when a new law is enacted that makes the initial terms impossible to perform due to illegality. Occurs frequently in zoning issues.

is actually built, the municipality bans the operation of any bar or restaurant that serves alcohol within 500 yards of a school. If the bar was to be opened within 500 yards of a school, the contract must be discharged due to **supervening** illegality.

CASE ILLUSTRATION

Guided Reading Pointers

In *Cedyco*, the court discusses the meaning of a condition precedent and then makes a determination that the condition precedent must be satisfied to permit the sale of lot 26 by PetroQuest. Here the condition precedent requires Exxon to consent to the assignment. Exxon did not consent to the assignment. Because Exxon did not consent to the assignment, the condition precedent was not satisfied. The act or conduct that is the condition precedent must occur prior to the promised performance under the contract. Because the condition precedent was not satisfied, Petroquest did not have an obligation to perform.

Cedyco Corp.
v.
PETROQUEST ENERGY LLC
497 F.3d 485 (Fifth Cir. 2007)

In this diversity case, PetroQuest Energy, LLP ("PetroQuest") appeals the district court's grant of summary judgment and award of damages in favor of Cedyco Corporation ("Cedyco") on Cedyco's claim that PetroQuest breached a contract to sell its working interest in two oil wells . . .

PetroQuest is a company engaged in oil and gas exploration and production. In November 2001, PetroQuest offered its working interest in two Louisiana oil wells for sale by auction at the Oil & Gas Asset Clearinghouse ("Clearinghouse") in Houston, Texas. The wells were auctioned as "Lot 26." Prior to the auction, PetroQuest distributed a "Property Data Sheet" to potential buyers. This document contained a provision stating that Lot 26 is "subject to a consent to assign." This is because the mineral deed identified as Lot 26 was originally leased in 1945 to ExxonMobil Corporation ("Exxon"), then subleased to PetroQuest in 1991 under the condition that PetroQuest not sell or assign the mineral rights without first obtaining Exxon's written consent.

Cedyco was the only bidder for Lot 26 and won the auction with a bid-offer of $ 1,000. PetroQuest then asked Exxon for consent to assign Lot 26 to Cedyco, and Exxon replied that it would grant only a conditional consent, subject to PetroQuest's remaining obligated for the original sublease and agreeing to indemnify Exxon for any liability arising from Cedyco's operation of the lease. PetroQuest proceeded to investigate Cedyco's credit and regulatory compliance histories and found that Cedyco had a record of violating state regulations imposed on oil and gas producers. As a result, PetroQuest declined to accept Exxon's conditional consent to assign because Cedyco presented too high of a risk for PetroQuest to agree to indemnify Exxon. PetroQuest then notified Clearinghouse that it could not sell Lot 26 to

Cedyco because Exxon had given "an unacceptable 'conditional' consent to the assignment." Within three weeks of the auction, Clearinghouse informed Cedyco that Exxon had not consented and refunded Cedyco's bid money and auction fees. Almost two years later, PetroQuest sold Lot 26 for $125,000.

Cedyco sued PetroQuest in Texas state court for breach of contract, specific performance, and conversion. . . . Applying Texas law, the district court granted summary judgment in favor of Cedyco. Its reasons were brief: "The sale at the auction was final. Title to Lot 26 passed to Cedyco." After a bench trial to determine damages, the district court denied Cedyco's claim for specific performance and awarded Cedyco $290,205 in damages and $37,250 in attorney's fees. The parties cross-appealed. . .

[W]e agree with PetroQuest's alternative argument that the contract contained a condition precedent that Exxon consent to the assignment. A condition precedent is an act or event that must take place before performance of a contractual obligation is due. *Hohenberg Brothers Co. v. George E. Gibbons & Co.*, 537 S.W.2d 1, 3 (Tex. 1976); *see also Texas Dep't of Hous. & Community Affairs v. Verex Assurance*, 68 F.3d 922, 928 (5th Cir. 1995). While Texas does not generally favor reading conditions precedent into contracts, *see Sirtex Oil Indus. v. Erigan*, 403 S.W.2d 784, 787 (Tex. 1966), the inclusion of words "such as 'if,' 'provided,' 'on condition that,' or some similar phrase of conditional language" indicate that the parties intended there to be a condition precedent. *Criswell v. European Crossroads Shopping Center, Ltd.*, 792 S.W.2d 945, 948 (Tex. 1990).

Here, the auction documents contain the requisite conditional language indicating that Exxon's consent was a condition precedent to the sale. The "Property Data Sheet" informed all potential buyers that Lot 26 was "subject to a[] consent to assign." "Subject to" means "likely to be conditioned, affected, or modified in some indicated way[, and] having a contingent relation to something and usually dependent on such relation for final form, validity or significance." WEBSTER'S UNABRIDGED DICTIONARY 2275 (3d ed. 1993). Thus, the language of the auction documents expressly indicates that the sale of Lot 26 was conditioned on Exxon's consent. . . . PetroQuest included the language "consent to assign required" in the "Property Data Package Update," in a handwritten cover page to the "Property Data Package Update," in the "due diligence inquiries" section of the Property Data sheet that was physically posted at the auction, and in large bold letters on a sign at the auction. Cedyco acknowledged and agreed to all disclosed conditions when it signed the "Bidder/Buyer's Terms and Conditions."

Cedyco's arguments that the auction documents did not contain a condition precedent are entirely without merit. For one, its assertions are belied by the plain language of the auction documents. Furthermore, Cedyco's argument that a condition precedent is an event that must occur before a contract is formed—and because a contract was formed at the close of the auction, there no longer existed a condition precedent—is circular and finds no support in Texas contract law. . . . condition precedent may be "those acts or events, which occur subsequently to the making of the contract, that must occur before there is a right to immediate performance and before there is a contractual duty." . . . Here, Exxon entertained a request for consent after knowing the identify of the buyer from the auction; thus, the condition precedent was to occur after the contract was formed but before PetroQuest's obligation to sell Lot 26 came due.

Because we find that the contract for the sale of Lot 26 contained a condition precedent, the critical question is whether the condition precedent was met—i.e., whether Exxon consented to the assignment . . . PetroQuest argues that Exxon did not consent; Exxon only *conditionally* consented. Cedyco responds that PetroQuest was obligated under the contract to obtain consent by accepting Exxon's conditions. In other words, neither party argues that the term "consent" is ambiguous; rather, the parties disagree over the legal meaning of the term. . .

Were we to interpret the contract as imposing on PetroQuest the duty to obtain consent by accepting all of Exxon's terms, then the contract's condition precedent would be superfluous, that is there would be no need include a "consent to assign" provision in the contract at all as PetroQuest would be required to obtain consent under any circumstances. We decline to adopt such a construction, as we must ensure that each provision of the contract is given effect and none are rendered meaningless . . .

The summary judgment record contains evidence only that Exxon consented to the assignment under the condition that PetroQuest comply with Exxon's terms. Because PetroQuest was not obligated by the contract to accept Exxon's terms, Exxon's response was not a "consent" under the terms of the contract, and the condition precedent was never satisfied. As a result, PetroQuest's obligation to perform under the contract never came due. We therefore vacate summary judgment, and reverse and render judgment in favor of PetroQuest . . .

Guided Reading Questions

1. What was Cedyco trying to purchase or bid on?

2. Why did Exxon require that the party comply with its terms?

3. Why is the condition at issue?

4. How does the fulfilling of a condition precedent impact performance under a contract?

■ THE U.C.C. AND PERFORMANCE AND DISCHARGE

In contracts for the sale of goods and in contracts between merchants, the Uniform Commercial Code applies. The rules in the Uniform Commercial Code differ from the common law rules for performance and discharge because of the recognition for the need to facilitate commerce.

Under U.C.C. §2–601, when the goods delivered fail to conform to the contract in any respect, and if the parties did not agree otherwise in the contract, a buyer has the right to:

(a) reject the whole; or
(b) accept the whole; or
(c) accept any commercial unit or units and reject the rest.

This differs from the common law material breach where the injured party is discharged from his duties under the contract.

However, under §2–602, a merchant must reject the nonconforming goods within a reasonable time after they are delivered and also under the U.C.C. the seller may obtain conforming goods, or replace or repair defective goods.

There are instances when a buyer is unsure that the seller will perform. This is called insecurity. Under §2–609, the Uniform Commercial Code states that a party has a "Right to Adequate Assurance of Performance."

U.C.C. rules on anticipatory repudiation, in §2–610, allow a party to a repudiated contract to await performance within a commercially reasonable time and, regardless, to resort to any remedy for breach of contract even though he or she may have put the breaching party on notice that he or she is awaiting performance.

U.C.C. §2–615 also has rules pertaining to the failure of certain conditions to performance due to commercial impracticability and supervening illegality. In these instances, delay in delivery or nondelivery, when in good faith, will not constitute a breach. Also, the seller can partially perform. The seller must give the buyer adequate notice, if possible, of the inability to deliver all or part of the goods.

■ WHAT A PARALEGAL NEEDS TO KNOW

A paralegal must be aware that the determination of whether a contractual obligation is discharged or if the party breached the agreement is a legal decision to be made by the attorney. A discharge relieves a party of his or her obligation under the contract. In contrast, a breach of contract occurs when a party fails to perform as promised. Once the attorney instructs you as to whether there is a breach or a discharge of obligations under the contract, then you can proceed to contact the client. After the attorney makes this determination, be sure to contact the client promptly because she will want to exercise her rights as soon as feasible.

The parties must use careful drafting to anticipate if an event occurs subsequent to the time that the agreement is finalized, in which case the party is excused from performance and there is no breach. This basically requires the parties to think ahead, to anticipate who will bear the risk when economic conditions change, when future events may occur that impact the contract's purpose, the event of an act of God, or when the law changes so that the contract no longer complies with the law.

This is a legal determination made by the attorneys negotiating the agreement.

CHAPTER SUMMARY

This chapter explored the concepts of performance under a contract and when the obligation to perform is discharged. A contract is performed when both parties comply with and follow through with the terms of the agreement. You have learned that sometimes there are conditions to performance or conditions that extinguish the duty to perform. Also, you have learned that a failure to comply with the terms is a breach. A breach is material or immaterial depending on whether a party did not receive a substantial portion of the bargain agreed to. The chapter also explored the many instances of when a party's obligations under the contract may be discharged. These include: release, novation, discharge by agreement, anticipatory breach, accord and satisfaction, impossibility of performance, commercial impracticality, and commercial impracticability. As a paralegal, be aware of any material breach, any condition that may impact a duty to perform, and any situation that may discharge a party's duties under the contract.

Performance and Discharge

Performance	Performance occurs when the parties comply with the terms of the contract that they agreed to
Breach—Material and Immaterial	According to the Restatement (Second) of Contracts §241, to determine if the breach is material, examine: "(a) the extent to which the injured party will be deprived of the benefit which he reasonably expected" An immaterial breach occurs when a party receives a substantial portion of the benefit reasonably expected
Substantial Performance	Substantial performance occurs when the party to perform under the contract performs a significant portion, a material portion, of his or her obligation When the injured party receives a substantial portion of the benefit from the agreement, the breach is immaterial and the injured party is not relieved from his or her duty to perform under the contract
Conditions	Can be express, implied in law, or implied in fact Timing—condition precedent, condition concurrent, condition subsequent
Discharge of Obligation, Generally	Generally, a discharge of obligation under the contract occurs when a party is excused from performing There are various ways to discharge the duties under the contract The easiest and simplest way to discharge obligations is to perform the agreement according to its terms The second simplest is to mutually agree to rescind the contract
Common Situations Where a Party May Attempt to Be relieved of His or Her Obligation to Perform	Release; novation; termination; discharge by agreement; anticipatory breach; accord and satisfaction; impossibility of performance; commercial impracticality; commercial impracticability

The U.C.C. and Performance and Discharge	The U.C.C. strives to facilitate commerce Partial performance is permitted at the buyer's discretion even when a party does not perform as agreed Also, even if there is an anticipatory breach, the nonbreaching party can resort to any remedy for breach of contract even though he may have put the breaching party on notice that he or she is awaiting performance Lastly, the code discharges obligations, if in good faith, if performance as agreed has been made impracticable by the occurrence of a contingency that was assumed to not occur when the contract was made, such as frustration of purpose or supervening illegality
The Paralegal's Role	A decision as to performance or discharge of obligations is a legal decision to be made by an attorney You should be aware of any material breach and alert the client, under the attorney's direction Also, become familiar with any instance that would impact a party's ability to discharge his or her obligations under the contract

REVIEW QUESTIONS

1. Define *condition subsequent*.
2. Name two reasons why a contract can be discharged.
3. What is commercial impracticality?
4. What is a release?
5. Define *accord and satisfaction*.
6. What is a novation?
7. What is the easiest way to discharge an obligation under a contract?
8. List two instances of when performance is impossible.
9. What is a supervening illegality?
10. What is an act of God, and how does this impact performance?

SKILL-BUILDING APPLICATION EXERCISE

Read the following provisions from the Ocean Cruise Lines contract. Indicate if the provision is a condition and whether it is a condition precedent or condition subsequent. Identify any language that discharges Ocean Cruise Lines obligations or discharges the passenger's obligations under the contract.

. . . Carrier is not liable for death, injury, illness, damage, delay or other loss to person or property of any kind caused by an Act of God; war, civil commotions; labor trouble; terrorism, crime or other potential sources of harm; governmental interference; perils of sea; fire; or any other cause beyond Carrier's reasonable control; or any other act not shown to be caused by Carrier's negligence.

(Continued)

Passenger's Obligations . . .

Before you board the ship, you must:

1. Pay your full fare.
2. Familiarize yourself with the cruise contract.
3. Bring your passport and all minors' passports in your charge with you to board.
4. Arrive two hours prior to scheduled sailing time on day of departure. . .

SIMULATED LAW OFFICE ASSIGNMENT

The supervising attorney mentioned a client's situation during a meeting with the paralegals in your department. The client, Joe's Pizza, is a wildly successful restaurant chain that specializes in wood-oven-baked pizzas. Joe Rigglio has opened six restaurants with his partner Tom Smith. Joe and Tom want to enter into a buy-sell agreement where in the event of Joe's death or incapacity to work, Tom will purchase Joe's interest in the business. Joe's death or incapacity to work will trigger Tom's right to purchase Joe's half of the business.

What type of condition arises in this fact pattern?

Find a form for a buy-sell agreement.

DRAFTING EXERCISE

Draft a release based on the sample release in this chapter. Incorporate the following facts:

EasyChair Corporation, doing business as CHAIR Co., markets its chairs with an extra-heavy-duty fabric that can withstand any family wear and tear. The fabric is called ToughStuff. Sage Furniture Company wants to use ToughStuff fabrics on its upholstered products, including couches, chairs, and loveseats. Your firm represents EasyChair. Sage Furniture is willing to pay EasyChair for the use of the ToughStuff fabric. However, EasyChair wants Sage to sign a release, releasing EasyChair from any liability that may arise from Sage's use of the fabric. EasyChair seeks to be released from any and all claims that may subsequently arise, based on Sage's use of the ToughStuff Fabric, including any claims for physical damages, wear and tear, staining, abrasions, fire damage, water damage, and any other possible damage to the material. Additionally, EasyChair seeks to be released from any obligation to replace the material and/or the furniture and any obligation for any labor required to replace the furniture and/or the material.

DEVELOPING CRITICAL THINKING SKILLS

Read *Cedyco Corp. v. Petroquest Energy LLC* reprinted in this chapter. What type of condition is at issue in the case? Write a paragraph legally describing the condition discussed in the case.

PORTFOLIO ASSIGNMENT

You are working with an attorney to perform the legal work for a large construction project in Indianapolis. Your firm represents Acme Development Corporation. Acme has developed the Indianapolis Subdivision, which consists of a group of 200 single-family homes and town homes. Acme contracted with Beta Roofing to roof the homes. Beta mixed recycled shingles with new shingles on the structures. Acme is eager to finish the project but asserts that the value of the mixed shingles is less than all-new-shingle components. Originally, the parties agreed that Acme would pay Beta $100,000 to roof all of the structures in the Indianapolis Subdivision. Acme asserts now that the value of the roofing and materials is $75,000 due to the mix of shingles. Acme wants to pay Beta $80,000 for the entire project because the project required the same amount of labor and because Acme does not want to punish Beta. Acme feels that although it did not receive roofing as contracted for, Acme wants to be able to do business with Beta in the future.

Based on your reading of this chapter, can Acme discharge its obligation under the contract?

How would Acme discharge its obligation?

Write a letter to Beta stating Acme's offer to pay $80,000 for the work and the reasons for the payment of $80,000.

Remedies

CHAPTER 10

INTRODUCTION—REMEDIES IN GENERAL

The purpose of remedies is to compensate the injured party when a contract is not fulfilled as promised. The injured party can seek to be made whole or at least put in the position he or she would have been in if the contract had been performed as agreed or to be put in the position he or she was in prior to entering into the contract. The basic goals of all remedies are either to make a party perform or to financially compensate the nonbreaching party. Courts will fashion a **remedy** when the **breach** is **material** to create the value that the injured party would have received under the terms. The court's objective is to compensate the injured party either by imposing a remedy that pays him back for any benefit that the other party obtained from the breached contract (restitution interest), placing him in the position he would have been in if the contract had been performed as agreed (expectation interest), or restoring, to the nonbreaching party, the benefit that the breaching party received when the nonbreaching party acted in reliance on the contract (reliance interest).

There are two major classifications of remedies—legal and equitable. Legal remedies are derived from the common law and from statutes, such as a state's adoption of a U.C.C. provision, and are granted as a matter of legal right to the injured party. Equitable remedies are granted according to the court's discretion and are directed at achieving a fair result without the constraints of common law rules. Common law remedies for breach of contract are generally damages, which

LEARNING OBJECTIVES

After studying this chapter, you will be able to:

1. Discuss the purpose of remedies.
2. List several common law remedies.
3. Discuss equitable remedies.
4. Know the difference between equitable and legal remedies.
5. Define *liquidated damages*.
6. Discuss unjust enrichment.
7. Define *cover* under the Uniform Commercial Code.

Remedy
A way to redress a wrong.

Breach
Not performing, without any permitted legally permitted excuse, a contract as agreed by the parties.

Material
significant.

Liquidated
An amount made definite and certain by the parties' agreement. Generally, stated in the contract's terms, an amount for damages.

Nominal damages
Not significant. Sometimes only mentioned to indicate a party's obligations or rights but not assessed a dollar amount.

Restitution
A way to restore a party to the position he or she was in before being wronged.

Specific performance
A remedy. Specific performance puts the injured party in the position he or she would have been in if the contract had been performed.

are commonly measured in monetary amounts. In particular, the categories of damages in common law pertaining to contracts are: compensatory, consequential, incidental, **liquidated**, **nominal**, and punitive. Punitive damages are only ordered when there is wrongdoing, which generally is not usually the case in contracts. Equitable remedies for contracts disputes are: rescission, **restitution**, injunction, and **specific performance**.

■ THE GOALS OF COMMON LAW REMEDIES

The Restatement (Second) of Contracts §344 states that court-imposed, common law remedies have one or more of the following three goals:

- to protect the promisee's "'expectation interest,' , which is his interest in having the benefit of his bargain by being put in as good a position as he would have been in had the contract been performed," . . .
- to protect the promisee's "'reliance interest,' which is his interest in being reimbursed for loss caused by reliance on the contract by being put in as good a position as he would have been in had the contract not been made," . . .
- to protect the promisee's "'restitution interest,' which is his interest in having restored to him any benefit that he has conferred on the other party."

Furthermore, according to Restatement (Second) of Contracts §345, remedies for aggrieved parties can take one or more of the following forms:

1. Money
2. Specific performance (requiring a party to perform as agreed)
3. Requiring or enjoining the contract's nonperformance
4. Requiring the return of an item to prevent unjust enrichment
5. Tendering money to prevent unjust enrichment
6. Stating the parties' rights
7. Carrying out an arbitration award

■ BREACH

The need for a remedy arises when a party does not perform one or more terms of a contract as agreed. When a contract is not performed as agreed, the aggrieved party can sue for breach of contract. A breach is a failure to perform the agreement according to the terms. The court will always look at the language of the agreement to see if it has been fulfilled. When drafting a contract, it is important to be sure that the terms express the precise agreement between the parties and their expectations from performance.

Sometimes only a portion of the agreement is breached; this is a partial breach. Sometimes the entire contract is not performed as agreed; this results in a total breach. Often, a contract will contain a provision regarding what will constitute a breach and also state directly the remedies that are expected if the contract is not performed as agreed. However, if remedies are not stated in the agreement, an injured party has the right to pursue any available legal remedy and if the legal remedies are inadequate, the injured party can pursue an equitable remedy.

Material

A material breach is a failure to fulfill one or more of the essential terms of the agreement. The essential terms are basically the basis of the bargain, the heart of the agreement. This can be determined by asking: What induced the party to enter into the agreement? What did each party expect to receive? If the breach went to the essence of the agreement and impacted its purpose, the injured party then has the right to pursue damages for the entire agreement.

Example: Jane Jones contracted with New York Design for the shipment of twenty-five (25) red dresses, short sleeved, knee length, at $35 per dress, by June 25. If New York Designs fails to ship any dresses to Jane Jones, then the contract is materially breached. If New York Designs ships the dresses and the dresses arrive a day late, then this is not a material breach, unless the contract states that the dresses are required for a fashion show on June 26.

Immaterial

An immaterial breach occurs when a party, though injured, receives nearly all of what was agreed to or receives what was essential under the agreement. In an immaterial breach, performance received can be incomplete, an incomplete amount, or the quality is not what was agreed to but it is still capable of being used for the purpose intended. Courts look at the agreement itself to determine what the party anticipates to receive under the contract and if performance falls short of the expected benefit. If performance falls short, but the essence of the contract is performed and the promisee still receives a benefit, then the breach is immaterial. A party can still recover damages even if the breach is immaterial. Sometimes in the instance of an immaterial breach, the damages are nominal, meaning not significant or only mentioned to indicate a party's obligations or rights but not assessed an amount.

Example: If New York Designs ships the twenty-five red dresses, short sleeved, knee length, to Jane Jones by June 25 but the dresses have loose buttons, then the essential terms of the contract are fulfilled but the condition of the dresses is not what was anticipated by the parties. If the altered condition is not so great that it impacts significantly the goods' value and the promisee received a substantial portion of the bargain, then the breach is immaterial. However, the nonbreaching party can still seek a remedy even if the breach is immaterial.

■ WHAT A PARALEGAL NEEDS TO KNOW ABOUT BREACH

The determination of whether a breach is material or immaterial is a legal decision. This requires an examination of the contract's terms, the expectations of the parties, and a determination of whether the injured party received most of the expected benefit from the performance, even if that gain was not the full benefit anticipated. When the rights of an injured party are at issue, this is a legal matter to be determined and evaluated by the supervising attorney who will in turn direct your actions.

The Paralegal's Role in a Breach of Contract

First, as a paralegal you should keep detailed records of when performance under an agreement is due and when performance actually occurs. You should keep the supervising attorney informed.

Second, when performance fails to occur by the agreed date, a paralegal should, upon instruction of the supervising attorney, send a letter to the nonperforming party that performance was due by a certain date, performance has not occurred by the required date, and that performance is requested.

Third, if the attorney determines that the contract has in fact been breached, as a paralegal you may be required to draft a letter communicating the breach to the party that failed to perform and demanding performance. The supervising attorney will determine if he or she should sign the letter or if you may sign the letter.

Sample demand letter communicating breach of contract:

Jane Jones
Jones Dress Store
125 Central Street
Des Moines, Iowa

August 13, 2010

Mr. Steven Good
New York Designs
357 W. 38th Street
New York, N.Y. 10011

Re: Breach of Contract

Dear Mr. Good:

This letter is to inform you that we failed to receive the 25 red, knee length, short sleeved dresses, at $35 per dress, by June 25. We contacted you regarding the shipment of the dresses on June 26, July 5, July 18, and July 25. Our agreement provided that we would require the dresses for our fall fashion show, to be held on September 15.

We require the dresses four weeks prior to the fashion show so that they can be steamed, accessories can be selected, and models can be chosen.

We are informing you that you have materially breached this contract because you did not deliver the dresses that you agreed to provide in time for our fall fashion show. At this point, we demand complete refund of the $875 we paid you for the purchase of the dresses plus an additional $1,000 to purchase substitute dresses. If you do not reply in 5 days to this letter, a complaint will be filed.

Sincerely,

Jane Jones
Jones Dress Store

Examine this letter. The letter puts the party that failed to perform on notice that the agreement has been breached. The letter also seeks to rescind the agreement and to set a remedy to make the injured party whole, or to place the injured party in the position she would have been in if the contract had been performed as agreed. This remedy may have been provided by the terms of the contract or it may be the remedy that places the injured party in the position she would have been in had the other party performed as agreed. If the breaching party does not agree to the terms set out in the letter, then a lawsuit will ensue.

■ COMMON LAW REMEDIES

Damages

Generally, damages are a monetary amount given to the injured party with the intent to put him in the position he would have been in had the contract been performed or to compensate him economically or legally for the injury arising out of the contract's breach. The remedy of monetary damages was requested in the demand letter dress example.

Damages are not provided for a loss that was not anticipated or contemplated within the value of the contract. Also, damages are not open ended and are generally determined by the value that the party anticipated to receive if the contract had been performed as agreed.

Damages should approximate the injured party's expected value to be received under the agreement. According to the Restatement (Second) of Contracts §347, damages are generally measured as follows:

- Loss measured by the value not received due to the breaching party's deficient or failed performance
- Plus any other loss arising out of the breach, which can include consequential or incidental expenses or loss
- Minus any cost that the nonbreaching party has avoided or saved

$$(\text{Loss of value not received} + \text{Incidental and consequential expenses/losses}) - \text{Expenses avoided} = \text{Damages}$$

The common law and the Restatement (Second) of Contracts §346 permit the nonbreaching, injured party to receive damages when the contract is not performed as agreed unless the language of the agreement states otherwise. Nominal damages, or a small amount of damages, are still awarded if the breach does not cause any harm, economic or otherwise.

Compensatory Damages

Compensatory damages compensate the nonbreaching party for her loss with the goal of placing her in the position she would have been in had the contract been performed as agreed.

Example: The Raleigh Department Store planned its annual Fashion Show at the West End Club. The Fashion Show is a large source of profit for the store. Each year, many customers place orders for clothing at the fashion show. For the past two years, Raleigh had a profit of $100,000 per year from the event. Additionally, Raleigh paid fifteen employees a total of $5,000 to work the Fashion Show. To launch the show, Raleigh sends out engraved invitations to its best customers. The invitations cost $8,000. Raleigh pays West End $10,000 for the use of the Club's facilities and for sparkling water, wine, and cheese.

One week prior to the show, West End alerted Raleigh that the Club was inadvertently double booked for the McCall wedding and would not be able to fulfill its agreement to use the Club for the fashion show. West End would refund Raleigh's $10,000 for the use of the Club. What damages could Raleigh expect to receive from West End Club's breach?

Remember that damages are calculated as follows: Damages based on the expected gain from performance due under contract = (loss of profit due to other party's failure to perform or deficient performance + the value of any incidental or consequential loss due to the breach) − any expense or loss the nonbreaching party avoided by not having to perform. In essence, damages are calculated by tallying total losses and subtracting out any expenses that are avoided due to the breach.

Damages due Raleigh based on expected gain from performance under contract = ($100,000 loss of profit because of West End's failure to perform + $5,000 incidental costs for employees + $8,000 incidental costs

Compensatory damages
category of damages awards in a breach of contract with the goal of compensating the nonbreaching party for her loss with the objective of putting her in the position she would have been in if the contract had been performed as agreed.

for invitations) − $10,000 expenses avoided for catering due to reimbursement by Club.

$113,000 − $10,000 = $103,000. Raleigh would be entitled to $103,000 in damages because of West End's breach of contract.

Damages are not open ended and must be established with reasonable certainty and must be justified. Also, if a party's reliance on performance is established, then the nonbreaching party may be entitled to damages based on relying to his or her detriment on the promise.

Incidental Damages

Incidental damages arise from the breach and include any expenses that would be incurred in carrying out the agreement.

The U.C.C. and Incidental Damages
The U.C.C. provides examples of incidental damages as including shipping costs, transportation, and storing and warehousing goods. U.C.C. §2–715 states:

(1) Incidental damages resulting from the seller's breach include expenses reasonably incurred in inspection, receipt, transportation and care and custody of goods rightfully rejected, any commercially reasonable charges, expenses or commissions in connection with effecting cover and any other reasonable expense incident to the delay or other breach.

Consequential Damages

Consequential damages are damages that arise because of a party's failure to perform, resulting from the breach. These are generally limited to damages arising from not meeting the nonbreaching party's expectations as they were known at the time of contracting. They are damages that arise as a consequence of the breach.

The U.C.C. and Consequential Damages
Section 2–715 of the U.C.C. states:

(2) Consequential damages resulting from the seller's breach include
   (a) any loss resulting from general or particular requirements and needs of which the seller at the time of contracting had reason to know and which could not reasonably be prevented by cover or otherwise; and
   (b) injury to person or property proximately resulting from any breach of warranty.

Example: Mr. Thomas had a leak in his gas tank. Thomas had his car repaired at Ace Car Repair. Mr. Thomas communicated to the manager at Ace that he needed his gas tank repaired and was concerned with the gas leaking onto his garage floor. His neighbor's house caught fire due to gas leaking on the garage floor, and Mr. Thomas wanted his gas tank repaired to avoid a possible fire. Ace did not repair the tank adequately and gas leaked from the car onto Mr. Thomas's garage floor. Mr. Thomas's son was smoking a cigarette in the garage and threw the butt on the garage floor. A fire started and burned down the garage. This is a consequential damage since the garage burned down as a consequence of the failure to repair the leaking gas tank.

However, if Mr. Thomas parked his car at work and it was hit by hail during a storm, this would not be a consequential damage for it does not arise from the failure of the parties to perform based on the nonbreaching party's requirements communicated at the time the contract was entered into.

Punitive damages
damage award with the objective of punishing for a wrong committed. Rarely used in a breach of contract.

Punitive Damages

Punitive damages are usually not assessed for a breach of contract. A punitive damages award requires that the nonbreaching party was wronged or injured, which is an action in tort. This does not happen often in contract cases. Punitive damages are rarely recovered in breach of contract cases because generally compensatory and incidental damages are sufficient to compensate the injured party.

Example: The Millers contracted with Smith Funeral Homes for the funeral of Mrs. Miller's mother. The Millers' contract with Smith provided for a mahogany casket, preparation of the deceased, a closed-casket viewing for two days, funeral, and burial. Before the funeral service, Mrs. Miller requested to have one last look at her mother. The undertaker opened the casket and instead of Mrs. Miller's mother in repose, there was an elderly man. Mrs. Miller may file a complaint for breach of contract and a tort action for the infliction of emotional distress. For the breach of contract, Mrs. Miller may request compensatory damages and she may request punitive damages for the emotional distress experienced. The punitive damages would be a tort remedy and are separate from the remedies available under her breach of contract claim.

Liquidated Damages

A contract may set out in the agreement a specific amount for damages if the agreement is not performed according to its terms. This amount must be reasonable and must reflect the loss that would be due to the nonbreaching party for the failure to perform the contract as agreed. Many contracts contain a liquidated damages clause. You can find forms for the language in most formbooks and in sample contracts at your place of employment.

Example—Sample Liquidated Damages Clause:

The parties to this contract agree that if Morgan Architects breaches its promise, to build the home at 123 Main Street, Williams, Mississippi, according to plan and to comply with Williams Village Code, by failing to construct the home as planned and by failing to comply with the Williams Village Code, then Morgan Architects shall pay the sum of $100,000 to Mr. and Mrs. John Rogers as liquidated damages.

The U.C.C. and Liquidated Damages   According to U.C.C. §2–718:

(1) Damages for breach by either party may be liquidated in the agreement but only at an amount which is reasonable in the light of the anticipated

or actual harm caused by the breach, the difficulties of proof of loss, and the inconvenience or nonfeasibility of otherwise obtaining an adequate remedy. . .

(2) If the seller justifiably withholds delivery of goods or stops performance because of the buyer's breach or insolvency, the buyer is entitled to restitution of any amount by which the sum of the buyer's payments exceeds the amount to which the seller is entitled by virtue of terms liquidating the seller's damages in accordance with subsection (1)

    (a) the amount to which the seller is entitled by virtue of terms liquidating the seller's damages in accordance with subsection (1), or

    (b) in the absence of such terms, twenty per cent of the value of the total performance for which the buyer is obligated under the contract or $500, whichever is smaller.

(3) The buyer's right to restitution under subsection (2) is subject to offset to the extent that the seller establishes:

    (a) a right to recover damages under the provisions of this Article other than subsection (1), and

    (b) the amount or value of any benefits received by the buyer directly or indirectly by reason of the contract.

(4) Where a seller has received payment in goods their reasonable value or the proceeds of their resale shall be treated as payments for the purposes of subsection (2); but if the seller has notice of the buyer's breach before reselling goods received in part performance, his resale is subject to the conditions laid down in this Article on resale by an aggrieved seller . . .

Rescission

Rescinding the contract is a remedy that a party can choose. Rescinding a contract takes away the agreement between the parties and puts them in the place they were in prior to entering the contract. Once a contract is rescinded, though, there can be no action for breach for there is no longer an agreement. A rescission can be mutual or one party may elect to rescind the agreement due to impossibility of performance or due to fraud, for instance.

The Restatement (Second) of Contracts §283 states:

(1) An agreement of rescission is an agreement under which each party agrees to discharge all of the other party's remaining duties of performance under an existing contract.

(2) An agreement of rescission discharges all remaining duties of performance of both parties. It is a question of interpretation whether the parties also agree to make restitution with respect to performance that has been rendered.

Example: Mr. Wainwright wants to open a bar in New York City. Mr. Wainwright leases the property for $3,000 per month. Mr. Wainwright then tries to obtain a permit to operate the bar and tries to obtain a liquor license. Wainwright had to engage a law firm to assist him in obtaining the permit and the liquor license. In the interim, Wainwright was approached by the Saturdays chain to partner in the lease of the property. Wainwright agrees to enter into a partnership with Saturdays, so they split the rent at $1,500 each for one year. They also agree that either party can assume the lease. After three months, Wainwright expended $8,000 per month for legal fees, for a total of $24,000. Wainwright still had not obtained the permit or the liquor license. At this point Wainwright believes that he will spend more money to obtain the liquor license and the permit than he would spend on his half of the rent for the next nine months (9 × $1,500 = $13,500). Wainwright asks Saturdays to rescind their partnership agreement in the lease of the property and Saturdays agrees and assumes the lease.

Example: Sue Smith contracted to hold a reception at the Akron Club. The Akron Club and Smith entered into a binding contract to have the reception on August 2 at a total cost of $3,000. On July 3, the Akron Club burned down due to a fire. The Akron Club could rescind the contract due to impossibility.

Cover

Buyer's Rights under the Uniform Commercial Code

Cover

The right of a buyer, when the seller breaches, to obtain or purchase substitute goods and to recoup the difference, monetarily, between the original goods and the substitute goods, plus any incidental or consequential damages minus any savings that may occur in the process.

Cover is addressed in U.C.C. §2–712 and differs from common law remedies. Cover is the buyer's right, after the seller breaches, to purchase goods in substitution for the goods contracted, as long as this is done in good faith and in a timely manner.

Section 2–712 states:

(1) After a breach . . . the buyer may "cover" [sic] by making in good faith and without unreasonable delay any reasonable purchase of or contract to purchase goods in substitution due from the seller.
(2) The buyer may recover from the seller as damages the difference between the cost of cover and the contract price together with any incidental or consequential damages as hereinafter defined, but less expenses saved in consequence of the seller's breach.

Cover protects the buyer when the buyer must obtain substitute goods when the seller fails to deliver the goods promised or fails to deliver the goods. The goal is to protect the buyer by providing a remedy to obtain the goods contracted for but to acquire the goods from another party. The buyer, then, is entitled to damages equal to the difference between the contracted price and the cover price. Additionally, the buyer may be entitled to incidental damages, due to procuring the goods elsewhere, and consequential damages if determined. However, if the buyer saves money by obtaining the goods elsewhere, this amount will be subtracted from the damages. Also, for the buyer to effect cover, the buyer must either reject the goods or revoke acceptance, or the seller must fail to deliver the goods. There are many cases concerning when the buyer put the seller on notice that the goods were not delivered as promised and the buyer had to obtain goods elsewhere.

Duty to Mitigate Damages

A party will not receive damages for costs that can be avoided with modest efforts.

According to Restatement (Second) of Contracts §350, the injured party cannot recover damages for losses that could be avoided without onus, inconvenience, or shame.

Example: Marty Moore was the village manager of Winn. Moore hired Company A to plow the snow in the winter for the village for $20,000. Company A was having financial problems and its fleet of snow plows was very old and run down. In January, Company A alerted Moore that it was going out of business and would not perform the remainder of the contract. Moore received many mailings, over the past twelve months, from Company B stating that Company B would provide snow plow services for the village for $17,000. In January, Moore contacted Company B and Company B agreed to provide snow plow services for the village for the prorated amount of $15,000, since it was the end of January. At this point Moore cannot recover damages for the loss of Company A's snow plowing services for he could avoid the resulting damages without inconvenience.

Election among Remedies

Section 378 of the Restatement (Second) of Contracts states:

> If a party has more than one remedy . . . , his manifestation of a choice of one of them by bringing suit or otherwise is not a bar to another remedy unless the remedies are inconsistent and the other party materially changes his position in reliance on the manifestation.

CASE EXAMPLE—BREACH OF CONTRACT

Guided Reading Pointers

This case is on appeal. The trial court held for Triad Drywall in an action for breach of contract against Building Materials Wholesale and awarded Triad $160,000 in damages and $14,480 in attorney fees. The appellate court reversed the trial court's holding, stating that the evidence did not support the jury's award of damages, and the appellate court remanded, or sent back, the case to the trial court to reexamine the damage award. The evidence shows that Triad never signed its subcontract with Aviation and never provided evidence of lost profits. This case is interesting because it provides an example of how a court analyzes the facts to ascertain damages.

Building Materials Wholesale, Inc. v. Triad Drywall, LLC

653 S.E.2d 115 (Ga. App. 2007)

Triad Drywall, LLC sued Building Materials Wholesale, Inc. ("BMW") for breach of contract. A Fulton County jury awarded Triad $160,000 in damages and $14,480 in attorney fees. BMW appeals from the judgment entered in accordance with the verdict. For the reasons that follow, we reverse and remand for a new trial on the issue of damages for breach of contract and Triad's attorney fees claim.

. . . Triad is in the business of installing drywall, metal studs, and acoustic ceilings in commercial and large residential building projects. Triad purchased materials from a number of suppliers, including BMW. . . .

In May 2003, Triad received a letter from Aviation Constructors, Inc.in which Aviation expressed its intent to hire Triad as a subcontractor on the Bartow Center, Phase I, Floyd College project (the "Project"), conditioned upon Aviation receiving a construction contract for the Project. As part of its preparation, Triad solicited quotes from material suppliers. Through its salesman, David Dye, BMW submitted a "project quotation" for the "Floyd College Campus Phase I" which, along with a price schedule, indicated a "Bid Date: 10/22/2003," "Expires: 4th quarter 2004," and notation at the bottom that "Prices good until next manufacturer[']s increase." Triad's operation manager, Ziv Gal, contacted Dye and told him that Triad would be purchasing its material through BMW.

According to Dye, BMW's price quote was good until the end of the fourth quarter of 2004. Dye agreed that the verbal notification from Triad was an acceptable method of notifying BMW that Triad accepted the proposal, and typical in the industry. Dye also agreed that BMW expected, based on Triad's commitment, that Triad would purchase the materials.

During the Second week of January 2004, Dye informed Gal that there was a shortage of materials and market prices were going up. Dye asked Gal to place an order for the materials so that BMW could, in turn, buy the materials and avoid a cost increase to BMW. On January 20, 2004, Triad submitted a purchase order specifying the quantity of materials it needed for the Project which further stated: "As you requested, this is the material list for Floors 1 & 2. Please stock it and we will take delivery mid-February."

On January 29, 2004, BMW principal Mike Gist submitted an adjusted price schedule to Gal, stating that manufacturer price increases for building materials made the adjustments necessary and asking whether Triad wanted BMW to proceed with the order based on the adjusted prices. Gal responded that Triad expected BMW to honor its commitment to sell the material at the originally quoted prices. Gist reiterated BMW's position in a letter dated February 9, 2004, and Dye, Gal, and Gist subsequently met at Triad's office to discuss the matter. Gal informed Gist and Dye that Triad would ask Aviation for an increase in BMW's contract price to defer the rise in material costs, but otherwise Triad expected BMW to honor the original quote. After the meeting, Gist and Dye discussed "why we should sell [the material] for this amount when we can sell it for more to someone else."

Triad started work on the Project during the first week of March 2004 performing the jobs that it could while waiting for delivery of the majority of the materials. Before that time, BMW obtained liability insurance and a performance and payment bond in accordance with its agreement with Aviation.

On March 15, 2004, Aviation's project manager wrote to Triad declining Triad's request for additional monies for steel studs, and expressing his irritation at Triad for having brought the subject up after the request had been previously discussed. Aviation then indicated that Triad could sign its subcontract agreement that day and provide written confirmation of the steel stud delivery date, or Aviation would contract with another company to do the work.

Triad maintained daily contact with Dye to check on the status of the materials, which BMW received on March 17, 2004. After the materials were delivered to BMW, Gal called Aviation to schedule a delivery to the job site, but there was a delay due to several days of rain. Triad informed BMW that it was not ready for the materials, but never said that it did not want the materials. Three or four days later, BMW sold the materials to another drywall company, AFM Interior Systems, Inc., for over $ 48,000 more than had been originally quoted to Triad. Triad was unable to do its work on the Project without the materials, and Aviation awarded the Project subcontract to AFM. . .

. . . BMW challenges the jury's $ 160,000 damage award on the ground that "Triad never got a subcontract for the Floyd College project through no fault of BMW." . . . It is apparent, however, that BMW contends that the evidence was insufficient to support a recovery for consequential damages for breach of the contract between BMW and Triad arising out of Triad's inability to perform its agreement with Aviation. . .

. . .The evidence shows that Triad never signed its subcontract with Aviation. BMW argues that Triad never had a signed subcontract with Aviation because Aviation resisted Triad's attempts to "blackmail" Aviation for more money, and that Triad's loss of the subcontract could not be attributed to BMW. . . [T]he jury was authorized to find that there was an agreement between Triad and Aviation for Triad to work on the Project, and Triad was unable to perform the work because BMW breached its contract to supply materials to Triad.

. . . BMW further contends that the jury's $ 160,000 damage award was not supported by any evidence because Triad did not prove the amount of its lost profits. We agree. Typically, a plaintiff who is seeking to recover lost future profits argues that such profits would have been derived from a transaction that was never completed because of a contract breached by the defendant or a tort committed by him . . . it is incumbent on the plaintiff to show what revenues he would have obtained from the transaction, as well as the expenses he would have incurred in generating those revenues. The plaintiff must prove both anticipated revenues and expenses with reasonable certainty in order to recover.

Since Triad was seeking to recover lost profits from a transaction that was never completed, Triad was required to prove both its anticipated revenues and expenses with reasonable certainty. Evidence showed that Triad's anticipated revenue on the Project was $ 998,800, which was the amount of the contract between Triad and Aviation. Triad did not, however, show its anticipated expenses on the Project other than the cost of materials from BMW and certain insurance and payment bond costs. Rather, Ziv Gal testified that he anticipated $300,000 in profits from the Project based on a planned profit margin of 30 percent. According to Gal, "the profit that [Triad is] asking for here [is] based on the history of Triad's profit based on other jobs in the prior few years," Gal testified to the contract price, cost, and profit of four specific projects in which Triad's profit, as a percentage of the contract amount, ranged from 29 percent to 33 percent. According to Gal, Triad's average profit margin was 36 percent, although the exhibit introduced into evidence which listed Triad's profit on its various projects in 2004 and 2005 showed that profits ranged from 16 to 63 percent of project revenues. Gal also testified that Triad used all labor, material, equipment, and some overhead costs in determining its profit, but did not testify as to the anticipated amount of those costs as it related to the Project. When BMW's counsel asked Triad principal Gadi Gal if he could give the cost figures for the Project, Gal responded that "I don't have that in front of me."

Triad contends that because it had established a "track record" of profits that it could establish its lost profits by evidence of its past earnings. As a rule, anticipated profits are too speculative to be recovered, but where the business has been established, has made profits and there are definite, certain and reasonable data for their ascertainment, and such profits were in the contemplation of the parties at the time of the contract, they may be recovered even though they can not be computed with exact mathematical certainty. *Nonetheless*, to recover lost profits one must show the probable gain with great specificity as well as expenses incurred in realizing such profits. In short, the gross amount minus expenses equals the amount of recovery.

. . .Thus, evidence that Triad was a well-established, profitable business was relevant to show that it was entitled to a recovery, but Triad was also required to introduce evidence of expenses associated with its work on the Project. "[Triad] having failed to put up any evidence of [its] anticipated expenses, [its] proof of lost profits was insufficient as a matter of law." . . .

. . . In view of the foregoing, we conclude that the evidence was insufficient to sustain the jury's damage award. BMW is entitled to a new trial on the issue of damages for breach of contract. . . .

In sum, the judgment of the trial court is reversed, and the case is remanded for a new trial on the issue of damages for breach of contract and attorney fees.

Guided Reading Questions

1. What damages did Triad allege?

2. Why did BMW assert that Triad could not support its allegations of damages?

3. Are lost profits important in assessing damages? What else did Triad have to demonstrate?

Equitable Remedies

A court has the discretion to grant an equitable remedy. The goal is to achieve fairness. Equitable remedies are resorted to when there is no adequate remedy at common law. There are rules that determine when a court may grant an equitable remedy.

Doctrine of Unclean Hands

This doctrine states that a party is not entitled to relief, in **equity**, if he or she was deceitful, committed fraud, or was dishonest in the action where he or she is requesting relief, even if the other party breached the contract. A person cannot receive an equitable remedy if he or she had "unclean hands."

Laches

Equitable remedies are not available when a person or a party requesting them has sat on their rights by waiting an excessive amount of time before requesting a remedy.

Quantum Meruit

Quantum meruit is a doctrine in equity that provides that the party that performed is entitled to receive the value of his or her performance. This prevents the party that benefited under the agreement from being unjustly enriched. This is often used as the basis of a claim in equity, often called a claim in quantum meruit, stating that the party who performed is owed a reasonable amount for the value, in the form of labor and/or materials, supplied without a contract.

Adequate Remedy at Law

If there is a common law remedy available or where damages would compensate the injured party, then a party cannot seek an equitable remedy.

Equitable Remedies

Injunction, specific performance, rescission and restitution, reformation, quasi-contract remedies of quantum meruit and promissory estoppel, and waivers are equitable remedies.

What a Paralegal Needs to Know about Equitable Remedies

The determination to seek an equitable remedy is a legal decision that must be made by the supervising attorney. Most frequently, the nonbreaching party will seek common law remedies and will be awarded damages. Equitable remedies are only sought when there are no remedies available at common law or when damages will not compensate the nonbreaching party. You need to know the types of equitable remedies available in contracts disputes and the vocabulary used.

Specific Performance

Specific performance is an equitable remedy, imposed for the sake of fairness, to force a party to fulfill his or her specific obligations under the agreement. Generally, specific performance is used when the subject of the contract is unique. Examples include the sale of land, art, and antiques.

However, personal services are rarely considered so unique as to require specific performance, except maybe with an artist of the fame of, for example, Elton John.

Specific performance is not ordered by the court if the aggrieved party can obtain damages that would compensate him for his expectation interest under the contract.

Equity
A branch of the legal system that permits aggrieved parties to seek judgments on the basis of fairness and not according to the common law rules.

Example: In 2009, the remedy of specific performance was used by condominium developers in Chicago. The developers used the remedy of specific performance to require that buyers perform their obligations under the purchase contracts or at least that the developers recover the earnest money and the cost of the upgrades in finishing the condo units.

The U.C.C. and Specific Performance

Under the Uniform Commercial Code §2–716, specific performance is permitted if the buyer cannot obtain substitute goods because the goods are unique such as art or a collectible, such as a rare stamp.

Injunction

Injunction is a remedy that forbids the breaching party from doing an act or compels the breaching party to perform the act that it agreed to carry out. Often, you will hear about an injunction when there is a strike and the strikers must work.

Injunction
An remedy, in equity, used to require a party to perform or to bar a party from acting.

Reliance Issues

Detrimental Reliance

A party relies that an agreement it makes with another party will be carried out and often expends money or makes a change on the basis of the contract's successful performance. When the contract is breached or when the performance is less than anticipated and the nonbreaching party made sacrifices to enter into the agreement, then he or she is entitled to compensation. Sometimes a court of equity will impose damages when there is no contract in existence but when a party acts or performs and another party benefits, under the theory of detrimental reliance. Basically, the court as a remedy will fashion a contract and impose damages based on one party's promise and the other party's reliance on that promise to his or her detriment. Sometimes this is called a quasi-contract because the court creates a contract from the party's actions. The court sets damages in this instance to avoid a party's unjust enrichment. Under the theory of detrimental reliance, the enforcement of a promise is allowed without consideration and without a contract.

Damages for reliance are set by the court and are measured by the value that the party expected to gain when depending on the promise minus any loss, that can be reasonably proved, that the injured party would have incurred if the promise had been performed.

Restitution

Restitution puts the injured party in the position he or she would have been in prior to entering the contract. The damages are measured by the amount it would take to put the injured party in the position he or she would have been in prior to entering the agreement. However, the amount granted is limited to the benefit received, by partial performance, value, or reliance, by the uninjured party.

The Restatement (Second) of Contracts states in § 384, that:

(1) Except as stated in Subsection (2), a party will not be granted restitution unless
   (a) he returns or offers to return, conditional on restitution, any interest in property that he has received in exchange in substantially as good condition as when it was received by him, or
   (b) the court can assure such return in connection with the relief granted.
(2) The requirement stated in Subsection (1) does not apply to property
   (a) that was worthless when received or that has been destroyed or lost by the other party or as a result of its own defects,
   (b) that either could not from the time of receipt have been returned or has been used or disposed of without knowledge of the grounds for restitution if justice requires that compensation be accepted in its place and the payment of such compensation can be assured, or
   (c) as to which the contract apportions the price if that part of the price is not included in the claim for restitution.

CHAPTER SUMMARY

In this chapter you learned about the various ways that an injured party, due to a contract not being performed as agreed, can be compensated, can force the other party to perform, or can be restored to the position he or she was in prior to the agreement. There are various remedies available to the non-breaching party. Possible remedies include: damages, specific performance, injunction, rescission, and restitution. The nonbreaching party has the duty to mitigate or lessen the damages. The Uniform Commercial Code provides that the nonbreaching party effect cover, or procure substitute goods, if possible. Once a remedy is determined by the attorney, damages can be calculated. Equitable remedies are granted when there are no common law remedies available.

Remedies

Remedies in General	The purpose of remedies is to compensate the injured party when a contract is not fulfilled as promised
Breach	Material and immaterial
Damages	Generally, damages are a monetary amount given to the injured party with the intent to put him in the position he would have been in had the contract been performed or to compensate him economically or legally for the injury arising out of the contract's breach
Types of Common Law Damages for Breach of Contract	Nominal, compensatory, incidental, consequential, liquidated

Rescission	Rescinding a contract takes away the agreement between the parties and puts them in the place they were in prior to entering the contract as if no contract existed A rescission can be mutual or one party may elect to rescind the agreement due to impossibility or due to fraud, for instance
Cover	Addressed in U.C.C. § 2-712 and differs from common law remedies Section 2-712 states: "(1) After a breach . . . the buyer may 'cover' [sic] by making in good faith and without unreasonable delay any reasonable purchase of or contract to purchase goods in substitution due from the seller"
Principles of Equitable Remedies	Equitable remedies are granted according to the court's discretion and are directed at achieving a fair result Equitable remedies are used when common law remedies do not adequately compensate the nonbreaching party and when damages are unavailable
Equitable Remedies—Injunction and Specific Performance; Common Equitable Remedies Used in Contracts	Injunction—to forbid the breaching party from doing an act or to compel the breaching party to perform Specific performance, an equitable remedy, imposed for the sake of fairness, to force a party to fulfill his or her specific obligations under the agreement

REVIEW QUESTIONS

1. Is a party suing for breach of contract and damages entitled to punitive damages?
2. What are incidental damages?
3. What are consequential damages?
4. List one or more of the goals of an equitable remedy.
5. Define *cover*.
6. List two goals of remedies.
7. Define *specific performance* and state an instance when specific performance is available.
8. If a party rescinds a contract, can he avail himself of any remedies?
9. What is a party's restitution interest?
10. What is the difference between a material and an immaterial breach?

SKILL-BUILDING APPLICATION EXERCISES

Read the following fact pattern. Based on your reading of this chapter, what damages can be asserted? Write a paragraph that lists the types damages that the museum may allege and your reasons why the museum can support its claim for damages.

The Stream Museum is a major natural history museum with an esteemed board that raises millions of dollars annually for the museum. One of the board's recipients of fundraising is the New Men in Science Program. The New Men in Science Program selects two promising young men annually to perform research and to present their research findings at the Board Spring Luncheon. The New Men in Science participants each also develop an exhibit for the museum based on their research. The recipients know that future fundraising goals are supported by the success of the research and the popular presentation. The museum attracts many donors and donations because of this program. Often after the annual lecture, many donations are made due to the excitement this stirs. William Williams was selected to be one of the two New Men in Science for the 2009 calendar year. William Williams's research concerned the growth of grasses in different environments and the cellular adaptivity of grasses. Mr. Williams gave a terrific presentation and was extremely well received. The donations to the museum soared following Mr. Williams' presentation. The museum received $3.2 million dollars in donations on the basis of Williams' presentation. However, upon returning to his office, Mr. Adlai Johnson decided to research Mr. Williams and his work. It turned out that research demonstrated that Mr. Williams was suspended from high school three months before graduation due to breaking and entering the college counselor's office. Mr. Williams in fact never graduated from high school. Mr. Johnson alerted the entire board as to this information regarding Mr. Williams. The donors withdrew the entire $3.2 million in donations.

SIMULATED LAW OFFICE ASSIGNMENT

Frederick Investment Company entered into an agreement with Chicago Party Supply for chairs, tables, and linens for an investment seminar to be held at the Missouri Club on April 27. Frederick Investments relies on investment seminars to attract new clients. Frederick Investments sent out invitations for the event to 200 guests and received positive replies from 150 individuals planning on attending. On April 20, Frederick Investment Company contacted Chicago Party Rental to cancel the order because the company was under federal investigation for fraud and was barred from operating as an investment company.

What effect did this cancellation have on the contract between Frederick Investments and Chicago Party Rental?

DRAFTING EXERCISE

Write a demand letter informing the breaching party that the agreement has not been fulfilled as promised and that your firm's client will seek damages. Use the letter to Mr. Good, in this chapter, as an example. The letter should be based on the following facts:

Your firm's client is Bentley Park Crafting Custom Metals. Bentley Park has experienced tremendous growth in manufacturing due to the weak dollar. Many companies overseas that are in countries using the euro and British pound want to buy American products due to the favorable exchange rate. Bentley Park received an order from the French Company for 600 aluminum chassis used in telecommunications equipment. Bentley would receive $1,200,000 for the chassis. Bentley received the order for the chassis on March 1 and the French Company requires the chassis by September 30. As soon as Bentley received the request for the chassis but prior to accepting the order, Bentley contacted Star Aluminum Supply to make sure that Star could supply the necessary aluminum to manufacture the parts. Bentley and Star agreed that Star would provide the aluminum by June 30 and Bentley would pay Star $300,000. Bentley communicated to Star that the aluminum is necessary to fulfill an order for the chassis and that the chassis must be shipped by mid-September so that French Company receives the items by September 30. Bentley paid Star $150,000 and the remaining $150,000 is payable upon Bentley's receipt of the aluminum. Bentley did not receive the aluminum from Star on June 30. Bentley decided to wait two weeks before contacting Star. By July 15, Bentley still had not received the aluminum. Bentley's president contacted Steve Banks, an attorney at your firm, about this matter. Bentley wants Star to know that the contract was materially breached. Bentley wants the $150,000 returned. Bentley also seeks an additional $200,000 to purchase the aluminum elsewhere and $50,000 to pay for overtime for the factory workers to complete the order on time. Banks requests that you write the letter incorporating this information.

DEVELOPING CRITICAL THINKING SKILLS

Read *Building Materials Wholesale v. Triad Drywall*, reprinted in this chapter. What are the issues in the opinion, as stated by the court?

PORTFOLIO ASSIGNMENT

Northberg Public Library had seepage in the basement of the library building. The basement housed over 25,000 volumes and the library director wanted to protect the books from water damage. Northberg Library hired SureSeal Basement Specialists to make the basement watertight and to guard against future seepage and flooding. Northberg paid SureSeal $9,000 to make the basement watertight. Two weeks after SureSeal finished work, the town of Northberg was hit by a major rainstorm. Four inches of rain fell within three hours. The sewers in town could not handle the deluge of water. The library's basement flooded and all of the books were damaged by the water. The damaged books would cost approximately $3.00 per book to replace for a total of $75,000. However, the library was planning on hiring a service to weed the outdated volumes from the basement. The service would charge $1.00 per book to remove the titles. There were 2,000 outdated books to be removed.

How would the damages be measured by Northberg Library? Are there any consequential or incidental damages?

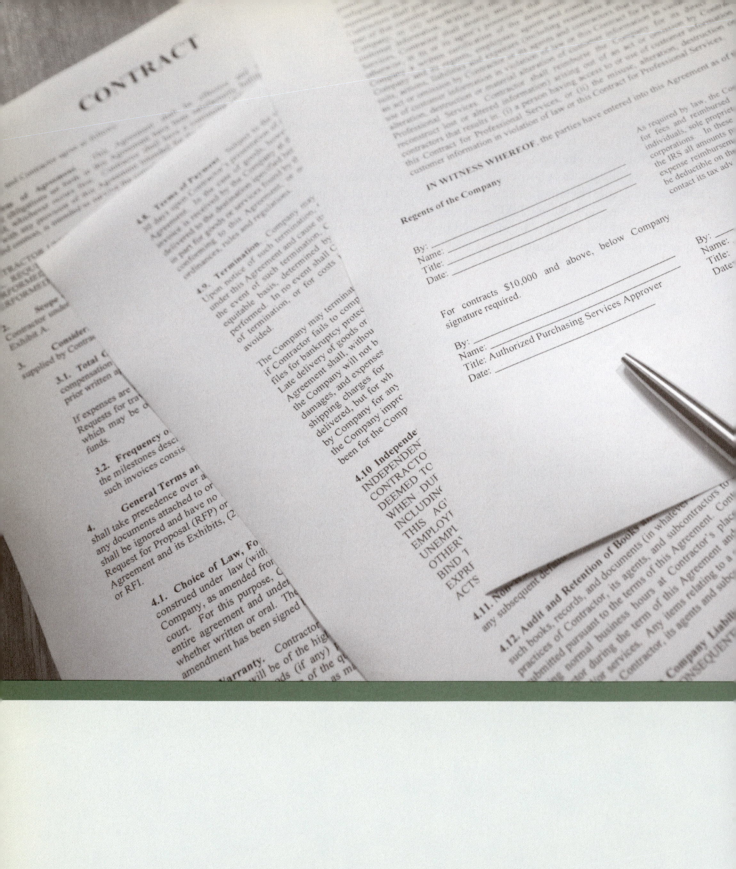

Researching and Drafting Contracts

CHAPTER 11

INTRODUCTION—RESEARCHING AND DRAFTING CONTRACTS IN GENERAL

The ability to research and draft effective, accurate contracts is a skill that is developed throughout one's career. Legal professionals are always refining their research and writing skills. As a paralegal, you will draft many documents and learn that your best writing is achieved after careful pre-writing and planning and after skillful editing and revising. This chapter will introduce you to the many skills and resources that you will need to research and to draft contracts. Since there are an unlimited variety of contracts, and each contract uniquely represents the particular deal reached by the parties, one model will not suffice. However, knowing that you can find forms and applicable authority, knowing that you will ask the supervising attorney for direction, and knowing that you will employ skills required for professional drafting, you will have an excellent start for completing a polished, accurate contract.

■ RESEARCHING CONTRACTS

Researching to locate the appropriate form to be used to draft a contract is actually the first step in drafting. As you sift through all of the available information, you are analyzing what is relevant and what can be incorporated into the contract

LEARNING OBJECTIVES

After studying this chapter, you will be able to:

1. Find sources to obtain contract forms.

2. Understand that the form selected and the document drafted sets out the parties' legal rights and obligations and must be approved by a supervising attorney.

3. Locate U.C.C. provisions in the relevant state statutes.

4. Write professionally, accurately, and clearly.

5. Understand that you must be aware of all facts pertaining to the agreement, address all issues presented, and anticipate any issues that may arise.

6. Use plain English when drafting.

so that the document reflects the agreement reached by the parties and protects their respective interests.

Material for drafting contracts is available on the Internet, in proprietary websites, in books, in looseleaf services, and in firm files. You must evaluate the value and the accuracy of the form that you select. Also, the supervising attorney should review the form to be sure that it conforms with all requirements for the particular jurisdiction. This may be even more complex when you are working in Ohio, for example, yet the parties reside in Indiana and the terms of the agreement will be carried out in Indiana as well. This will require a decision that Indiana law applies to the agreement and that if there is a dispute, then the parties will submit to the jurisdiction of Indiana courts to resolve it. This of course is a legal decision, yet as a paralegal you should note and draw the attorney's attention to any information regarding the parties' state of residence and the place where the agreement will be carried out.

Selecting the form and the resource is really the start to drafting the document. Also, researching which terms to include to capture the parties' precise agreement sets out the respective party's legal rights and obligations. For instance, choice of law affects which state's law governs the agreement. For example, some states are more lenient or liberal in certain areas of the law. Credit card companies often have credit card contracts comply with the law of South Dakota because of the favorable laws for issuers of credit cards there. Proper drafting also involves anticipating how any dispute may be handled in the event that the contract is not performed as agreed.

Forms are extremely valuable when drafting contracts. Forms provide checklists and language so that you do not have to take the time to create a contract from scratch. Forms also ensure that the contract will contain all of the necessary provisions. However, a form only goes so far in creating the contract that the parties will sign. Each form must be reviewed and customized to a certain extent to represent the unique facts and the unique agreement reached by the parties. Sometimes an excellent form only goes so far; you still must insert the unique facts that pertain to the client's agreement: the parties' names, the parties' names as doing business as (dba), the parties' addresses, date of agreement, price, quantity, and time for performance. This will usually vary in each situation no matter how routine the transaction. As a paralegal, you will obtain all of this information and check its accuracy.

■ WHERE AND HOW TO FIND FORMS

Sources for Forms

Am. Jur. Legal Forms and *West Legal Forms*, both published by Thomson-Reuters, are terrific, comprehensive, multi-volume sets with forms for almost every conceivable contract. The indices are easy to search. Additionally, the blanks provide checklists for information that you need to obtain to complete the form. Review the information that you obtained from the parties and the supervising attorney, then examine the appropriate form to be used for the contract. See if you have all of the information necessary to complete the form. Sometimes, you will not have the information that you need to complete the form, and you will have to ask the supervising attorney or the client for the missing data.

State practice guides and continuing legal education materials are also terrific resources for contracts forms. The state practice guides will often have annotations and commentary noting particular issues concerning state law. The state practice guides also have tips for practitioners.

Remember that the contracts in many form books, state practice guides, and continuing legal education materials can serve as good checklists. You can list the categories of information that must be filled in on the form and work backwards to see if you have the necessary terms and facts.

Westlaw and Lexis

Using forms and checklists obtained from Westlaw and Lexis is not only convenient but also is quite efficient. You can copy and paste a form into a Word document and then customize the form. You have enhanced search capability and you are not restricted by the access points in a printed index. You can use any term or connector that you and the supervising attorney feel is appropriate and will retrieve relevant material or hits.

Furthermore, *Am. Jur. Legal Forms* and *West Legal Forms* are available on Westlaw. On Westlaw, you will see them listed under the Forms heading on the first page of the database directory. You can use a terms and connectors query to search for forms rather than rely on an index when searching for forms online. Also, the forms are up to date and you can click on related practice aids. When researching on a proprietary databank such Lexis or Westlaw, you access the other resources published by the company. For instance, on Westlaw, when searching in Am. Jur. you will have references to *West Legal Forms*, relevant practice aids, statutes, cases, and the Uniform Commercial Code, if relevant.

On Lexis, under "Legal," then "Secondary Legal," then "Forms and Agreements," you can select either "All Transactions LexisNexis Forms" or "LexisNexis Transactions and Regulatory Checklists." Under "All Transactions LexisNexis Forms," you can check the "Contracts Law" heading and create a terms and connectors search to obtain relevant forms. You can also check the "Contracts Law" heading when searching in the "LexisNexis Transactions and Regulatory Checklists" file.

Form File

Almost every law firm and corporation has contract forms that have been used in the past. Always ask the supervising attorney if there has been a similar transaction and if you can review the contract drafted. Often, the forms are on the firm's internal computer network and they are searchable. This will provide a template for the contract that you are assigned to draft, or at least you will be able to copy and paste the wording for some provisions. Additionally, you will see the terms and provisions required for a similar contract, the type of language used, and the level of detail employed to describe the agreement. You will also have samples of the supervising attorney's drafting style for you to follow.

The Internet

You can construct a Google or Bing search to find relevant forms. It is challenging to evaluate the quality of websites and the currency of the contents. Additionally, because the sources on the Internet are quite vast, it is time consuming to sift through the incredible amount of information and some sites will charge for each form. You can start your search for a form by looking on the Internet, although this is not the most expedient way to find a form. Also, sometimes you have to pay for the form. Many sites have sample contracts that you can use as a template for the contract you are drafting. Whenever you find a sample or a form on the Internet, have the supervising attorney review it before completing the assignment. A supervising attorney must evaluate the contracts to determine if the provisions reflect current law and that the provisions comply with the law of the appropriate jurisdiction.

The Paralegal's Role

It is always best to have the supervising attorney review the form that you select. The attorney will know if the form complies with the jurisdiction's law as well. A supervising attorney must always review any contract selected, because the document you draft will capture the parties' agreement and will set out the parties' legal rights and remedies.

■ FINDING STATE LAWS

Most state laws concerning contracts are rooted in the common law if the contract does not involve merchants and the sale of goods. Common law contracts research is performed most quickly by starting with the index to the state legal encyclopedia. Also, many legal encyclopedias, both national and state, are on Lexis and Westlaw. The two national legal encyclopedias are: *American Jurisprudence*, 2nd edition, commonly called *Am. Jur. 2d*, and *Corpus Juris Secundum*, or C.J.S., both published by Thomson-Reuters. All of the research skills that you acquire in a legal research class will assist you in finding relevant state law.

Example

You want to research forms for personal service contracts. You can start your research on Westlaw in the *Am. Jur.* database, which has the full text of *American Jurisprudence*, 2nd edition. Your search is: contracts w/p personal w/1 service. This means that the term "contracts" will appear in the same paragraph as the words "personal" and "service." Also, to maintain the context, the terms "personal" and "service" will appear within one word of the other. As you scroll through the search results, you see a relevant entry on the cite list. Click on it and bring the section from *Am. Jur.* up in full text. You will see many citations to cases. Scan the citations to find cases from the jurisdiction required for your project. Also, remember that often the case listed in the encyclopedia has the broadest, most general rule from the jurisdiction. Be sure to read the actual decision if you are going to rely on it. Additionally, update and validate any case, to see if it is still good law and to see where more recent courts have cited it, by Shepardizing or KeyCiting the reference. Many publishers bundle their resources, as noted earlier. For instance, on Westlaw, when searching *Am. Jur.*, you can click on "References" and you will see many related West publications, including *Am. Jur. Legal Forms.* You will see sample forms and form drafting guides for particular contracts.

You can also find the relevant discussion in the state legal encyclopedia in the hard-copy sets and on Lexis and Westlaw. In the state legal encyclopedia, in hard copy, you will notice that there are citations to cases and often references to practice aids, including formbooks.

The Martindale Hubbell United States Law Digest is a good source for state statutory information and provides access to statute sections so that you can then consult the state statute set for more information.

Don't overlook state practice guides for sample forms as well as checklists.

Uniform Commercial Code

The easiest source to use to find relevant U.C.C. provisions is the Cornell website, www.cornell.edu/ucc/2. This website is a searchable, updated, free website for the full text of the Uniform Commercial Code, Article 2—Sales.

Where to Find State-Specific U.C.C. Provisions

Since the particular Uniform Commercial Code provision must be adopted by the respective state, you must search the appropriate state statutes to find the relevant U.C.C. provision. Forty-nine states have adopted the U.C.C. but have placed the provisions within their state statutes. The easiest and least expensive way to find the relevant U.C.C. provision is to use the following website: topics.law.cornell.edu/wex/table_ucc.

■ DRAFTING

All of the rules of good legal writing apply to drafting contracts. Review the writing mechanics covered in your legal writing class. Some general tips to keep in mind when drafting:

1. Maintain a professional voice, formal yet not pretentious.
2. Avoid the use of the first person, "I."
3. Avoid ambiguous terms, when a word has more than one meaning.
4. Avoid vague terms, when the word's meaning is unclear.
5. Use short paragraphs and include a single provision in each paragraph.
6. More time spent in the pre-writing stages of obtaining information, selecting a form, outlining, and reviewing, results in a more polished document.
7. Determine the purpose of the document, ask the attorney for a form or research to obtain a form, research to obtain checklists, have the

supervising attorney review them, complete the form, and have the supervising attorney review it prior to signing.

When drafting a contract, remember that the written agreement must capture the deal that the parties made and include all of the necessary facts and details. Always ask the supervising attorney questions about anything that you are confused by or if you need more information. Proper supervision and guidance from the supervising attorney will not only help you draft a better contract but will also avoid any issues concerning the unauthorized practice of law. Review the notes from the client conference carefully to be sure that there are adequate details. Always ask the supervising attorney for a form or a model contract that he or she would like you to use. If the firm or company does not have a model, then use a formbook. Most forms have checklists, and this will help you determine that the information is complete or if you have to obtain more information from the client. For instance, if Mr. Ray contracts with Iceland Construction to erect a wall, the contract would include such details as the date the contract was signed, identification of the parties, the date of performance, time for performance, the price, the size of the wall, its location, the thickness and length, and the materials the wall is to be composed of. If the contract merely stated that Iceland was to build a wall without any other specific terms and that the parties would work out the remaining details later, this contract would not adequately capture the deal that the parties made nor protect the parties. Your job in drafting is to be aware of all of the facts and information, address all aspects of the agreement, and anticipate any issues and eventualities that may arise.

Aware, Address, Anticipate

Be aware of all facts pertaining to the agreement, address all issues that are presented by the parties and the transaction, and anticipate any issues that may arise. With the example concerning the wall, be aware of each party's goals and terms; you must address all of the terms in the contract posed by Ray and Iceland and must stipulate the time of performance, the materials requested to build the wall, the location of the wall, the size and thickness, and the price to be paid, the consideration. If Iceland agrees to the terms offered by Ray, then a contract is formed. Issues that are presented might concern number of workers and pay per hour versus pay for the job. For instance, if this is a contract for the sale of goods, which it is not, then the Uniform Commercial Code would apply. Since this is a construction project, the parties may need to address insurance issues, and if the construction requires the workers to enter the neighbor's land, then a temporary easement may be required. The issues that parties may anticipate concern the failure to perform and types of damages. Issues to anticipate are: if the parties cannot perform due to an act of God, force majeure, or because it is commercially impractical because the price of the materials is extremely expensive so that it would be an undue hardship. Other issues that are anticipated are which state's law controls if there is a dispute, or if the parties decide that the dispute would be resolved by binding arbitration, and how damages, in the case of breach, would be calculated.

Writing Mechanics

When writing, use clear, simple, precise sentences to express the points in the contract. Always take a step back and ask if the reader, who may not be familiar with the transaction, would be able to clearly identify the parties, their roles, and the terms after reading the contract once. Although the contract is drafted to represent the parties' agreement, others may read it to enforce it. Always draft the contract so that the unfamiliar reader understands the document. Use simple language that is precise. Avoid vague terms, which are unclear, and avoid ambiguous terms, which have more than one meaning. Sometimes a contract will be in effect longer than you are employed at the firm, so draft the contract so that subsequent paralegals and attorneys can easily understand the terms and provisions. Sometimes you need to include definitions for some terms to avoid ambiguity. Use modern, formal English that is appropriate for the business environment. Avoid archaic terms and pretentious language. Additionally, be sure that the sentences are short and do not contain too many clauses. Finally, the paragraphs can also be quite short to address only a single topic in the contract; for instance, a single paragraph can contain the contract provision regarding choice of law and another paragraph will contain a provision on damages.

Sometimes you can include provisions, which have set language, called boilerplate. For example, a provision, using boilerplate language, stating that the nonbreaching party is entitled to liquidated damages is as follows: The parties to this contract agree that if Morgan Architects breaches its promise to build the home at 123 Main Street, Williams, Mississippi, according to plan and to comply with Williams Village Code, by failing to construct the home as planned and by failing to comply with the Williams Village Code, then Morgan Architects shall pay the sum of $100,000 to Mr. and Mrs. John Rogers as liquidated damages.

Archaic Contract Terms—Legalese

There are certain words and terms that appear in many contracts. In the attempt to avoid the use of legalese, many of these terms can be written in simple modern English. However, some terms, although sounding of legalese, are used because of their unique characteristics, and a single word can be used instead of a phrase—for instance, "heretofore" means previously or prior in time.

The following are common terms used in contracts that sound of legalese. Sometimes, using one of the archaic terms is more concise than writing out the meaning in plain English. Always determine if the contract is easy to follow and understand. Ask yourself if the word or term adds to the meaning or enables the reader to more clearly understand the term or provision. If not, then use plain English even if you need to substitute a phrase for a single word. See "heretofore" (previous paragraph) as an example of using a phrase in lieu of the single term. Substitute plain English whenever the reader's comprehension of the agreement will be facilitated.

Common contract terms that can be written in plain English

Foregoing—can be replaced with "already stated."
Hereof—can be replaced with "regarding this" or "from this."
Heretofore—can be replaced with "previously" or "prior in time."
Hereunder—can be replaced with "in this agreement."
Said use—can be simply conveyed as "the use of the _____ for the _____."
Therewith—can be substituted with "in connection with" or "arising from."
Whereas—means "in fact" or "this is the fact." You can just leave "whereas" out and start the sentence with the provision, for the provision itself states the point.
Wherefore—can be replaced with "that which" or just the provision itself. Often, when "wherefore" is used in a provision, just state the provision and omit "wherefore." For instance: "Mr. Tom Jones and Mr. Simon Garfunkel enter into this agreement on May 10 wherefore they agree" could be simply stated as "Mr. Tom Jones and Mr. Simon Garfunkel enter into this agreement on May 10th and agree . . ."

Find the Flaws

In the following contract, how can the sentences be revised to state the agreement in clear, modern, professional language? What is missing from the contract?

EDSEL MOTORS SAFETY TEST DRIVE WAIVER AND RELEASE

I, _____, the undersigned do hereby release, discharge, indemnify, and hold harmless Edsel, and any of their subsidiaries, officers, agents, and employees, from all claims, demands, actions, or liabilities of whatever kind and nature, including but not limited to bodily injury, death, or property damage arising from, or in any way connected to, the undersigned's use, operation, inspection, or testing of said automobile or automobiles. This also includes all costs, losses, or expenses in connection therewith arising from, or by reason of, any property damage arising out of any accident or occurrence during, or in connection with, said use, whether negligent or otherwise.

I acknowledge that I have read and fully understand all of the foregoing, and that no officer, agent, or employee of Edsel is authorized to vary the terms or provisions of this instrument, or make any representation contrary to the provisions hereof. I assume complete responsibility for all risks and for injuries, death, and/or property damage that may occur as a result of those risks, even if such injuries, death, or property damage occurs in a manner that is not foreseeable at the time I sign this release. I make these representations with the full understanding that you are relying on these representations.

I certify that I have a valid driver's license and I am authorized to drive in the state in which the Event is being conducted; I have valid automobile insurance throughout the testing period; I and all passengers in my vehicle will use available seat belts while the vehicle is being operated; I am not aware of any medical condition or other circumstance that may effect my ability to participate in the Event; and I have not consumed any alcoholic beverages or illegal substances prior to participating in the Event.

I certify that I am 21 years of age or older, with a valid driver's license.

_____ _____ _____

Print Name   Signature   Date

_____   _____

Event Location   Driver's License No.

First, look at the language and the voice here. Also, when drafting it is important to select words that precisely convey the meaning intended. Notice that legalese has been used several times. Avoid legalese and write in plain English. There is no need for "do hereby," "therewith," "said use," or "hereof." "In connection with" can be substituted for "therewith." "Said use" can be simply conveyed as "the use of the vehicle for the Event." Instead of using "hereof," the writer can directly and simply state: "to the provisions of this agreement." Remember that the parties to the contract may not think of every single term. When drafting the agreement to be signed, be sure to be clear, protect the parties, capture the agreement reached, and anticipate any issues that may arise. Be aware of the precise facts and terms of the deal, know which state law applies, or ask the supervising attorney. Clear, plain language goes a long way toward describing each party's rights and obligations.

Second, think of the components required for a valid contract—offer, acceptance, consideration, meeting of the minds, and definite and certain terms. Consideration is not mentioned in this contract. Simply adding: "I, _____, in consideration of driving/riding in one or more automobiles at the From Edsel With Love Event do hereby release, discharge, indemnify, and hold harmless Edsel, and any of their subsidiaries, officers, agents, and employees, from all claims, demands, actions, or liabilities of whatever kind and nature, including but not limited to bodily injury, death, or property damage arising from, or in any way connected to, the undersigned's use, operation, inspection, or testing of said automobile or automobiles."

Third, a date of performance is also essential. Signing the contract with a date is necessary, but also the contract should state the specific date of participation or performance.

Fourth, the use of "effect," in the third paragraph, is incorrect here. It should be "affect," which means to influence.

Polish Your Draft—the Process

Follow these pre-writing and editing steps to polish your draft.

Pre-writing and Editing Summary

1. When you receive the assignment:
   A. Clarify the purpose of the assignment.
      i. Determine the type of contract that you will draft and which state's law will apply.
   B. Audience—Generally, write succinctly, precisely, and directly. Assume that the reader is very busy yet unfamiliar with the facts and the authorities. Ask yourself if the following readers will understand the contract, even several years later.
      i. Attorney
      ii. Judge
      iii. Client
      iv. Party to the contract
   C. Clarify the assignment task—what are you writing about? Ask questions.
      i. Refine the precise question or questions you are to examine and points to include.
2. Create an outline.
   A. List the points you are to address or provisions you are to examine.
   B. Perform research—find relevant forms; find state statutes if relevant.
   C. Summarize research and facts from the client under each relevant point to be included in the contract. Compare your information with the checklist and the blanks on the form. Obtain additional information if necessary.
      i. Make sure that your citations, if applicable, are completely accurate so that the reader can find the information in the source.
      ii. Write the information, derived from the source, in your own professional voice.
      iii. Summarize the information accurately.
3. Write a rough draft using short paragraphs, where each paragraph contains a single provision.
4. Print out the draft of the contract in hard copy. Read the hard copy after taking a break from the project so that you review the document with fresh eyes.
5. Create an after-the-fact outline.
   A. Examine each paragraph.
      i. Note the point of each paragraph in left margin.
      ii. Note how each paragraph captures a facet of the agreement in the right margin.
      iii. Is the paragraph short and does it contain a single tenet of the agreement?

B. Is the authority, if applicable, accurately summarized and cited? Controlling state statute or U.C.C. provision accurately cited?

C. Is the authority relevant to the provision?

D. Do you provide adequate factual/legal context for the contract?

E. Do you include the relevant facts from the parties? Are the parties and their roles clearly identified? Are addresses and titles up to date and accurate?

F. Are the terms definite and certain?

G. Is time for performance clearly stated?

H. Is the consideration clearly identifiable?

I. Are all the portions of the form filled in with information derived from the parties?

J. Is the contract dated?

K. Did you only use precise terms and avoid ambiguous and vague terms?

L. Do you need to go back to the supervising attorney or to the client to obtain additional information?

6. Revising

A. Examine the after-the-fact outline. Write the point of each paragraph in order and insert how each paragraph conveys the components of the contract.

   i. Do the points of each paragraph present a logical statement of the agreement?

   ii. Does each paragraph advance the components of the agreement and draw the reader to the next point?

B. Do you use headings to guide the reader and to capture the point of the section or paragraph that follows? Think of the headings as you would use a table of contents to find information in a book.

C. Check the authority used. Make sure it is current.

D. Are the language, terms, and provisions clear for the unfamiliar reader?

E. Writing mechanics—read the document to check English usage and edit accordingly.

   i. Sentence fragments

   ii. Modifiers—do modifiers appropriately modify the subject of the sentence? Is this clear?

   iii. Clauses—main clauses and subordinate clauses

   iv. Diction—word choice. Are you writing in plain English?

   v. Appropriate use of legalese

   vi. SpellCheck and proofread. SpellCheck will only show where words are misspelled, but if you use "then" instead of "the," for example, you will find this only by proofreading.

F. Ask the supervising attorney to review the final draft before presenting the contract to the client.

Example–Simple Contract and Its Components

DERMATOLOGY PROFESSIONALS INDEPENDENT PHYSICIAN AGREEMENT

This Physician Agreement ("Agreement") is effective as of **January 1, 2011** (the "Effective Date"), by and between DERMATOLOGY PROFESSIONALS, LLC, a Connecticut limited liability company ("Practice") and **Nina Cray, M.D.** ("Physician"), sometimes referred to collectively as "the Parties."

Pursuant to this agreement:

1. The physician is an independent medical practitioner, specializing in the field of dermatology;

2. Practice is a professional medical practice that provides dermatology diagnostic services;

3. Practice desires to engage Physician as an independent contractor in accordance with the terms and conditions of this Agreement; and

4. Physician is agreeable to such engagement.

In consideration of the above recitals and other good and valuable consideration, the receipt and sufficiency of which are acknowledged by the parties, the parties agree as follows:

1. <u>**Provision of Services; Payments**</u>

    1.1 <u>Provision of Services</u>. Physician shall serve as the President and principle executive officer of the Practice, and shall additionally provide on request professional dermatology services such as diagnoses, consultation, and surgery as needed.

    1.2 <u>Payment for Services</u>. In full consideration for all Services performed by Physician, Practice agrees to pay Physician the Compensation and Professional Fees in the amount of $144,000 annually, disbursed, via electronic fund transfer, to physician's bank of choice, monthly in the amount of $12,000. Practice shall reimburse Physician for all expenses necessarily or incidentally incurred in his or her performance of duties under this Agreement.

    1.3 <u>Licensing Fees</u>. Practice also agrees to pay all fees, including initial application, renewal, or similar fees, necessary to secure, re-establish, or renew Physician's right to practice in Connecticut.

2. Professional Qualifications and Physician Independence

2.1 <u>Professional Qualifications and Obligations</u>. At all times during the Term of this Agreement (defined below), Physician: (a) shall maintain permanent residence in the United States (b) shall maintain Physician's status as a board certified dermatologist and (c) shall maintain his or her license in the state of Connecticut.

2.2 <u>Clinical Privileges</u> Physician shall obtain clinical privileges ("Clinical Privileges") for each medical facility requested by the Practice within a reasonable time following Practice's request. Practice agrees to provide Physician with reasonable assistance, including the preparation and submission of applications necessary to obtain Clinical Privileges at each hospital, or other medical facility designated by Practice in its sole judgment to permit Physician to provide Services at such facility.

2.3 <u>Compliance with Professional Standards</u>. Physician shall perform all Services contemplated by this Agreement in accordance with the standards of professional ethics and practice as may from time to time be applicable to the fields of medicine and dermatology, in the United States and in the state of Connecticut in which Physician holds a License, including standards promulgated from time to time by the American College of Dermatology for the practice of dermatology.

2.4 <u>Independent Contractor.</u>

a. Physician is and shall at all times remain an independent contractor to Practice. Nothing in this Agreement shall create, or be construed to create, any relationship between Physician and Practice other than that of an independent contractor. Physician hereby consents to Practice identifying Physician among Practice's independent contractor physicians on Practice's, or Practice's management company's, website.

b. Physician's obligations under this agreement relate primarily to the provision of Services as President and principle executive officer of Practice.

c. Physician acknowledges that the Health Insurance Portability and Accountability Act of 1996 and related regulations (45 C.F.R. Pts. 160 and 164 (2010)) ("HIPAA") requires Practice to establish and follow written procedures pertaining to the protection of patient information and the provision of health care services.

3. Term and Termination

This Agreement between Physician and Practice will have an initial term of three years from the Effective Date. The Agreement shall automatically renew for subsequent two year periods after the expiration of the initial period.

4. Insurance

4.1 <u>Professional Liability Coverage</u>. Practice agrees to have and maintain a policy of professional liability insurance naming Physician as an additional insured with coverages of at least the amount of Five Million Dollars ($5,000,000) per claim and Seven Million Dollars ($7,000,000) in the aggregate annually (the "Insurance"). The Insurance shall cover Physician for malpractice claims made during the term of this Agreement, based on conduct alleged to have occurred based on Services provided during the Term. Such coverage will apply only to the practice of medicine performed for Practice and specifically excludes any other practice of medicine or professional services that the Physician may engage in outside the Agreement.

4.2 <u>Separate Insurance</u>. Physician agrees to provide certificate(s) of insurance (or other proof of coverage) to Practice, upon its request, for all policies carried by Physician relating to the practice of medicine or any other professional services conducted by Physician outside of this Agreement, and agrees to provide Practice thirty (30) days prior written notice of any change in, or termination of, such separate coverage.

5. Confidentiality and Prohibition against Competition

5.1 Physician shall abide by the provisions relating to confidentiality and noncompetition as are set forth is the separate Employment Agreement between Physician and Dermatology Professionals.

6. Warranties, Indemnification, and Limitation on Damages

6.1 <u>Disclaimer of Warranties</u>. Except as otherwise expressly provided in this agreement, all services or products provided by Practice are provided without warranty of any kind, whether express, implied or arising from custom, course of dealing or trade usage, any implied warranties of non-infringement, merchantability or fitness for a particular purpose.

6.2 <u>Indemnification</u>. Each party agrees to indemnify and hold the other harmless from any and all claims, liabilities, damages, taxes, fines, repayment obligations, or expenses, including court costs and reasonable attorney fees (collectively, "Claims"), arising from any act or omission by the indemnifying party or its employees or agents (excepting the indemnified party), or from the indemnifying party's material breach of this Agreement. Without limiting the generality of the terms already stated, Physician expressly agrees to indemnify and hold Practice harmless from any and all Claims arising from any other professional services provided by or on behalf of Physician or any other work Physician may engage in outside of this Agreement.

6.3 <u>Limitation of Liability</u>. Neither Practice nor Physician shall be liable for, nor shall any measure of damages include, any indirect, incidental, special, exemplary, punitive, or consequential damages or amounts for loss of income, profits, or savings, loss of data arising out of or relating to its performance or failure to perform under this Agreement, even if the party against whom liability is sought to be imposed has been advised of the possibility of such damages or loss; provided, however, that the limitations of liability set forth this paragraph shall not apply to (i) Practice's failure to make payments to Physician for services rendered, (ii) Physician's obligations set forth in this agreement, or (iii) the reciprocal obligations of indemnification as stated in this agreement.

7. Miscellaneous

7.1 <u>Force Majeure</u>. Neither party shall be responsible for any damages, delay in performance, or failure to perform by Physician or Practice, if caused by any act or occurrence beyond its reasonable control such as embargoes, changes in government regulations or requirements (executive, legislative, judicial, military, or otherwise), acts of war or terrorism, power failure, electrical surges or current fluctuations, lightning, earthquake, flood, the elements or other forces of nature, delays or failures of transportation, or acts or omissions of telecommunications common carriers.

7.2 <u>Amendment</u>. This Agreement may be amended only by a writing that is signed by both parties.

7.3 <u>Assignment</u>. Practice may, in its sole discretion, assign this Agreement to any entity that succeeds to some or all of the business of Practice through merger, consolidation, or sale of some or all of the assets of Practice, or any similar transaction. Physician acknowledges that the services to be rendered to Practice are unique and personal and therefore Physician may not assign any rights or obligations under this Agreement.

7.4 <u>Successors and Assigns</u>. Subject to Section 7.3, the provisions of this Agreement shall be binding upon the parties hereto, upon any successor or assign of Practice, and upon Physician's heirs and the personal representative of Physician's estate.

7.5 <u>Waiver</u>. Any waiver by either party of compliance with any provision of this Agreement shall not operate or be construed as a waiver of any other provision of this Agreement or of any subsequent breach by a party of the same or another provision of this Agreement. Any delay or failure by either Party to assert a right under this Agreement shall not constitute a waiver by said Party of any right hereunder, and either Party may subsequently assert all of its rights hereunder as if the delay or failure had not occurred. No waiver by Practice shall be valid unless in writing and signed by an authorized representative of Practice.

7.6 <u>Severability</u>. If any one or more of the provisions (or portions thereof) of this Agreement shall for any reason be held by a final determination of a court of competent jurisdiction to be invalid, illegal, or unenforceable in any respect, such invalidity, illegality, or unenforceability shall not affect any other provisions (or portions of the provisions) of this Agreement, and the invalid, illegal, or unenforceable provision shall be deemed replaced by a provision that is valid, legal, and enforceable and that comes closest to expressing the intention of the parties.

7.7 <u>Governing Law, Arbitration</u>. This Agreement shall be governed by and construed in accordance with the laws of the State of Connecticut without reference to the conflict of law provisions. Any dispute, claim, or controversy arising out of or related to this Agreement shall be resolved by binding arbitration by a single arbitrator in Connecticut, in accordance with the Commercial Arbitration Rules of the American Arbitration Association then in effect. Judgment upon the arbitration award shall be final, binding, and conclusive and may be entered in any court having jurisdiction. If for any reason Physician performs Services under this Agreement outside of the United States, Physician agrees to submit to the jurisdiction of, be accountable to, and remain in compliance with all applicable state and federal law, rules, regulations, or executive orders of any U.S. or foreign government, agency, or authority, and accreditation authorities.

7.8 <u>Counterparts</u>. This Agreement may be executed by facsimile signature and by either of the parties in counterparts, each of which shall be deemed to be an original, but all such counterparts shall constitute a single instrument.

7.9 <u>Notices</u>. All notices, requests, or other communications hereunder shall be in writing and either transmitted via facsimile, overnight courier, hand delivery, or registered mail, postage prepaid and return receipt requested, to the parties at the address listed below their respective signatures or such other addresses as may be specified by written notice. Notices shall be deemed to have been given when received or, if delivered by registered mail, five days after posting.

7.10 <u>Equitable Relief</u>. The parties acknowledge that their remedies at law for any breach or threatened breach of this Agreement may be inadequate. Therefore, a party shall be entitled to seek injunctive and other equitable relief restraining a party from violating this Agreement, in addition to any other remedies that may be available to it under this Agreement or applicable law.

7.11 <u>Entire Agreement</u>. This Agreement, including any attached Exhibits, schedules, and appendices (which are hereby incorporated into the Agreement), constitutes the entire agreement between the parties hereto with respect to its subject matter and there are no other representations, understandings, or agreements between the Parties relating to such subject matter.

7.12 <u>Services Provided Prior to Effective Date</u>. Except with respect to compensation, the Parties acknowledge that any Services provided by Physician prior to the Effective Date of this Agreement are covered by the terms herein. Physician acknowledges that any compensation owed for Services performed prior to the Effective Date of this Agreement shall be covered, if at all, by separate agreement.

I have witnessed that the parties have executed this Agreement effective as of the Effective Date.

_____

Sandra Smith, Witness   Date

Notary Seal_____

DERMATOLOGY PROFESSIONALS, LLC,

A Connecticut limited liability company

By: /s/ Nina Cray
           Sean O. Casey, M.D., President
Date:

Address:
12 Colonial Way
Danbury, Connecticut 06811
203-756-6565

■ MISCELLANEOUS PROVISIONS THAT APPEAR IN MOST CONTRACTS

As the previous example indicated, when a provision is characterized as miscellaneous, it is still important and affects the rights and obligations of the parties. The clauses fall into the miscellaneous category because they are stated after the specific terms of the particular contract. Often, people call these provisions "boilerplate" because the wording of the provision, or the language, is standardized and the parties do not have to draft unique language to express the particular term, such as submitting to arbitration, for example. However, remember that the decision to include any or all of the miscellaneous provisions available is a legal decision to be made by the supervising attorney because it will impact a party's legal rights.

Sample Miscellaneous Provisions Using Boilerplate Language

Example–Arbitration

If a dispute arises out of or related to this agreement, the parties to this contract agree first to try in good faith to settle the dispute by mediation under the Commercial Mediation Rules of the American Arbitration Association.

If there is any remaining unresolved controversy or claim, it shall be settled by arbitration in accordance with the Commercial Arbitration Rules of the American Association, and judgment shall be binding, replacing the right to go to court.

Example–Breach

The following constitutes a "breach" of this contract: (1) Buyer fails to pay Seller any moneys when due as required by this agreement; or (2) Buyer ceases to conduct its operation in the normal course of business, voluntarily files a petition in bankruptcy or makes a general assignment for the benefit of creditors, a receiver is appointed for Buyer or a petition in bankruptcy is filed against Buyer, or Buyer becomes insolvent or fails to pay indebtedness when due.

Example–Choice of Law and Submission to Jurisdiction

This agreement shall be governed by, and construed in accordance with, the law of the State of _____. Each party consents to personal jurisdiction and venue in the state and federal courts located in _____ with respect to any actions, claims, or proceedings arising out of or in connection with this agreement.

Example–Indemnities

Except as otherwise expressly provided in this contract or any attachment to this contract, Seller shall indemnify and hold Buyer and the property of Buyer, including the assets, free and harmless from any and all claims, liability, loss, damage, or expense resulting from Seller's ownership of the assets or Seller's operation of the assets, including any claim, liability, loss, or damage arising by reason of the injury to or death of any person or persons, or the damage of any property, caused by Seller's use of the assets, the condition of the assets when owned by Seller, or the defective design or manufacture by Seller of any product or products.

Example–Integration, Sample 1

This instrument with its attachments constitutes the entire agreement between Buyer and Seller respecting the assets or the sale of the assets to Buyer by Seller, and any agreements or representation respecting the assets or their sale by Seller to Buyer not expressly set forth in this instrument are null and void.

Example–Integration, Sample 2

This contract is intended by seller and buyer as the complete, final expression of their agreement concerning its subject matter. It supersedes all prior understandings or agreements between the parties and may be changed only by a writing signed by seller and buyer. No course of dealing, or parole, or extrinsic evidence shall be used to modify or supplement the express terms of this contract.

Example–Liquidated Damages Clause

The parties to this contract agree that, if Morgan Architects breaches its promise to build the home at 123 Main Street, Williams, Mississippi, according to plan and to comply with Williams Village Code, by failing to construct the home as planned and by failing to comply with the Williams Village Code, then Morgan Architects shall pay the sum of $100,000 to Mr. and Mrs. John Rogers as liquidated damages.

Example–Severability, Sample 1

If any provision of this contract is found to be illegal, invalid, or unenforceable, that provision shall be enforced to the maximum extent permitted, but if fully unenforceable, that provision shall be severable, and this Contract shall be construed as if that provision had never been a part of this Contract, and the remaining provisions shall continue in full force and effect.

Example–Severability, Sample 2

If any provision of the agreement is found invalid, the remainder of the agreement will remain in effect.

Example–Term

The Term shall begin on the date of this agreement and shall end at midnight on _____ Date _____.

Example–Termination

Either party may terminate this agreement in writing with sixty (60) days or more notice to the other person. In addition, either party may terminate this agreement immediately on written notice in the event that the other person violates any law, state or federal, or files for bankruptcy.

Example–Effect of Termination

On termination or expiration of this contract, each party's rights and obligations, as stated and established in this contract, shall be extinguished.

Example–Waivers

No claim or right arising out of a breach of this contract can be discharged in whole or in part by a waiver or renunciation of the claim or right unless the waiver or renunciation is in writing, is signed by the aggrieved party, and is supported by bargained-for consideration.

Example–Warranties

The Seller disclaims all warranties, guaranties, and requirements to which the goods under this contract must conform, including any express or implied warranty concerning these goods, warranties for title, merchantability, and fitness for a particular purpose.

■ TICKLER SYSTEM

After the contract is approved by the supervising attorney and after the agreement is signed, a paralegal should set up a tickler system. The tickler system has all necessary follow-up dates stated in the agreement, including contingencies and conditions of performance. Also in the tickler file is all contact information for the parties to the agreement, including current addresses, email addresses, telephone numbers, and fax numbers.

■ RESOURCES AND REFERENCE SOURCES

Books to Consult

Basic Legal Writing for Paralegals, 3rd ed., by Hope Samborn and Andrea Yelin (WoltersKluwer, 2009).

Legal Research, Analysis & Writing, 3rd ed., by Joanne Banker Hames (Pearson Prentice Hall, 2008).

Legal Research and Writing Handbook: A Basic Approach for Paralegals, 5th ed., by Andrea Yelin and Hope Samborn (WoltersKluwer, 2009).

Legal Writing in Plain English, by Bryan A. Garner (University of Chicago Press, 2001).

Modern Legal Drafting: A Guide to Using Clearer Language, by Peter Butt and Richard Castle (Cambridge University Press, 2006).

Real World Document Drafting: A Dispute-Avoidance Approach, by Marvin Garfinkel (ALI-ABA, 2008).

CHAPTER SUMMARY

One of the primary goals of your research is to find a usable form and to modify it to reflect the agreement reached by the parties. You can consult in-house form files, you can ask the supervising attorney for a similar contract to mark up, you can consult *Am. Jur. Legal Forms* and *West Legal Forms* in hard copy and on Westlaw, you can consult practice guides and state continuing legal education materials, and you can search Lexis to find forms. Remember that any form selected must be approved by the supervising attorney because the selection of the form will legally impact the parties, as it sets out the parties' legal obligations and rights.

When drafting a contract, be sure that the terms express the precise agreement between the parties and their expectations from performance. Use simple, clear language. Avoid legalese. Assess the contract's purpose, research to find forms and checklists, consider your audience, outline, edit, and revise. Leave time for the supervising attorney to review the final draft.

Researching and Drafting Contracts

Researching Contracts	Common law sources of authority—to locate, use national legal encyclopedias such as *Am. Jur. 2d* and *C.J.S.*, both published by Thomson-Reuters For specific state common law, consult state legal encyclopedias For statutory authority: state statutes; Martindale Hubbell United States Law Digest; U.C.C. provisions adopted by the particular state—Cornell website, www.cornell.edu/ucc/2
Paralegal's Role	Find forms, update and find accurate information, fill in form, have attorney review draft
Drafting	Mechanics—use professional voice, avoid legalese, use plain English, use simple sentences, use short paragraphs, avoid vague and ambiguous terms, use headings
Editing	Consider your audience—would the reader understand the contract after a single reading? Create an after-the-fact outline Check if authority is accurately summarized and cited Are all facts relevant? Are all parties identified accurately, with current addresses? Are the terms definite and certain? Is time for performance clearly stated? Is the consideration clearly identifiable? Are all the portions of the form filled in with information derived from the parties? Did you only use precise terms and avoid ambiguous and vague terms?

Revising	Present provisions logically
	Writing mechanics—read the document to check English usage and edit accordingly
	
	  i. Sentence fragments
	  ii. Modifiers—do modifiers appropriately modify the subject of the sentence? Is this clear?
	  iii. Clauses—main clauses and subordinate clauses
	  iv. Diction—word choice. Are you writing in plain English?
	  v. Appropriate use of legalese
	  vi. Spellcheck and proofread.
	
	Ask the supervising attorney to review the final draft before presenting the contract to the client

Goals in Drafting Contracts	Be aware of all facts, legal authority, issues, and terms Address all points raised by the parties to reflect the agreement reached Anticipate any eventuality that may realistically arise
Tickler System	Follow-up dates Contingencies and conditions All contact information for parties to contract

EXERCISES

Note that the following exercises, designed to reinforce your drafting skills, depart from the format used in earlier chapters. These exercises are designed to help you understand and use the knowledge that you have acquired.

SKILL-BUILDING APPLICATION EXERCISE

Read the following hypothetical situation carefully. Establish a list of terms that the parties agreed to. Evaluate whether the parties have a contract, use a form book to find a template for an applicable contract, and draft a contract that reflects the parties' agreement.

Dan White purchased a computer from Computer Services for $2,000 on January 15, 2010. The computer came with a warranty that the computer would be fixed without charge for one year from the time of purchase. Additionally, Computer Services provides lessons to the purchaser on the use of the system for as long as the purchaser requires lessons. Mr. White purchased the computer system from Computer Services based on these promises. Mr. White could have purchased the computer for less money elsewhere but wanted the one year of repairs and the indefinite number of lessons. Computer Services made this promise and has this information about the repairs and lessons on the receipt. Computer Services accepted $2,000 from Mr. White and Mr. White received the computer.

Accepted

_____

Mr. Blake Shaw

CONSULTING SERVICES AGREEMENT USED WORDS, LLC

FROM BEADS TO BLING

This Consulting Services Agreement (the "Agreement") is dated as of December 19, 2009, by and between Beads to Bling ("Contractor") and Craft Store ("Client") (collectively the "Parties").

The Parties agree as follows:

1. **SERVICES:**
   Contractor will perform the consulting services described below (the "Services"): Beads to Bling Representative will provide a two-hour workshop from 6:00 P.M. to 8 P.M. on November 1, 2010, at Craft Store instructing workshop participants on the creation of a beaded project. Other services to be arranged as agreed, etc.

2. **TIME OF COMPLETION:** *(mark the applicable provision)*
   The Services shall be commenced on or before November 1, 2010.

3. **EQUIPMENT:** *(mark the applicable provision)*
Client shall provide the following equipment for Contractor's use when performing the Services: <u>LCD projector and screen for PowerPoint presentation, sound system.</u> Contractor will provide all other equipment necessary to perform the Services.

4. **PAYMENT:** *(mark the applicable provision)*
Client shall pay Contractor for the material and labor to be performed under this Agreement the sum of <u>Two thousand five hundred Dollars</u> (<u>$2500.00</u>). Full payment is due within thirty (30) days.

5. **OTHER EXPENSES/ACCOMMODATIONS:** Client shall reimburse Contractor for the following expenses: <u>Travel expenses November 1–2, 2010.</u>

Client shall be responsible for providing only the following accommodations to Contractor in connection with Contractor's performance of the Services: <u>Accommodations November 1, 2010: One nonsmoking room with Internet access.</u>

6. **GENERAL PROVISIONS:**
   (a) Contractor is an independent contractor and not an employee of Client.
   (b) Any changes to this document must be signed by both Contractor and Client.
   (c) This Agreement shall be construed in accordance with the laws of the state of Washington.

IN WITNESS WHEREOF the Parties have executed this Agreement on the date first written above.

CLIENT: **CONTRACTOR:**

_____   _____
Signature   Signature

_____   _____
Name (please print)   Name (please print)

_____   _____
Title (if applicable)   Title (if applicable)

_____   _____
Date   Date

What could be added to this contract to indicate that the parties anticipate any issues that could arise? How can you revise this contract in plain English?

SIMULATED LAW OFFICE ASSIGNMENT

An attorney in your office requests your assistance with the following situation. Mr. Shaw, a firm client, wants to have a deck built on the back of his house. Shaw contacted American Carpenters to have a custom deck built. American Carpenters sent an estimator to look at the project and to derive a price for the work and materials. Shaw wants the patio furniture that he currently owns to fit on the new deck. Shaw also wants the work to be completed by Memorial Day so that he has the entire summer to enjoy the deck.

American Carpenters sent the following letter to Shaw to be signed and returned. Please read over the letter and insert additional provisions that capture the agreement between the parties. Also, revise the agreement to reflect Shaw's expectations at the time of the contract.

March 15, 2011

American Carpenters
900 Michigan Avenue
Detroit, Michigan

Dear Mr. Shaw:

The purpose of this letter is to put into writing the agreement we reached regarding the construction of the deck at your home. To begin work, I require a $1,000 deposit prior to construction to purchase materials. The entire job will cost $5,000. The $5,000 includes labor, materials, site preparation, and pouring the concrete base.

According to our discussion at your home, we can begin work on the deck on April 21 as long as the ground is not frozen. The entire construction process should take ten (10) business days. We plan on completing the project on May 2. We will comply with local ordinances and not begin work prior to 7 A.M. on weekdays, 8 A.M. on Saturdays, and 12 noon on Sundays. Additionally, we will fence in the entire work site.

The proposed deck will measure 10' by 15'; an have an elevation of 14'. The composition shall be redwood and have a concrete poured base on each pillar.

American Carpenters insures our workers fully. American will cart any debris and leave the premises completely clean after the finished job.

Cancellation of this job within five (5) days of performance will require forfeiting the deposit.

All cancellations must be done prior to April 16. Payment of the outstanding $4,000 is due upon completion of the deck.

If you are in agreement with the terms contained in this letter, please sign and return the enclosed copy of this letter to American Carpenters, together with your check for $1,000.

Sincerely,

Joe Fern
d/b/a
American Carpenters

Accepted

_____

Mr. Blake Shaw

DRAFTING EXERCISE

Use the following fact pattern to draft a simple contract containing the terms agreed upon for both parties to sign. Use a formbook to find a form to use to draft the agreement.

Mr. Bussell has a Colorado Closet Company that specializes in designing and organizing closets.

Mr. Bussell hired Sam Michaels as a carpenter to work daily from 3 P.M. to 7 p.m. installing custom closets. This time was selected due to many customers' work schedules. Mr. Michaels would be paid $25.00 per hour and work twenty (20) hours per week. Mr. Bussell would not provide any benefits for Mr. Michaels. Mr. Bussell and Mr. Michaels agreed that Mr. Michaels would work for a total of twenty (20) weeks beginning on January 2, 2008. Mr. Bussell would provide the tools, materials, transportation, design, and customers. Mr. Michaels would install the closets according to the design provided by Mr. Bussell.

Your firm represents Mr. Bussell.

DEVELOPING CRITICAL THINKING SKILLS

Review the following publishing agreement. Insert additional provisions reflecting the expectations that each party had at the time of entering into the contract.

Mr. Steven Young was contacted by XYZ Publishers to write a marketing textbook. Mr. Young wants to write the book and XYZ needs the title for its list. Mr. Young met with Mr. James Andrews, Acquisitions Editor for XYZ Publishing, to discuss the agreement and the proposed textbook.

Mr. Young requested that XYZ would provide a $6,000 grant to write the text. Mr. Young asked that the grant be paid upon signing the contract. Additionally, Young requested that any research and travel expenses incurred to write the text be reimbursed by XYZ. Mr. Andrews discussed Young's requests with senior management at XYZ and then emailed Young to say that the terms would be included in the contract. Young received the agreement but the additional terms were not included. Please revise the agreement to add the additional terms.

PUBLISHING AGREEMENT

This agreement, made and entered into as of this 20th day of May, 2010, by and between XYZ Publishers ("XYZ"), a Delaware corporation, having offices at 3000 Berkeley Road, Chicago, Illinois 60610, and the following author Steven Young (the "Author"). The Author and XYZ declare each declare the desire to act under this Agreement in an atmosphere of mutual respect and cooperation in an effort to achieve the professional standards and commercial success that each party deserves.

1. Grant of Rights. Steven Young agrees to prepare a work on Business Marketing. You grant and assign exclusively to XYZ this work and all rights to this work and its component parts, revisions, and subsequent editions that are now in existence or are created in the future in all languages and in all forms, for the full term of the copyright. This grant includes the exclusive rights to reproduce, print, distribute, promote, publish, sell, license, broadcast, or transmit, in all channels and media developed currently or in the future.

2. Delivery. Steven Young agrees to deliver the text, Business Marketing, in complete final form ready for production by September 1, 2010. Steven Young and XYZ agree that the text will consist of 300 pages.

3. Royalty. Based on the net cash received by XYZ or its affiliate from the sale of the Work, XYZ will pay Steven Young a royalty of 20%.

4. Royalty Statement. XYZ will furnish Young with a royalty statement on or about March 31 and September 30 of each year for the six-month period ending in December or June of each year respectively. With each statement XYZ will pay Young the royalties due for the respective six-month period.

Signature

_____

_____

Steven Young, Author   XYZ Publishers

Date _____   James Andrews, President

                                          Date _____

PORTFOLIO ASSIGNMENT

The attorney you work for requests that you examine the following scenario. The attorney wants you to list the terms of the contract, from the facts presented, and to tell the attorney if the contract appears to be a gratuitous promise or truly a contract. Please draft a short memo stating your findings.

Mr. Paul Gain of Gain Electric purchased a photocopier, from Copier Universe, for the office of Gain Electric. The copier was new when purchased. Mr. Gain did not sign a purchase agreement and did not purchase any extended warranties. Additionally, Mr. Gain did not purchase a service agreement at the time of the sale. The copier came with a 90-day warranty for parts and labor.

Mr. John Shaw sold the copier to Mr. Gain on July 10, 2009. When Shaw sold the copier Shaw assured Gain that the copier was a terrific machine and extremely dependable. The machine was so dependable that an extended warranty was not necessary. Additionally, because the copier was so reliable a service agreement was also unnecessary. Shaw stated that since this copier was so sturdy and reliable that Copier Universe would repair the copier, in the unlikely event that a malfunction should occur, for the first two years of operation. Mr. Gain tried to make a copy on January 2, 2010. Gain turned on the machine and after the machine warmed up, Gain heard clicks. The clicking would not stop and the machine would not make copies. Gain immediately called Copier Universe and requested that the copier be repaired, at no cost, as promised by Shaw. Greg Jones, owner of Copier Universe, spoke with Gain. Jones informed Gain that Shaw no longer worked for Copier Universe. Jones inquired if Gain purchased a service contract when he procured the copier. Gain stated again the assurances that Shaw made at the time of purchase.

Shaw said that Copier Universe would be willing to repair the copier at a cost of $50 per hour for labor plus parts. Shaw felt badly for Gain and offered to pick up and deliver the copier at no charge. Gain asked the attorney at your firm to evaluate the situation to see if he had an agreement for service.

This appendix provides a sample click-and-accept agreement in full, and descriptions of two other sample contracts for commonly encountered agreements. All of the agreements share a single feature in that they are all contracts of adhesion. A contract of adhesion requires that the offeree must accept the terms tendered and has no bargaining or negotiating rights.

■ CLICK AND ACCEPT

Many contracts on the Internet, particularly for software and for credit card purchases, require a click to accept the terms of the agreement rather than the traditional signature and reply. The click-and-accept format does not allow for any negotiation or for any modification of any term or condition. Most states now allow assent, particularly by a consumer, to the terms of the contract by clicking "accept" by pushing a button or clicking a mouse.

The following is a sample click-and-accept agreement. Individuals must sign agreements of this type to purchase goods and to use software. Note that the offeree has no choice as to the terms and cannot make a counteroffer with different terms.

StayInn Motels Pre-paid Stay Agreement

Advance Purchase, $169.00 U.S.D. per night, plus applicable local taxes, for 2 Queen Beds—1 room, June 19, 2011, Arrival, June 20, 2011, departure.

Complete Restrictions and Rules

FULL PAYMENT IN ADVANCE/NO REFUNDS: FULL PAYMENT IS REQUIRED FOR THIS RESERVATION AT THE TIME OF BOOKING; YOUR CREDIT CARD WILL BE CHARGED IMMEDIATELY IN U.S. DOLLARS FOR THE TOTAL AMOUNT QUOTED FOR THE ENTIRE STAY AS RESERVED AND NO REFUNDS OR CREDITS WILL BE ISSUED. CHARGES CANNOT BE APPLIED TO OTHER STAYS, SERVICES, OR MERCHANDISE. NO PRICES OR HOTEL AVAILABILITY ARE GUARANTEED UNTIL FULL PAYMENT IS RECEIVED. EVEN AFTER FULL PAYMENT HAS BEEN RECEIVED, WE RESERVE THE RIGHT TO CANCEL A RESERVATION WITHOUT NOTICE IF WE BECOME AWARE OF OR ARE NOTIFIED OF ANY FRAUD OR ILLEGAL ACTIVITY ASSOCIATED WITH THE PAYMENT FOR THIS RESERVATION.

RESERVATION CANNOT BE MODIFIED: PRICE QUOTED APPLIES TO EXACT DATE(S)/NIGHTS/STAY BOOKED. MODIFICATIONS TO

YOUR RESERVATION (INCLUDING BUT NOT LIMITED TO NAME CHANGES, DATE CHANGES, ETC.) ARE NOT PERMITTED.

EARLY DEPARTURE/CANCELLATION: IF YOU DEPART EARLY OR YOU CANCEL OR FAIL TO HONOR THIS RESERVATION FOR ANY REASON, YOU WILL NOT RECEIVE ANY CREDIT OR REFUND.

EXTENDING YOUR STAY: EXTENSIONS WILL REQUIRE A NEW RESERVATION FOR THE ADDITIONAL DATE(S), SUBJECT TO AVAILABILITY AND PREVAILING RATES AND THIS RATE SHALL NOT APPLY.

PRICE DOES NOT INCLUDE: THE PRICE YOU SELECTED IN-CLUDES ROOM RATE AND APPLICABLE TAXES ONLY AND DOES NOT INCLUDE ANY APPLICABLE SERVICE CHARGES OR CHARGES FOR OPTIONAL INCIDENTALS (INCLUDING BUT NOT LIMITED TO GRATUITIES, FOOD AND BEVER-AGE, PARKING, MINIBAR CHARGES, AND OTHER OPTIONAL INCIDENTALS).

OTHER RESTRICTIONS: THIS RATE IS NOT COMBINABLE WITH ANY OTHER OFFERS AND PROMOTIONS AND IS NOT AVAILABLE TO GROUPS. THIS RATE IS NON-COMMISSIONABLE. IF YOU FAIL TO ARRIVE AT THE HOTEL ON THE SCHEDULED ARRIVAL DATE, YOUR RESERVATION WILL BE CANCELLED AND YOU WILL NOT RECEIVE ANY REFUND OR CREDIT.

| By pressing CLICK–This Button, I accept the rules and restrictions of this offer and agree to have my credit card charged $169.00 plus the applicable taxes. | **Click and Accept** |

Following is a brief outline of the typical contents of a credit card agreement. The full agreement is available at www.pearsonhighered.com/yelin.

■ CARDMEMBER AGREEMENT

Acceptance of This Agreement

This agreement governs your credit card account with us referenced on the card carried containing the card for this account. Any use of your account is covered by this agreement. Please read the entire agreement and keep it for your records. You authorize us to pay for and charge your account for all trans-actions made on your account. You promise to pay us for all transactions made on your account, as well as any fees or finance charges. If this is a joint account, each of you, together and individually, is responsible for paying all amounts owed, even if the account is used by only one of you. We may require that you pay the full amount owed without first asking the other person(s) to pay. . . .

USING YOUR ACCOUNT
Types of Transactions:
Billing Cycle:
Authorized Users:
Credit Line:
International Transactions:
Refusal to Authorize Transactions:
Refusal to Pay Checks:
Lost or Stolen Cards, Checks, or Account Numbers:

PAYMENTS

FINANCE CHARGES
Grace Period and Accrual of Finance Charges:
Transaction Fees for Cash Advances:

OTHER FEES AND CHARGES
Annual Membership Fee:
Late Fee:
Overlimit Fee:
Return Payment Fee:
Return Check Fee:
Administrative Fees:

DEFAULT/COLLECTION
CLOSING YOUR ACCOUNT
ARBITRATION AGREEMENT
CHANGES TO THIS AGREEMENT
CREDIT INFORMATION
NOTICES/CHANGE OF PROFESSIONAL INFORMATION
TELEPHONE MONITORING AND RECORDING
INFORMATION SHARING
ENFORCING THIS AGREEMENT
ASSIGNMENT
GOVERNING LAW
YOUR BILLING RIGHTS
RATES AND FEES TABLE

Following is a brief outline of the typical contents of a leasing agreement.
The full document is available at www.pearsonhighered.com/yelin.

RESIDENTAL LEASE

Property Address:

Tenant(s):   SSN: Lessor:

APPLICATION AND OCCUPANCY NOTICE TO TENANT

Tenant acknowledges that this Lease has been extended to Tenant pursuant to
an application therefore submitted by Tenant. The accuracy of the information
therein contained is a material condition of Lessor in extending this Lease

to Tenant. Tenant warrants that all information given by Tenant in applying for this Lease is true and acknowledges that providing false information is a material breach of this Lease. Occupancy by more persons as set forth in this Lease or application shall constitute a material breach of this Lease.

NOTICE OF CONDITIONS AFFECTING HABITABILITY

Tenant hereby acknowledges that Lessor has disclosed any code violations, code enforcement litigation, and/or compliance board proceedings during the previous twelve (12) months for the Apartment and common area and any notice of intent to terminate utility service, copies of which, if any, are attached to this lease.

ASSENT TO AGREEMENT

On this date, as set forth above, in Chicago, Illinois, in consideration of the mutual agreements and covenants set forth below and on all pages attached hereto, including the "Rider to Lease" (all of the same being fully included as part of this Lease), Lessor hereby leases to Tenant and Tenant hereby leases from Lessor for use in accordance with Paragraph 8 hereof the Apartment designated above, together with the fixtures and accessories belonging thereto, for the above Term. All parties listed above as Lessor and Tenant are herein referred to individually and collectively as Lessor and Tenant respectively.

SIGNATURES

TENANT(S)   **LESSOR**

_____   _____

_____

LEASE COVENANTS AND AGREEMENTS

1. RENT:
2. LATE AND RETURNED CHECK CHARGES:
3. SECURITY DEPOSIT:
4. POSSESSION:
5. CONDITION OF PREMISES:
6. LESSOR TO MAINTAIN:
7. TENANT'S DUTY TO INSURE/LIMITATION OF LIABILITY:

8. USE OF PREMISES:

9. TENANT TO MAINTAIN:

10. UTILITIES:

11. APPLIANCES:

12. ALTERATIONS, ADDITIONS, FIXTURES, APPLIANCES, PERSONAL PROPERTY:

13. SECURITY GATES OR BARS:

14. DISTURBANCE:

15. RULES AND REGULATIONS:

16. ACCESS TO PREMISES:

17. FIRE AND CASUALTY:

18. EMINENT DOMAIN (CONDEMNATION):

19. SUBLET OR ASSIGNMENT:

20. HOLDING OVER:

21. ABANDONMENT:

22. FORCIBLE DETAINER:

23. LIABILITY FOR RENT:

24. SUBORDINATION OF LEASE:

25. MECHANIC'S LIEN:

26. BINDING EFFECT:

27. TERMINATION AND RETURN OF POSSESSION:

28. NOTICES:

29. ATTORNEY'S FEES:

30. LESSOR'S REMEDIES:

31. REMEDIES CUMULATIVE, NON-WAIVER:

32. PROMISES OF THE PARTIES:

33. SEVERABILITY:

34. OTHER PROVISIONS:

RULES AND REGULATIONS

RIDER TO LEASE

1. Lease can be cancelled by Lessor 120 days after written notice is given by Lessor to Tenant if Building is to be refurbished, demolished, etc.

GLOSSARY

acceptance   Consenting to the terms of an offer

accord   An agreement.

adequate   Sufficient.

adhesion contract   A contract that does not permit the promisee to negotiate the terms. Basically, it requires the promisee to "take it or leave it."

arbitration   The resolution of a dispute by a third party, usually a mediator rather than in a courtroom by a judge.

assignment   To transfer the benefits or rights under a contract to another party who is not an original party to the agreement.

assumpsit   A common law action to recover damages for not performing; the non-performance of a contract.

bargain   A mutually agreed and negotiated agreement.

beneficiary   One who will obtain the advantage or value from the contract.

benefit   Gain.

bilateral   Both parties bound where there is a contract composed of a promise for a promise.

breach   A failure by one or more parties to an agreement to honor the terms of the accord.

capacity   The capability to understand one's obligations.

certain   Distinct, clear, and free from ambiguity.

choice of law   Selecting which jurisdiction's legal authority will control the contract.

codes or statutes   Rules of law enacted by governmental bodies such as the U.S Congress on the federal level or the state legislature. Once the rules are enacted by the legislature, the rules are then added to the jurisdiction's code, also called statutes. The process of inserting legislation into the code is called codification. Codes are commonly called statutes.

collateral   Either personal or real property that is used as security for a loan.

common law   Legal rules derived from judicial opinions or cases.

compensatory damages   Category of damages awards in a breach of contract with the goal of compensating the nonbreaching party for her loss with the objective of putting her in the position she would have been in if the contract had been performed as agreed.

condition   An event that is to happen or has happened that affects or triggers a legal obligation.

consideration   The value sought by the parties to enter into a contract that cements the agreement and binds the parties. Value given to induce a promise; sometimes the value is forsaking something.

contract   A binding agreement between two parties, who have the capacity to contract, that has a valid offer, acceptance, and adequate consideration.

counteroffer   An offer made in reply to an offer. A counteroffer is made in response to an offer but has different terms than the original offer.

course of dealing   In a business transaction, or in a contract between merchants, the parties' prior conduct is used to understand the parties' conduct in the current exchange or transaction.

covenant   An agreement or promise made between two or more parties.

cover   The right of a buyer, when the seller breaches, to obtain or purchase substitute goods and to recoup the difference, monetarily, between the original goods and the substitute goods, plus any incidental or consequential damages minus any savings that may occur in the process.

definite   Exact and precise.

delegation of duty   Transferring the duty owed to a party under a contract to another.

detriment   Harm or sacrifice or personal cost.

detrimental reliance   When a promisor makes a promise that leads the promisee to depend, with resulting harm, on that promise.

detrimental   Causing great harm.

discharge   Relieving a party's obligations under a contract, either by performance or by other means such as impossibility.

equity   A branch of the legal system that permits aggrieved parties to seek judgments on the basis of fairness and not according to the common law rules.

executory A contract that has not been performed.

expectation What a party plans to receive from entering into the contract.

express Stated directly, usually in writing but can be communicated orally.

forbearance agreement The agreement to not enforce a right or the agreement to not do an act.

forbearance To not do something or to not act. Agreeing to not sue is an act of forbearance.

formal Historically, a formal contract is under seal; currently, it involves observing the formalities surrounding formation.

formation Creating the contract.

fraud or fraudulent Intentional misstatement or misrepresentation, designed to purposely induce another's reliance, with the intent to cause the individual to part with property or to give up a legal right.

gratuitous An offer or a promise tendered without any value, or consideration, to support it.

illusory promise A promise where there is no recourse for either party's failure to perform or performance is at the party's discretion.

implied Not directly stated in an agreement. Sometimes the law will intervene and create a contract on the basis of the parties' conduct, for example, when one party is unjustly enriched by the situation. This is an instance of an implied contract because the parties did not expressly create one.

incapacity Lacking the mental ability to understand the ramifications of a particular situation. Usually determined by age, for if the individual is a minor, he or she does not have the capacity to contract, nor do the mentally impaired.

informal Not a formal contract but the agreement has all of the contract components.

injunction An remedy, in equity, used to require a party to perform or to bar a party from acting.

integration in contracts The written agreement, adopted by parties to a contract, that represents the complete and final statement of their bargain.

jurisdiction A particular court's right to hear and to decide a case.

lapse When an offer expires due to failure to accept the offer, or failure to exercise the right in the offer, within the stated time frame.

legal precedent Court opinions that are used to guide the analysis of legal issues that arise subsequently that are similar to the prior decision in law and fact.

liquidated An amount made definite and certain by the parties' agreement. Generally, stated in the contract's terms, an amount for damages.

manifest or manifestation To indicate directly and plainly.

manifestation To be indicated as obvious.

material Essential or important to the agreement. The material terms usually concern price, quantity, timing, and condition. An immaterial term may concern how the shipping labels are placed on a package, for example. Goes to the essence or the subject of the offer. Terms in a contract are material if they concern the essence of the agreement.

meeting of the minds When both parties have the same intentions regarding the agreement and both parties agree to the substance and the terms.

memorialize Formal way of stating that a contract or a note, such as a certificate of deposit, is put into writing.

modification Alteration that changes some components of a contract or agreement.

mutual assent Where both sides have a meeting of the minds, in which they agree on the intent and the terms.

mutuality of obligation Requires that both parties are bound to the agreement.

nominal damages Not significant. Sometimes only mentioned to indicate a party's obligations or rights but not assessed a dollar amount.

novation The act of substituting a new agreement or contract for an existing one. This must be done only when the parties to the original contract agree.

obligee The recipient of the obligations under a contract.

obligor The party that is obligated to perform under a contract.

offer A clear indication that a party wants to enter into an agreement

offeree The person or party receiving the offer.

offeror The person or party extending or tendering the offer.

performance Actually doing the action that one promises in a contract.

privity Rights to the agreement. Used in relation to contracts, where the parties to the contract have rights under the agreement. Under the Uniform Commercial Code §2–318, the rights created under this relationship, privity, are now extended to subsequent purchasers of goods. Each state has laws in the respective state statutes concerning privity between the merchant and original purchaser and to the extent that the warranties for the goods are extended to household members, remote purchasers, and other users of the goods.

promisee The person or party who receives the promise.

promisor The person or party who makes the promise. With an offer, the promisor is usually the party extending the offer.

promissory estoppel A court will enforce a promise made, when that promise reasonably led a party to rely on it, if the failure to enforce the promise will cause the promisee great harm. This bars the promisor's ability to reneg on the promise if justice can achieved by enforcing it.

promissory note   A written agreement in which a borrower agrees to pay back a specific amount of money to a lender according to a specific schedule with a stated rate of interest. A promissory note generally contains the total amount of the loan, the interest rate, payment schedule, time frame establishing when payments are late, and possibly collateral securing the loan.

provision   A point, part, condition, or paragraph in an agreement, contract, or statute.

public policy   Legal and societal objectives of the jurisdiction.

punitive damages   Damage award with the objective of punishing for a wrong committed. Rarely used in a breach of contract.

release   Agreeing to permit a party to be relieved from his or her obligations under the agreement. Usually a release is in writing.

reliance   When a party to an agreement acts because he or she trusts that the other party will perform as promised.

remand   When a court, usually an appellate court, sends a case back to a lower court, usually a trial court, to make a further determination.

remedies   When a party does not receive what was promised under the contract, a remedy is a right that the injured party can exercise. To fix a wrong or to redress a right that has been deprived.

render   To state judgment by a court.

rescind   To revoke or to invalidate.

restatements   A scholarly work with the goal of taking the rules from cases and organizing the rules in a way that works like a code. The goal is to provide a resource that will give legal professionals guidance and certainty regarding the legal rule, regardless of state, on

common law issues; the Restatement (Second) Contracts is used widely.

restitution   A way to restore a party to the position he or she was in before being wronged.

restrictive covenant   Language in a deed restricting certain uses for land or language in a contract restricting certain types of activities.

satisfaction   Performing to satisfy the obligation under the contract or tendering a substituted performance that will fulfill the terms.

security   Used by a lender in a loan to ensure that the loan is repaid; a security interest permits the lender to have a right to the borrower's property if the loan is not repaid. Also, another term for stock or share.

specific performance   A remedy. Specific performance puts the injured party in the position he or she would have been in if the contract had been performed.

stare decisis   A Latin phrase meaning "let the decision stand." It is used to indicate that the courts will follow cases that have been decided.

statute of frauds   Statutory provisions adopted by each state requiring that certain types of contracts be in writing. The most common types of contracts affected by the Statute of Frauds are: contracts that require a year or longer to complete, contracts for the sale of real estate, and contracts for the sale of goods over $500.

stipulate   To state precisely.

sufficiency   Used when determining if consideration was adequate or enough to support the promise made.

summary judgment   A party may move for summary judgment, depending on the Rules of Civil Procedure for the court where the case is being heard, if there is no issue of material fact and the party is entitled to judgment as a matter of law. This is a motion that is made prior to the completion of a case.

supersede   When an entirely new agreement comes into existence that replaces a prior agreement, the new agreement is said to supersede the prior contract.

supervening   Arising after the initial terms. For instance, a supervening illegality arises, after the initial terms of the contract are agreed upon based on existing law, when a new law is enacted that makes the initial terms impossible to perform due to illegality. Occurs frequently in zoning issues.

tender   To convey in a business transaction

third party   Not an original party to a contract, but a party that is either a beneficiary, intended or incidental, under the contract to whom one of the original parties assigns his or her benefit or delegates his or her duty.

unconscionable   An unconscionable contract is even more one sided than a contract of adhesion. A contract is unconscionable when it is oppressively one sided.

uniform commercial code (U.C.C.)   One of the Uniform Acts drafted with the goal to make a specific area of law uniform among the fifty states. Article 2 of the Uniform Commercial Code provides the legal rules concerning the sales of goods. Article 2 (commonly called "Sales") is important because contracts are made and goods are sold across state lines. Each state adopts the U.C.C. provisions, and once the state adopts the provisions it is part of the state's code. Forty-nine states, all states except Louisiana, have adopted Article 2 of the U.C.C., which concerns sales.

unilateral   Generally means one sided. A unilateral contract occurs when there is a promise without a return promise and generally there is a promise for performance.

valid   A contract that fulfills all of the legal requirements so that it is judicially enforceable and is binding between the parties.

void A contract without any force; a void contract is completely ineffective as a legal instrument.

voidable A contract where the aggrieved party still can obtain value but the wrongdoer cannot. For example, this occurs when a party is induced to enter into a contract on fraudulent terms. The party perpetuating the fraud cannot benefit under the agreement.

warranty A promise made in the course of the contractual agreement that can be the basis of the bargain. A promise that an assertion made is true. Generally used in the sale of goods to state a promise that the subject of the agreement will be of a certain condition.

INDEX